Romance of the Sea

Romance of the Sea

By J. H. Parry

Published by
The National Geographic
Society

Gilbert M. Grosvenor
President

Melvin M. Payne
Chairman of the Board

Owen R. Anderson
Executive Vice President

Robert L. Breeden
*Vice President, Publications
and Educational Media*

Prepared by
National Geographic
Book Service

Charles O. Hyman
Director

Staff for this book
Kenneth C. Danforth
Managing Editor

Verla Lee Smith
Editor

David M. Seager
Art Director

Anne Dirkes Kobor
Illustrations Editor

Susan Eckert Sidman
Chief Researcher

Thomas B. Allen
Edward Lanouette
David D. Pearce
Robert M. Poole
David F. Robinson
Margaret Sedeen
Jonathan B. Tourtellot
Editor-Writers

Melanie Ann Corner
Mary B. Dickinson
Suzanne P. Kane
Penelope A. Loeffler
Carol Bittig Lutyk
Elizabeth L. Newhouse
Lise M. Swinson
L. Madison Washburn
Anne E. Withers
Editorial and Research Staff

Molly Kohler
Illustrations Research

Paulette L. Claus
Teresita C. Sison
Editorial Assistants

Contributions by
Constance Brown Boltz
Gary W. Bradbrook
Polly Bryson
Seymour L. Fishbein
Thomas K. Hamburger
Jennifer Moseley
Towne W. Windom

Robert C. Firestone
Production Manager

Karen F. Edwards
Assistant Production Manager

Richard S. Wain
Production Assistant

John T. Dunn
Engraving and Printing

John D. Garst, Jr.
Virginia L. Baza
Lisa Biganzoli
Susanah B. Brown
Patricia K. Cantlay
Jerald N. Fishbein
Margaret Deane Gray
Gary M. Johnson
Susan M. Johnston
Alfred L. Zebarth
Geographic Art

Jeffrey A. Brown
Index

First edition 300,000 copies.

375 illustrations,
including 14 maps.

J. H. Parry
Gardiner Professor of
Oceanic History and Affairs,
Harvard University
Author and Chief Consultant

William Avery Baker
Frank Braynard
Derek Howse
Harold D. Huycke, Jr.
Sean MacGrail
David R. MacGregor

John J. McCusker
Andrew J. Nesdall
William W. Warner
Editorial Consultants

Foreword

"Hard alee. Back tops'l. Back t'gallant." Capt. Irving Johnson's voice barked above the distant drone of a foghorn. The brigantine *Yankee* was coming about in the fog-shrouded English Channel night, as a rhythmic diesel engine sounded louder and dangerously close at hand. The yards creaked and luffing canvas howled in protest as the *Yankee* swung around. The sails filled again and the howling ceased.

That one tense midnight maneuver made centuries of seafaring history and adventure tales come alive for me. I had just turned 16. My first night at sea. "Skipper" Johnson—who had circled the globe three times under sail—seemed just as excited. For six glorious weeks we sailed toward the New World. It was a fine crossing, the weather "like April in Andalusia," as Columbus once put it. The *Yankee,* a former North Sea pilot schooner, had just been refitted for round-the-world voyaging. We swung southward to catch the trade winds, following the ancient sailing routes to North America. We put in to the Azores, then Bermuda. Ever since that summer, like millions of other romantics, I have loved the sea and greatly admired the early explorers and the role that ships have played in linking together the far-flung peoples of the world.

In *Romance of the Sea,* the eminent maritime historian J. H. Parry and the National Geographic staff have assembled a word-and-picture chronicle of man's use of the oceans. It reaches back through the millennia to trace the development of ships—from ingenious animal-skin floats and dugouts to vessels capable of sailing wherever the winds blew and the channels led. It follows sea pioneers and traders, corsairs and conquerors, slavers and scientists. The legacy of seafaring is with us no matter where we go.

There are places where we can still feel the pulse of the past. I took up scuba diving mainly so I could explore shipwrecks. Bermuda, for instance, was once a crossroads of the Atlantic, and a lot of ships came to grief on its outer reefs. On one wreck site in one day I saw gold, silver, glass, porcelain—artifacts that had been locked in a time capsule for 200 years. Opening such a capsule gives us a fresh look at our culture. That's part of the romance of the sea.

Man's destiny has always been tied to sea power and waterways. Even in ancient times, whoever dominated a major sea-lane held a key to power. The Portuguese, Spanish, Dutch, British—all fought for control of the seas, and all knew the value of strategic waterways: the English Channel, Gibraltar, Hormuz. Hormuz has been a bottleneck since the Middle Ages, and even today our destiny is tied to that narrow strait: 60 percent of the West's imported oil is shipped by way of Hormuz.

In spite of the perfection of jetliners, the importance of seafaring has not diminished. Two hundred years ago the nation that ruled the seas ruled much of the world. Today we bounce messages and images around the globe by satellite, we move people faster than the speed of sound, but still our civilization is only as secure as the shipping lanes that oil-carrying supertankers ply in an endless procession. We remain as dependent upon ships and the freedom of the sea as at any time in our history.

Gilbert M. Grosvenor

From Boats to Ships

Long before man tamed beasts of burden or put wheels to carts, he had fashioned boats. First he used floats—logs, reed bundles, inflated skins, or hollow gourds—to cross bodies of water. Next, in various parts of the world, he shaped his buoyant materials into dugouts, rafts, and an astonishing range of simple but ingenious boats. Some, such as pottery and basket boats, contributed little to seafaring. But early man's efforts to master the waters also led to the planked hull, the oar, the sail, the rudder—and ultimately to the seagoing ship.

The course of history has been profoundly influenced by the efficiency and ingenuity with which competing civilizations could design a ship's hull, or rig up a piece of matting or cloth to harness the wind. The notion, for example, that the framework of a ship could be built before its outer shell, and not added afterward, revolutionized European maritime construction in the 15th century.

Down the centuries, the builders of watercraft usually have been conservative people, handing on their rule-of-thumb methods and tried, familiar designs. Innovation has been tentative and cautious. Traditional craft have persisted locally over long periods and still survive where Western industrial influence is small. Thus we can trace with reasonable confidence the geographical origin and spread—the lineage—of basic types of vessels.

Seaworthy boats and ships probably descend from three types of primitive craft: the raft made of logs fastened together, the dugout hollowed from a tree trunk, and the skin boat made of hide stretched over a frame of boughs. From these ancestral strains came wooden boats, and finally, the sailing ship that enabled man to venture from sheltered waters and make the sea his highway.

Poised at the prow of his dugout canoe, an Indian Ocean mariner faces the challenge of the open sea. From such craft evolved the modern ocean liner.

Indian reed boats resembling
the papyrus craft shown on a
4,000-year-old Mesopotamian
seal (opposite, upper) line
the shore of Lake Titicaca in
South America. The boats,
called balsas, are fashioned
of totora-reed bundles lashed

together with a continuous
spiraling cord. Paddles
or woven-reed sails propel them.
A larger version of the balsa
in 1970 successfully carried
Norwegian archaeologist Thor
Heyerdahl across the Atlantic
from Africa to the Caribbean.
    The origin of the boat is not
known. The oldest one so far
discovered, part of a dugout

The kind of craft found in a particular place depends on the nature of the weather, water, and available building materials. Rafts are usually warm-water craft because they float low and, except in calm conditions, their occupants are wet much of the time. Moreover, fast-growing tropical plants such as papyrus and ambatch provide buoyant reeds and boughs for raft-making.

Reed craft can still be found on Lake Chad in north central Africa, Lake Tana in Ethiopia, and Lake Titicaca in the Andes. Local Indians on Lake Titicaca, using tightly lashed, tapered bundles of totora reeds, have evolved a craft with sails made of reed matting that moves quickly in light wind and can carry two or three people. Log rafts are still used for ocean fishing in many parts of the world and, until the 1800's, also were employed as cargo carriers.

Before the Spanish conquest, Peruvian Indians conducted a considerable coastal trade in big sailing rafts. Francisco Pizarro found his first evidence of the rumored kingdom of the Incas in an encounter with such a raft. "This ship," his secretary wrote, "seemed to be of about thirty tons. The keel and bottom were made of reed stems as thick as posts, lashed together with sisal. . . . There were raised platforms made of lighter stems . . . on which the cargo was stowed and the people sat, to keep dry, because the hull was awash. It had . . . well-cut cotton sails . . . and stone anchors shaped like grindstones."

Although rafts can be made from a variety of materials, dugouts are always made of wood. A dugout big enough to be seagoing must be made from a fair-size tree—a problem for people without metal tools.

found in Holland, dates back
some 8,000 years. Wall carvings
from ancient Assyria (bottom)
show soldiers crossing a river
on goatskin floats about 2,800
years ago. A similar float,
made of water-buffalo hide,
even today buoys a native
on the Ganges River in India.

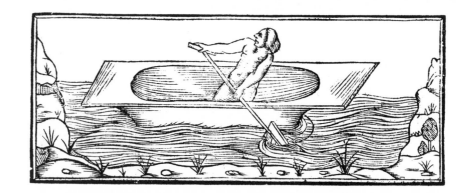

The wood must be soft enough to be worked but also strong enough to stand up to wear. It must be straight and free of branches for the required length and grow reasonably near the water. The log is hewn and whittled to the desired outside shape and the inside is hollowed, often by charring with a small fire and scraping with a stone or shell adz.

Dugouts have other shortcomings besides difficulty of construction. They are heavy and rigid, as well as narrow and shallow in proportion to their length, so that they ship water in any kind of a sea. Lacking keel or bilges, they are unstable, especially under sail. To overcome these drawbacks, a dugout can be expanded by softening the wood and wedging crossbars between the gunwales so that the sides flare out. The hull can also be extended by adding planks that run the length of the dugout. Adding outriggers or lashing together two hulls catamaran-style also improves stability.

A key development from the dugout began many centuries ago with the addition of planks to raise the sides of the hull. A planked hull evolved that was deep enough to keep out water even in a high sea and broad enough to possess stability under sail. When this stage was reached, hollowing out the original log became unnecessary. No longer a dugout, the log survived as a keel in the planked boat.

Boats developed from extended dugouts in many parts of the ancient world. There were differences from one region to another in the methods used to fasten hull planks, or strakes, to one another. In the Indian Ocean, strakes normally were stitched or lashed together with coconut fiber—called coir. The fiber was cheaper and more easily obtainable

"They have boats called canoes made of one single huge tree, hollowed out by the use of stone hatchets," wrote Magellan's chronicler of Brazil's coastal Indians. "They paddle with blades like the shovels of a furnace, and thus . . . they resemble, when paddling, the inhabitants of the Stygian marsh." Boats similar to those described and portrayed (above) by 16th-century voyagers still navigate the coasts and waterways of remote areas.

A dugout canoe (opposite), its sides built up with planks and reinforced with internal framing, crashes through the surf off the Caribbean island of Dominica. Tar daubed between the joints seals out water.

Venezuelan Indian boys (right) prepare to launch a bark canoe. Framing lashed to the gunwales gives the craft rigidity.

An Eskimo skin boat, or kayak, basks in the reflected hues of an iceberg near Jakobshaven, Greenland. Sleek, swift, and silent, such craft rank among the most ingenious hunting boats ever devised. Man and kayak become a single unit when the hooded jacket is tied tightly around face, wrists, and cockpit coaming. The hunter remains dry even when (as in the practice session opposite, below) he rolls his boat over.

Eskimo kayaks range in length from 15 to 25 feet and weigh 25 to 100 pounds—light enough for one man to carry. They are made of sealskins stretched tightly over a driftwood frame.

than iron, and the flexibility of a sewn hull, especially in the surf, could be an advantage. But the constant chafing of hull planks and rotting of stitches presented maintenance problems.

Sewn boats are almost extinct. A few small ones survive in out-of-the-way places in Oman and the Hadhramaut on the Arabian Peninsula. In a few small ports of southeastern India, *masula* boats, surfboats having sewn hulls without ribs or other internal support, are used for lightering cargo ashore.

In northern Europe, as in the Indian Ocean, when the dugout developed into the planked boat, the original dugout log was reduced to a solid keel. But northern Europeans developed a different method of construction and fastening: clinker-built or lapstrake. Almost all medieval northern European wooden boats and ships were built this way—an overlapping join is easier to make and stronger than an edge-to-edge join. Iron for fastening was available, and durable oak pegs could also be made. The result of lapstrake construction was a strong, yet light and resilient type of boat, well adapted to rough Atlantic seas. From these boats the tradition of Viking ships and their progeny developed.

Seagoing ships appeared in the Mediterranean by 3000 B.C.—perhaps before northern Europeans had graduated from dugouts. Unlike flat-keeled northern boats, Mediterranean craft had curved keels, except for some very early vessels with no keel at all. Curved endposts graced the boats fore and aft, and the sternpost rose much higher than the stern itself.

Planks on Mediterranean boats were joined edge to edge without overlapping, a construction method known as carvel-built. Thick stem-to-stern wales on

OVERLEAF: *Afloat on a murky sea off Iceland, the* Brendan, *a 36-foot leather-skinned boat, proved seaworthy on a 4,600-mile crossing from Ireland to Newfoundland. The voyage lent credence to sagas of a sixth-century journey to America by Saint Brendan.*

With sail lowered amidships, a Polynesian double canoe scuds through a Pacific storm. Wind-driven clouds part, revealing a star that enables this navigator to estimate his position with remarkable accuracy. Early seafarers committed to memory dozens of star patterns and positions to help guide the way through uncharted waters. A glimpse of the star usually sufficed. Then, by keeping wind and wave at a constant angle, a course could be set—at least until the elements shifted.

By such ingenious methods modern star-path navigators *(opposite)* in 1976 set out to steer a re-created double canoe 3,000 miles from Hawaii to Tahiti—a month-long voyage that successfully duplicated epic journeys taken by early Pacific wanderers.

the outside of the hull protected the planking. The craft was steered with an oar or rudder attached to the ship's quarter, the afterpart of its side, long after northerners had adopted rudders hung on the stern-post. The curved keel is practical in the almost tide-less Mediterranean; if a boat with a curved keel runs aground, it can often be refloated by shifting weight from bow to stern.

Hulls of these Indian Ocean, northern European, and Mediterranean vessels derived the greatest part of their strength from sturdy wooden shells. Shells came first, then frames were inserted if needed.

People living in treeless regions devised still another method of boat construction. Here the builder made his frame first, then covered it with a water-tight skin, as in the Eskimo umiak or the basketlike *gufas* still seen on the Euphrates River. In hide-covered *curraghs* Irish seafarers made long ocean passages in the sixth and seventh centuries A.D.

Curraghs, many now powered by outboard motors, are still used for fishing and coastal travel, but tarred canvas has replaced oxhide. Those of the Kerry coast in western Ireland carry six or eight people.

In areas where trees were plentiful, boats could be made of bark. Some, such as the birchbark canoes built by the Indians of eastern North America, were beautiful and sophisticated craft with internal frames that enabled them to take hard knocks. Less durable were the bark canoes of Africa, Australia, and South America—and the "woodskins" that still ply the backwaters of Guyana in South America.

Primitive man used boats of one sort or another for thousands of years before he invented the sail. The most rudimentary sail probably was a simple

Star positions, wind direction, and the flight habits of birds helped Pacific islanders find their way at sea. So did the waves themselves. A stick chart from the Marshall Islands uses shells to represent islands and atolls. Bent withes indicate the direction of swells caused by prevailing winds. Waves deflected by the islands often produced a confused sea that helped the primitive navigator sense his position.

square or rectangle laced to a horizontal yard which, in turn, was fastened to a mast set at right angles to the keel. Even today such sails can be seen from Lake Titicaca to Bengal and from Burma to the Marquesas. In its basic form the square sail is efficient only when running before the wind.

Another basic type is the lugsail, for many centuries the characteristic sail of China. The yard of a lugsail is hoisted from a point about one-third along its length, so that part of the sail rides before the mast. The sail, fastened to a boom along its foot, or bottom edge, is stiffened by a series of bamboo battens that give it a very flat set and a good performance heading into a wind. Battens also enable the sails to be promptly reefed or doused, a valuable attribute in the stormy waters of the China Sea.

The sail that now typifies Arab ships was called *lateen* by northern European mariners because they associated it with the Latin people of the Mediterranean region. It, too, is bent to a yard, but the yard is hoisted at an angle to the mast. The mast itself is short and is usually stepped with a pronounced forward rake. The cut of a lateen sail varies. In the Mediterranean it is triangular, with a high peak and a loose foot. This shape is carried to the extreme in the *gaiassas* that sail the lower Nile, the towering peak catching the wind above the embankments of ditches and canals. In the eastern Indian Ocean and western Pacific the lateen is again triangular, but has less of a peak, and the foot is laced to a boom, which in many cases curves upward at its forward end. The extreme form of this type of sail is the beautiful kite, or crab-claw, sail that propels many outrigger canoes.

Catching a fair wind (left), sailors of ancient Egypt raise a sail rigged to a bipod mast joined at the top. A kneeling crewman handles yardarm braces. Shipwrights (below) pursue their trade on a relief that decorates a 4,300-year-old Saqqara tomb. Workmen pound home doweled planks; others work with adzes.

OVERLEAF: *Broad-bottomed* gaiassas, *built to haul heavy cargo, parade beneath the cliffs of the Nile near Beni Hasan. Towering pyramids of canvas—lateen sails aided by jibs mounted on booms—propel the craft in airs that would barely stir a butterfly.*

In the western Indian Ocean, where the lateen rig may have originated, the sail has four sides. But its luff, or leading edge, is so short that the sail appears triangular from a short distance away. This "settee" sail is as characteristic of Islam as the crescent itself and may well represent the oldest form of the lateen, the form from which the triangular sail evolved.

Lateen sails spread westward in the wake of Arab invasions. By the 11th century they had almost replaced primitive square sails throughout the Mediterranean basin, as well as on the Atlantic coasts of Spain and Portugal as far north as the Tagus River.

The most noticeable feature of the lateen sail is the extraordinary length of the yard from which it is hung—a formidable spar that is often longer than the vessel and is usually made of two or three lengths lashed together. From the double thickness at the bunt, or center, the yard tapers toward each end. Under sail, it curves like a taut-strung bow. Arab vessels with their lateen rig and deep keel can sail close to the wind, very much better than vessels under square rig alone. They are at their best when reaching with a fair breeze on the beam, and in such conditions may show a remarkable turn of speed.

But the lateen is not a rig for running before the wind or for stormy waters. It can make a vessel yaw unpredictably with a following sea or with slight changes of wind. With such a rig an unexpected jibe, a sudden shift of the sail from one side of the vessel to the other, can be disastrous.

These basic sail and hull designs, then, were the building blocks that would enable man, through trial and error, eventually to turn boats into the ships that would make a highway of the open sea.

Lashed to the mast, Ulysses
resists Siren songs calculated
to lure mariners to grief
amid the rocks and whirlpools
of classical antiquity. This
ram-prowed ship, a combination
merchantman and fighting
galley, ranged Grecian waters
during the fifth century B.C.

Merchant ships race to rescue
a young man fallen from his
skiff at Rome's port of Ostia.
Brisk winds, choppy seas,
and imminent collision with
a ship entering the harbor
evidently thwarted the effort:
The scene, from the third
century A.D., embellishes the
sarcophagus of the victim.

Such vessels supported an
empire that reached from Egypt
to Britain. They hauled
bulk goods at no more than six
knots and, like Greek ships
before them, were built with
sturdy framing—added after
the hull itself was complete.

What is the difference between a ship and a boat? At a glance, size: Ships are big, boats are small. They also differ in function. Boats operate inland or near the coast; ships sail the open ocean, carrying people and goods safely over great distances. Most boats are open; ships are fully decked, with room for people between decks and space for goods below. Ships, unlike boats, are usually used for profit rather than for pleasure.

Boats have made long sea passages: William Bligh of the *Bounty* sailed 3,600 nautical miles from Tonga to Timor after the famous mutiny. But no seaman in his senses would seek to emulate Bligh.

Chance probably accounts for the success of the Polynesians in spreading themselves over the Pacific. From the Marquesas to Hawaii is more than 2,000 miles, to New Zealand farther still, and prevailing winds that favor the outward passage would hinder a return. In all likelihood the voyagers—in double canoes open to the weather except for a flimsy thatched cabin—aimed at nearer islands, missed, and were carried on and on, never to return.

Norse adventurers from the 9th through the 11th centuries did go back and forth over long distances. They were not sailing from one inconspicuous atoll or island to another as the Polynesians did, but between large, mountainous landmasses. Island-hopping from Bergen in Norway to Cape Farewell in Greenland, the longest open-sea distance is only 350 nautical miles. The Norseman ran less risk than the Polynesian voyager of losing the way.

Norse oceangoing vessels were far more substantial than double canoes, but not necessarily larger. The most complete surviving example is the 76-foot-long, ninth-century Gokstad ship now preserved in Oslo. Her solid oak keel, flexible frame, and clinker planking make her an inspired combination of strength and elasticity. She carried a crew of 32 to 35, pulled 16 oars a side, and boasted a substantial mast with a square sail whose yard was about

Reconstructing The Past At 15 Fathoms

The little ship never made it to port. Waylaid, perhaps, by a band of pirates within sight of the seaside town of Kyrenia on the island of Cyprus, she went down, sinking through the clear, blue-green water with her cargo of almonds, wine, and millstones. The ship came to rest on the sandy seabed, where she would lie undisturbed for 2,200 years.

The vessel, now known as the Kyrenia ship, was a battered Greek merchantman that probably had seen many long years of service before foundering. She was a tramp trader, sailing from port to port during the fourth century B.C.—the era of Alexander the Great—at no better than four or five knots. But to archaeologists who reconnoitered the wreck in 1967, the Kyrenia ship was a rare gift, a reliable witness that would reveal much about ancient seafaring.

Each piece of the wreck contributed to the story: Clay jars of 11 distinct styles traced the ship's ports of call from Samos to Kos to Rhodes; a coin minted during the reign of Demetrius the Besieger helped fix the date of the accident; lead sheathing on the pine hull indicated that shipworms were a constant bother; and a copper cauldron, along with the absence of other on-board cooking facilities, suggested that the ship's four-man crew put ashore to cook meals.

Taken separately, the fragments of the Kyrenia mosaic mean little. But pieced together, they form a picture frozen in time that provides hard evidence about ancient trade routes, shipbuilding, and life at sea. For that reason, nautical archaeologists continue to search the oceans for more wrecks like the Kyrenia ship. The Mediterranean, with a history of shipping that traces back 5,000 years to the Egyptians, has become the central focus of their attention, even

Bones of the Kyrenia ship, lost in the fourth century B.C., take shape—again—in the hall of a Crusader fort on Cyprus. Thousands of pieces of Aleppo pine dredged from the floor of the Mediterranean (opposite) had to be photographed, cataloged, and preserved before the 45-foot vessel could be reassembled— a task that took nearly three years to complete.

27

though many of the most accessible wrecks have been picked over by sponge divers and treasure hunters. Using the exacting standards of land-based archaeology and aided by modern photographic equipment, underwater historians are writing new footnotes to the saga of seafaring.

In Sicily archaeologists have found evidence that a third century B.C. Punic ship was designed for prefabricated construction, which would explain the speedy production of war vessels described in history texts. And the Kyrenia wreck, which has been exhumed and preserved, shows how ancient shipwrights worked, first piecing together the outer shell, or skin, of the hull, then buttressing it from within—exactly the opposite of modern ship construction, which adds the outer planking after the skeleton has been completed.

In Sweden scientists have recovered and restored the *Vasa,* an imposing relic of a 17th-century man-of-war. Like the Kyrenia ship, the *Vasa* was well embalmed in her underwater grave, partly because the hull was covered by silt after she sank. But even when well-preserved ships are resurrected and brought to land, they crumble into decay on contact with air. So scientists have developed methods to restore ships like the Kyrenia: Their aged timbers are impregnated with a waxlike compound that adds strength and prevents shrinkage.

Such advances are impressive, but underwater archaeology is still in its infancy. Although divers groped through Persian wrecks as early as 500 B.C., it wasn't until Aqua-Lungs became widely available after World War II that archaeologists could probe the deep in earnest. Because of the late start, an overwhelming amount of work remains to be done.

Lithe and graceful in repose at the Viking Ship Museum in Oslo, Norway, these vessels recall raids that terrorized medieval Europe from Britain to Byzantium. For two centuries beginning around A.D. 800, Norsemen raided—and traded

—in craft similar to the Gokstad ship (center), exhumed from a funeral mound in 1880. Its 76-foot hull, made of overlapping oaken planks, bore a sturdy pine mast and was pierced for 16 pairs of oars.

The ninth-century Oseberg ship (right), probably a pleasure craft, served as a sepulcher for a noblewoman.

The Viking love of ships is reflected in coins found in Sweden. The shield-rimmed boat carried raiders; the other, a bulkier knarr, *brought goods.*

A small, intricately carved animal head (left), found aboard the Oseberg vessel, may have decorated a bedpost.

37 feet long. With a 32-ton cargo capacity, the Gokstad ship probably was built for trading in either sheltered or open water. She is more ship than boat.

She is more of a ship, indeed, than the famous longships of the Viking marauders who, from about the end of the eighth century, made swift and savage raids on harbors, monasteries, and manor houses along the coasts of western Europe. Able to strike and run, seafaring people with such vessels had an immense advantage over more sedentary folk. Most longships were probably light, narrow, and small, although some, according to the sagas, were floating garrisons crammed with fighting men. Yet even King Olaf Tryggvason's *Long Serpent*, with her gilded dragon head and tail, probably could not have survived storms in the North Sea, to say nothing of the open Atlantic.

Norsemen sailed to Iceland, to Greenland, and briefly to parts of North America, not in longships but in the oceangoing *knarr*. The knarr was a sailing ship with oars that were used only when becalmed or during an emergency. She was beamier than the Gokstad ship and rode both deeper in the water and higher above it. With the development of this sturdy vessel, the transition from boat to ship in northern Europe was almost complete. Only full-length decks were lacking.

Ships developed from boats at different times in the China Sea, the northern Indian Ocean, the Mediterranean, and later, in northwestern Europe. But from very early times there were channels of contact between the regions. Commercial activities usually overlapped, though building traditions for ships, as for boats, were distinct.

GOKSTADSKIBET

GOKSTADSKIBET

Clanging armor and the crunch of wood mark the Battle of Guernsey in 1342, one of many Channel skirmishes during the Hundred Years War. French and English cogs grapple, forming a floating battlefield.

Round ships like these saw use mainly as channel traders, hauling wool, cloth, and herring, but could be pressed into service during time of war. Light, temporary castles at bow and stern—such as those displayed on Dover's seal (below) earlier in the century—have given way to stout fore- and aftercastles built

permanently into the hull. Rudders no longer hang over the quarter; now they swing from the sternpost. Masts have become strong enough and well enough stayed to support three or four men-at-arms in the fighting tops.

30·

The Mediterranean—an enclosed sea with islands conveniently spaced along much of its length—was a natural nursery for seafaring cultures. The earliest known records of seagoing ships, and the oldest surviving ship, are from Egypt. Egyptian vessels plied both the Mediterranean and the Red Sea. Carved reliefs in the temple of Deir el Bahri near ancient Thebes represent a fleet of five ships that Queen Hatshepsut is said to have dispatched on a trading mission to the "Land of Punt"—Somaliland or perhaps Yemen. The ships appear to have been keelless, the bottom planks rising in a graceful curve to a long, overhanging stern. They were propelled by oars and a single large square sail.

Contemporary with the first Egyptian dynasties, a purely Mediterranean sea empire flourished in Crete and undoubtedly traded with Egypt. The Minoan capital at Knossos, with its harbor, had no walls. The sea was its moat and ships were its defenses. But Minoans did not practice ship burial, and we know almost nothing about their vessels.

Nor do we know much about the ships of the Phoenicians, bold seafarers from the cities of Tyre and Sidon. From the 12th century B.C. to the 5th, the Phoenicians were the commercial carriers of the Mediterranean and founded colonies from Cyprus to Cadiz. They voyaged as far as southwestern Spain for silver, and to the "Cassiterides"—possibly the Scilly Isles or Cornwall—for tin.

The Phoenicians operated not only as merchants but also as naval mercenaries to the great powers of the area. Sennacherib, Xerxes, Alexander, all employed Phoenician transports and warships. The great Persian fleet that the Athenians defeated at Sa-

lamis probably was in large part Phoenician. Phoenician power and prosperity declined with the rise of Athens as a maritime rival.

We know much more about the Greeks as seafarers. Many volumes have discussed the Athenian war galley, the trireme, with its arrangement of tholes and benches, its oars and ram. Triremes did not carry cargo because the oarsmen took up too much room. The ships in which the Greeks traded and settled throughout the Mediterranean and the Black Sea were not triremes, but sailing ships. Paintings on vases, confirmed by the examination of sunken wrecks, suggest that the Greek sailing ships were open vessels with edge-joined planking and curved

keel, a single mast and a square sail. Some ships were carrying wine when they sank and can be roughly dated by the design of the amphorae in which the wine was stored. The earliest so far examined date from the sixth century B.C.

We do not normally think of the Romans as seafarers, but rather as warriors, engineers, and administrators. But the Romans gave the Mediterranean region political unity and their ships employed the seafaring peoples of the whole area. The Pax Romana encouraged a general flourishing of seaborne trade. Along with the expanding trade, we first read in Roman times of large-scale piracy, trade's dark counterpart. During the first century B.C., the Roman general Pompey earned great popularity for his vigorous and determined suppression of pirates in the Mediterranean.

Ancient Ostia at the mouth of the Tiber was a busy commercial harbor, as its ruins attest. Among the excavations, along what was once the waterfront, is a row of shipping offices. Some have mosaics of ships on their walls. The vessels show the characteristic curved keel, endposts, and quarter-rudders of earlier Greek ships. But the Roman ships were bigger: Evidence from wrecks reveals heavy, solid hull construction, each plank mortised and doweled along its entire length to those above and below. Square sails, one to a mast, were still in general use, but two and three masts were known. Early medieval descendants of these stout, multimasted vessels were carrying cargoes on the inland sea when the Vikings were spreading their reign of terror around northern Europe. With modifications in rig, such vessels characterized Mediterranean shipping

Evolution Of Nautical Transport

The saga of the sea is the story of the ship—from crudest dugout to sleekest liner. All descend from the humble log which, though transformed beyond recognition, today survives in nearly every ship as its keel.

The Björke boat of A.D. 100, named for the island in Sweden where it was excavated, has no keel proper. Instead, it has a bottom board hollowed from a log and tapered at both ends—clear proof of its kinship to the dugout carved 3,600 years earlier.

The Nydam boat, dug from a peat bog in southern Denmark, was built about A.D. 350. It has only a rudimentary keel, a plank slightly thicker and wider than the overlapping boards that form its sides. From this evolved the true keel, an example of which appears with the Kvalsund boat of A.D. 700, found in western Norway in 1920.

Evidence of sail makes an early appearance in northern Europe with the Gokstad ship, a Norse trader built about 150 years after the Kvalsund vessel. Note the ports for 16 pairs of oars.

Decks appear with the knarr, an ocean-going merchantman from about A.D. 900; and steering oars evolve into a stern-hung rudder like that seen on the Kalmar ship dated about 350 years later.

The 14th-century cog, clinker-built and fully decked, retains the square sail but now carries castles at stem and stern.

In the Mediterranean, meanwhile, lateen sails and hulls built with planks laid edge-to-edge characterize ship development from the trading vessel of A.D. 900 to the Venetian merchant ship of 1270 and the three-masted caravel of Columbus's day.

The mingling of regional shipbuilding methods gives rise, in the early 15th century, to the globe-girdling carrack.

Floating log; length indeterminate

Dugout canoe; length indeterminate

Björke boat; 24 feet

Nydam boat; 75 feet

Kvalsund boat; 60 feet

Gokstad ship; 76 feet

Knarr; 55 feet

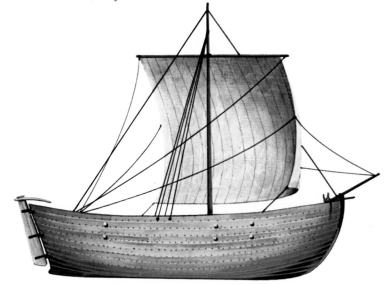

Kalmar ship; 37 feet

Hanseatic cog; 98 feet

Greek trader; 40 feet

Venetian merchant ship; 85 feet

Caravel; 75 feet

Carrack; 125 feet

throughout the Middle Ages. Less is known about the shipping of other areas because maritime historians and nautical archaeologists have been less active, not because there is less to know. For at least 500 years—from the 10th century to the 15th—Chinese ships were probably the biggest and most reliable in the world. From Sung times onward Chinese merchants voyaged far beyond their home waters. Berber historian Muhammad Ibn Batuta, traveling to India and China in the 14th century, wrote that Chinese ships carried on virtually all trade between South India and South China.

Between 1405 and 1433 the Chinese widened their maritime contacts greatly, although temporarily, through a series of seven expeditions organized by the Grand Eunuch Cheng Ho. The first fleet included 62 ships and "tens of thousands" of men. The voyages were intended to extend the influence and prestige of the Yung-lo emperor by conferring protection and gifts upon foreign rulers—and receiving their tribute. Chinese expeditions encompassed the northern Indian Ocean, including the entrances to the Persian Gulf and Red Sea, and the East African coast as far south as Madagascar. On the return passage of the seventh voyage, the fleet sailed from Hormuz to Calicut, about 1,450 nautical miles, in 22 days. Vasco da Gama, 65 years later, covered the 2,300 miles from Malindi to Calicut in 27 days, but he had the southwest monsoon behind him.

What were Chinese ships like? Contemporary descriptions are few and vague, drawings fewer still. We have to guess from surviving types. Many vessels described as junks after the 16th century incorporated some structural features imitated from foreign ships. But traditional junks, like sampans, probably trace their development from a raft ancestor. They are typically flat bottomed and have no keel, stempost, or sternpost. Planking closes in both ends, giving the vessel a flat, or transom, bow as well as a transom stern. These transoms form two of the stout bulkheads that give the hull strength and divide it into watertight compartments. A centerline rudder usually hangs aft. Seagoing junks are soundly constructed and may be 150 feet long. In earlier times they may well have been even larger. They are propelled by lugsails, one to a mast, with some of the largest junks having four or five masts. In the Middle Ages, Chinese seamen probably could have sailed around the world if they had been encouraged to do so. In fact, they were actively discouraged. After 1433, Chinese vessels no longer ventured into the Indian Ocean. Free mingling with foreigners was held a threat to morals and public order. Ming China withdrew to its own boundaries. From time to time imperial decrees forbade all foreign trade, although Chinese ships still traded as far west as Malacca, and were doing so when the Portuguese arrived there around 1500.

China's maritime retreat left the Indian Ocean chiefly in the hands of Arabs and Indian Moslems. Sickle-sailed ships, which Europeans call dhows, sailed regularly from Hormuz or Aden to the ports

36

along India's Malabar coast and often on to Malacca or farther east, timing their voyages to fit the alternating monsoon winds.

An appreciable number of dhows are still in service. They no longer cross the Indian Ocean but play a significant part in local coastal trade.

The rig of traditional Arab vessels has remained virtually unchanged for centuries. Medieval ships were lateen rigged, as dhows still are. But lateen rig, for all its elegant beauty, has disadvantages. Hoisting the long, unwieldy main yard is a laborious operation requiring the combined efforts of a large crew. There is a limit to the size of yard that can be handled, and this in turn limits the size of the ship. Nevertheless, medieval Arabs, like the Chinese, had ships able to sail round the world.

But they did not. Europeans did. The northerners had stronger motives for distant voyaging, but did they also have better ships?

In northern Europe the Viking knarr gave rise to the round-hulled, clinker-built sailing ship that carried most of the region's trade in the 13th century. A sunken merchant vessel of this type, found at Bergen in 1960, was 85 feet long and nearly 30 feet wide. The type survived for centuries.

As trade expanded in the 13th and early 14th centuries, a demand grew for ships of lighter, cheaper construction, with more space for cargo. The answer was the cog of late medieval northern Europe, of Germanic rather than Scandinavian origin. Cogs were simple, capacious cargo carriers, flush planked on the bottom and lapstraked along the sides. A later vessel, the hulk, is known only from brief mentions and sketchy drawings.

Lateen sail full and drawing,
a Kuwaiti dhow kicks up
a bow wave as it furrows
the Persian Gulf. Hoisting the
mainsail bent to a yard as
thick as a man's body requires
the efforts of the entire
crew—even the captain (right).

38   The cog derived its strength from its stoutly planked shell. Internal bracing, if any, was fitted only after the outer planking had been completed. It was a single-masted vessel, with a single square sail. This simple rig needed only a small crew, and was cheap to operate. Though seaworthy, the cog was not very maneuverable. Nor was it very big.

Mediterranean sailing ships in the later Middle Ages tended to be bigger—two or three masts—and they had lateen sails. The Mediterranean vessels, therefore, were somewhat more maneuverable and faster, though less seaworthy in heavy weather. Their hull construction was fundamentally different, too—flush planked over a preassembled frame.

No one knows where or when building a ship from the frame out originated—perhaps around 1400 in the Mediterranean area. It is thought that such preconstructed frames were used to build the big ships of the western Mediterranean. Certainly the effect of this innovation was profound.

Building the skeleton first is more sophisticated than adding it afterwards because the builder has to plot the exact lines of his ship, designing it rather than building it by eye. The element of calculation is increased, the element of chance reduced. Then, too, a preassembled skeleton permits heavier planking to be used, as well as shorter planks—important where big trees are scarce. Also, ships with preconstructed frames can be built much bigger than those in which the frames are later added.

By the middle of the 15th century, Venice's merchant fleet alone included, besides galleys, about 300 ships, some able to carry more than 250 tons of cargo. But these marine monsters also had their

Bangladesh dinghis *thread the winding Turag River near Dacca. The crescent-shaped boats— low in the bow, elevated at the stern—measure up to 40 feet long and haul goods and passengers among the myriad waterways of the Ganges delta. Their frames, like those of ancient Egyptian craft, are added after the hull is built.*

drawbacks. Their heavy construction probably made them sluggish sailers. They were expensive to build and maintain and, with three masts, required large crews to handle their huge lateen sails.

Until the early 1300's, shipbuilding in northern and southern Europe was as distinct as oil and water. But then the two regions began to trade by sea. Mediterranean seamen noted the simplicity of rig and low operating costs of the northern cogs and hulks that brought Baltic grain and herring; northern seamen admired the size, strength, and performance of southern ships with their lateen sails. It was an opportunity for mutual borrowing.

By the middle 1400's, multimasted ships were combining square and lateen rigs, with square sails on the forward masts and a lateen on the mizzen. The lateen gave maneuverability and performance heading into the wind, and the square sails provided driving power running before the wind, in addition to ease of handling. The square rig had another advantage: Two or more sails could be carried on a mast, one above the other, increasing canvas area while at the same time dividing it into manageable units. So was born the square-rigged ship or bark, which would become the basic oceangoing ship.

The new combination rig was first used in the big Mediterranean cargo carriers known as carracks and in smaller coasting vessels, particularly the caravels of southwestern Spain and southern Portugal. Probably the ships that today bear the nearest resemblance to a 15th-century caravel are the *fragatas* that ply the Tagus River. These modest and elegant little vessels do not now venture far, but their ancestors sailed halfway around the world.

Across the Boundless Sea

All the seas of the world are one. They are all connected and, except for icebound regions near the Poles, can be navigated. For skilled mariners with a good stout ship and adequate equipment, no country with a seacoast is inaccessible. The unity of the sea, which we so easily take for granted, first made possible our interlocking world society. Yet this vital knowledge was acquired only in relatively modern times.

Five hundred years ago no one knew whether the land area of the world surrounded the sea, or the sea the land. Nor did they know which was larger. Intelligent people could argue that the land, designed by Providence to support human life, *must* be bigger than the sea, in which people could not live. And, they contended, the area and weight of land in the Southern Hemisphere *must* equal that in the Northern, or the earth could not remain upright. According to Ptolemy's geography, the most widely accepted in 15th-century Europe, a great continental landmass at the south end of Africa joined it with Asia, landlocking the Indian Ocean. Of the Pacific, Ptolemy had no knowledge, nor had any European.

Not everyone swallowed Ptolemy's ideas entirely. Other people believed that Europe, Asia, and Africa made up a vast island in an encircling Ocean Sea. But that sea might be too immense, too hot in the tropics, or too cold near the Poles to be sailed.

A revolution from surmise to knowledge, from a land-dominated to a sea-dominated world, occurred in the 50 years or so after 1470. Western Europeans had developed oceanworthy ships. Expeditions sailed farther and farther from known waters, their sights on the treasures of exotic kingdoms half a world away. That amazing half century is known as the Great Age of Discovery.

In bluff and beamy carracks, Iberian mariners of the 1500's plied newfound sea roads to ancient landfalls of the fabled East.

The unfathomed seas teemed with monsters to menace man and vessel. So said yarns as old as seafaring. So said sober reports. And in an age when men sailed off the charts into oceans known only in theory, all things were possible. Sailors in small ships had good reason to be afraid of sea creatures of monstrous size.

A serpent might writhe up to snatch a human snack from deck or rigging. Off western Africa, tentacles of a giant squid could entwine the masts of a ship and threaten to careen it. Men spared a briny baptism told the story, inspiring the engraving (opposite).

42

Our planet is round, like the sun, the moon, and other heavenly bodies. Despite what many of us were led to believe as children, this knowledge did not originate with Christopher Columbus. Astronomers and other scholars had deduced that the earth is a sphere more than a thousand years before the first Iberian caravels weighed for the far lands of Asia. By that time the theory was well accepted. The few remaining flat-earth fundamentalists were looked on as cranks by educated Europeans.

As for seamen, they had little use for theories; they had eyes. And as the sails of their vessels filled in the wind, they had only to gaze over the stern and see the land sink behind the distant waves. As the Portuguese poet Luiz Camões wrote in *The Lusiads,* which became the nation's epic:

Little by little was exiled our sight
From hills of our own land that lay behind. . . .
Until at length all vanished utterly,
And we saw nothing but the sky and sea.
Thus we went forth to break those oceans through,
Where none before had ever forced the way.

But knowing that the sea curved around the globe did not make sailors eager to risk their lives exploring beyond the waters they already knew. It was not that they lacked courage. To people living on the tag end of the Middle Ages, the unknown world was full of marvels and menace. Seamen have always liked a good story. A large body of legend had been passed along through generations of mariners. From Scandinavian tales came the kraken, a sea monster with

thrashing "spikes or shining horns, which rear themselves like masts."

Saint Brendan, the sixth-century Irish voyager, told of meeting a sea creature so big his monks took it for an island. They landed on it and built a fire to cook dinner. At last the beast felt the heat, shook them off, and moved the island to a new location.

Accounts of travels to distant lands had a wide circulation in the 15th century. They often mingled fact and fiction. Among the most popular were those by Sir John Mandeville, an armchair traveler who combed and rewrote the journals of others, mixing in lies with such color and conviction that people did not know where fact left off and embroidery took over. Across his pages moved marvelously shaped folk—some without heads, others with a single foot so huge they used it as an umbrella. He described a well whose waters cured diseases and bestowed perpetual youth, a pepper forest inhabited by serpents and venomous worms, and enough gold, gems, and other trappings of wealth to help people overcome

their fear of the unknown and go searching for them.

Europeans took the initiative in sea discovery not just because they had adequate ships but because they wanted such things as gold and spices from the outside world. Until farmers began to grow root crops that would keep through the winter, they ran out of feed for livestock before pastures greened in the spring. They had to slaughter most of their herds in autumn, and salt or pickle the meat so it would keep. They needed spices to preserve it and enhance—or disguise—the flavor.

Spices came from tropical countries, those exotic faraway lands of wonder. Pepper grew in India and the East Indies, cinnamon in Ceylon, ginger in China, nutmeg and mace in the East Indies, cloves —perhaps the most costly of all—in the Moluccas.

The rajas of the spice lands were wealthy merchants with markets in many countries. The chain of distribution linked many kinds of ships. Chinese junks collected spices around the East Indian islands and carried them to the Malayan port of Malacca. Dhows of Muslim traders transported them to the flourishing ports of India's Malabar coast—Cochin, Calicut, Cannanore, Goa—where merchant firms of Persia, Egypt, and southern Arabia had warehouses run by resident agents called factors. From Malabar, Muslim shippers again loaded the aromatic and pungent cargoes, clearing for Aden at the mouth of the Red Sea or Hormuz at the mouth of the Persian Gulf. The spices eventually reached the hands of Venetians, who shipped them through the Mediterranean for distribution in Europe.

Every dealer and ruler along the way took his cut. Spices in western Europe were extremely expensive.

It got worse after 1453 when the Turks took Constantinople, a key distribution point. The only remaining way to Europe was through Egypt. The Egyptians made the most of their monopoly. Dealers pushed up prices and the sultan raised his duties. The Venetian middlemen, though distressed by this turn of events, eventually went along with it and passed the higher prices on to the spice consumers.

There seemed no escape from these middlemen—unless a new sea route could be found to the Indian Ocean. Even then, paying for spices would remain a problem. European products were crude by Oriental standards. Buying spices required gold, and European kingdoms had little of that.

Much of the gold coined in Europe came from trade with Morocco. It arrived there by camel caravan via handsome market towns—Gao, Djénné, Timbuktu—strung along the Niger River in western Africa. Europeans did not know where the gold was found, but they hoped to reach its source by coasting West Africa, using caravels instead of camels. This was how the Great Age of Discovery evolved, from searches for African gold and an indirect route to the Levantine-held spices that the gold would buy. There was no thought at first of rounding Africa. But perhaps there was a shortcut to the Red Sea spice realm by way of one of the rivers rumored to border the desert on the south and east.

They could expect Muslim opposition; but they might also find allies. According to legend, in the little known region south of Egypt and east of the Nile was a powerful Christian domain ruled by a priest-king whose title was Prester John. Long isolated from the rest of Christendom by Islam, he

At the crossroads of two seas, Portugal set the stage for the Great Age of Discovery. Royal direction came from Prince Henry—"the Navigator" to historians, though he was not a mariner. In this 15th-century court painting a somberly clad figure presumed to represent Henry stands between Lisbon's patron Saint Vincent and the future King John II, with Alfonso V kneeling below. Tradition says that an ascetic Henry forsook palace life for seagirt Cape Saint Vincent (right), making the stopover for ships into a gathering place for navigators and astronomers. Henry planned and promoted voyages until his death in 1460, prodding his seamen past a psychological barrier, Africa's Cape Bojador, the "land's end" of old Arab tales.

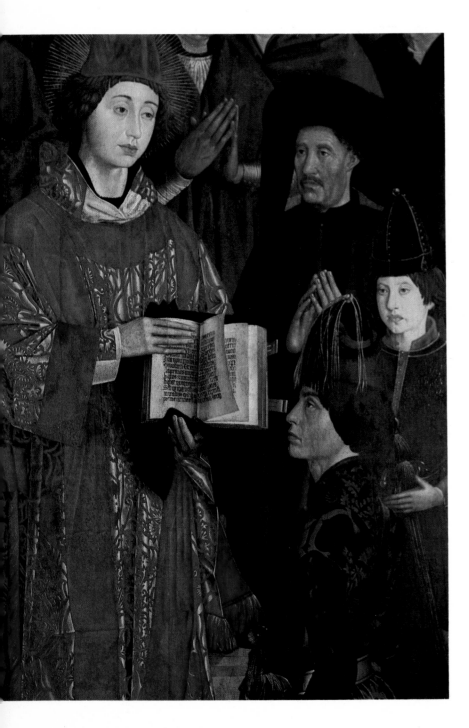

reigned from a gem-studded palace roofed with ebony, welcoming pilgrims to his emerald table supported by amethyst pedestals. If contact could be made with Prester John, a blow might be struck both for the Christian faith and for profit.

The initial pioneers were Portuguese. Theirs was a small, poor country, but of all in Europe it lay closest to the belt of steady easterly or northeasterly winds—later called the trade winds—that could carry a ship down the African coast with hardly a hand to sheets or braces the whole way.

Portugal had many seafarers, fishermen, and small coastal traders. It was the first European country whose royal family actively supported oversea exploration. At the helm between 1420 and 1460 stood the half-English younger son of John I, nicknamed Henry the Navigator, though he sailed no farther than neighboring Morocco. Prince Henry served as governor of the Algarve, the nation's southwestern province. Tradition links him with Cape Saint Vincent and its narrow promontory, Sagres Point. There is no real evidence to support the story of a formal school of astronomy and navigation there. Most of what we know of Prince Henry comes from court chronicles, full of the extravagant language of knightly make-believe. But the traditional picture of him gazing out to sea from his lonely headland still has power to fire the imagination.

Henry was a generous host and patron of seamen and cartographers. He financed expeditions, provided ships, placed gentlemen of his household in command of them. He demanded in return long voyages, detailed reports, captives to be converted or enslaved, and high returns. He gave energy and direction to a movement that might otherwise have dissipated itself in casual raiding.

In Portugal as elsewhere, commercial gain was a primary reason for exploration. The participation of princes and courtiers added other motives: crusading zeal, love of adventure, a longing for fame and reputation. These young noblemen often had to be enticed from the known excitement of raiding the harbors and ships of Morocco.

Sailors had to be lured past a place they called Cape Bojador. Beyond the dreaded "land's end" of old Arabian tales, ships would disappear, seamen would turn black from the sun or be devoured by savage creatures. Wary of the unfamiliar, sailors had other worries as well; when running before the northeast wind and with the Canary Current, they worried about getting back. Henry kept pushing them and eventually prevailed. But the cape's long sandspit was not passed until 1434. Smothered in spray and blown sand, it is dangerous enough, but 14 years for 800 nautical miles was slow going for a demanding prince.

The coast beyond the cape proved much like what came before, and the pace of exploration quickened: 1442, Cape Blanc and Arguin Island, site of the first European trading station in Africa; 1445, the green rounded hills of Cape Verde, and in its shelter Gorée Island, in later years the site of a big slave barracoon; 1446, the estuary of the Gambia; 1456, the Cape Verde Islands, some 300 miles offshore.

The Portuguese ships were caravels. Designed for coastal trade, they were well adapted for exploring near shore. They were of shallow draught, with an average length of 75 to 80 feet. They had two or

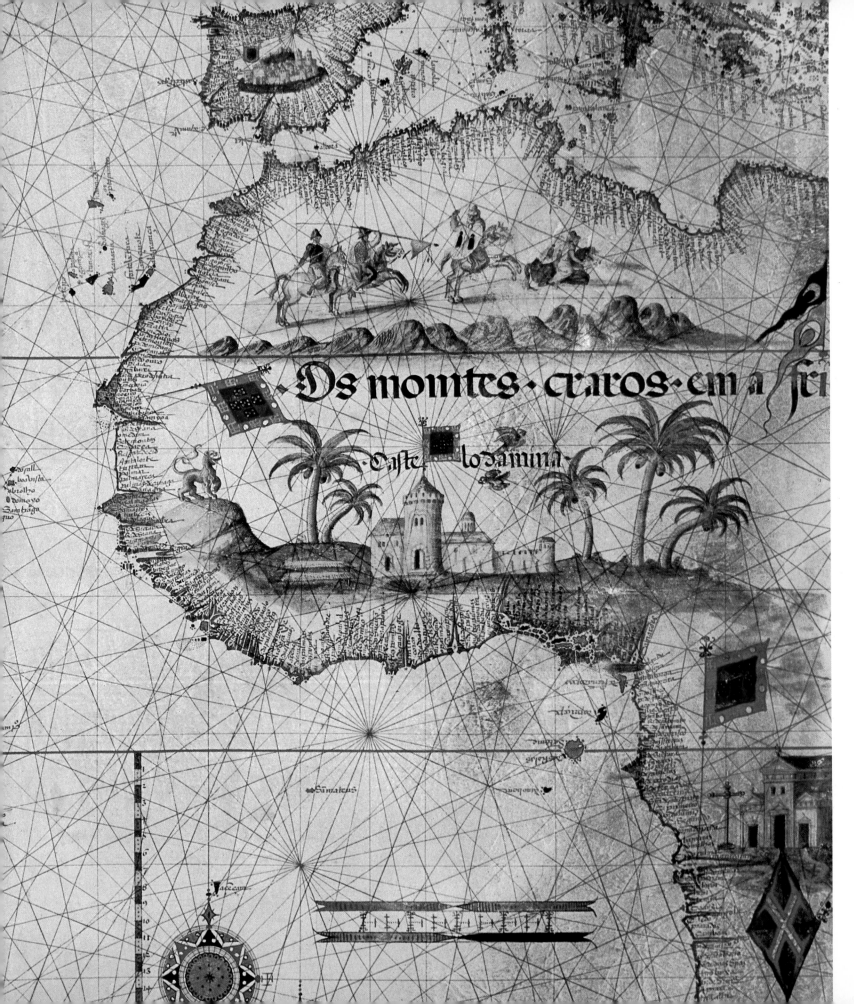

Os montes craros em a fri

Castelo damina

Iberian horsemen chase Moors across a 1558 map of Africa. With similar zeal the king's seamen crusaded for profit and power. From Portugal, ships brought dressed stone to Elmina to erect a fortified trading post, dealing in gold, slaves, and local pepper. Elmina Castle of today (opposite) dates from a period of Dutch domination.

three masts, lateen rigged in the first half of the 15th century; but later on they were often square rigged on the fore, and sometimes on the main.

The nimble little white-winged vessels amazed the West Africans. According to Azurara's chronicle of the voyages, they "marvelled much at the sight, for it seemeth they had never seen or heard speak of the like; and some of them supposed it to be a fish, while others thought it to be a phantom, and others again said it might be a bird." Four of them got into a dugout and paddled out far enough to see that there were men aboard the caravel. Then they fled.

The ships were carvel-built, Mediterranean fashion, but had a pronounced sheer, a straight keel, and a tall stem like some northern ships. The caravels had finer hull lines than most vessels at the time and were less bulky than earlier cogs and hulks. Caravels were fully decked. They had little or no superstructure forward. A humble poop contained the cabin accommodations and the steerage.

Even with a small crew of about 25, living conditions were cramped. There were no proper sleeping spaces besides the poop cabin and probably a few bunks in the steerage. Cables and gear took up even the tiny space beneath the forecastle deck. In good weather, most of the crew slept on deck; in foul weather they would crawl onto the cargo or ballast in the top of the hold. They built their cooking fires in an open sandbox, a system that worked only in fairly quiet, dry weather. In spite of the caravels' drawbacks, sailors handled them with confidence, and they proved to be tight and safe. Some mariners thought they were the most seaworthy craft of their age. They were also small enough to be replaceable,

48   a factor to be considered in any high-risk enterprise.

Between Cape Blanc and Cape Verde the desert ends. The coast is cut by rivers—Senegal, Gambia, Casamance, Geba. Cadamosto, a Venetian who traded with Prince Henry's license, described the people at the Senegal: "Beyond the river all men are very black, tall and big, their bodies well formed; and the whole country green, full of trees, and fertile: while on this side, the men are brownish, small, lean, ill-nourished, and small in stature: the country sterile." The brown-skinned Azanaghi of the desert "wear a handkerchief on the head with a flap . . . across the face, covering the mouth and part of the nose. For they say that the mouth is a brutish thing, that is always uttering wind and bad odours. . . . they never uncover it, except when they eat."

The Guinea rivers are so big that some geographers thought they might have a common source with the Nile, but efforts to explore them failed.

When Prince Henry died in 1460, Europeans had firsthand knowledge of the coast as far as Sierra Leone or thereabouts. The swampy coast ahead promised little reward, but exploring had become a habit and the voyages went on. The method was different. The Crown gave a trading lease to a private concern in return for an agreement to explore a hundred leagues of coast each year. The lessee kept the bargain. Eventually it paid off.

At Cape Three Points, reached in 1471, swamps give way to sandy, open coast with rocky headlands. This is the *Mina de Ouro,* the Gold Coast. The Portuguese, seeking trans-Saharan gold, had stumbled instead upon Ashanti gold. Hundreds of miles of forest cut off the Ashanti from the trading caravans.

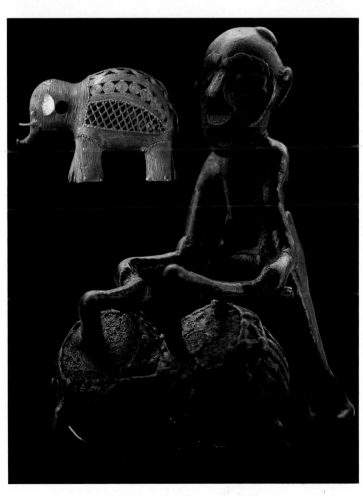

Gold caps a modern dignitary of the Ashanti people in Ghana and escalates the value of finely wrought art objects. Stylized lion (left) and elephant (inset, below) with intricate latticed flanks were cast in gold by the lost-wax process. Each stands less than four inches tall. The brass figure of an Ashanti drummer (below) was used as a counterweight for measuring gold dust. The desire to tap West Africa's gold supply at its source—along with the quest for spices—sent caravels of tiny Portugal inching boldly down the coast of the continent.

49

They accumulated most of their gold in lavish ornament. People of this golden kingdom would pay in gold for European textiles, beads, and hardware. As if that were not enough to excite the Portuguese, from Cape Three Points the coast trended steadily east and they wondered whether this might be southernmost Africa; whether they might not be able to sail on into the Indian Ocean and invest their Guinea gold in spices.

Fulfilling their contract, the caravels sailed on, past the lagoons of Yorubaland, past Lagos and its harbor, past the powerful kingdom of Benin, with its steady surplus of war captives to sell as slaves. East of Benin came the vast sodden sponge of the Niger Delta and the world's biggest mangrove swamp. Then the Cameroon River—River of Shrimps; the Bight of Biafra; the fertile islands of Fernando Po, Principe, and São Tomé; and the armpit of Africa.

Here, disappointment—the coast turns south. It trends south—though the Portuguese could not know it in 1474—for two thousand more miles.

At this point the Portuguese king had a choice to ponder. If the earth was round and the Ocean Sea stretched unbroken around the land, as theory said, it should be possible to reach eastern Asia by sailing west—if the distance was not too great. The leading academic cosmographer at that time, Paolo dal Pozzo Toscanelli in Florence, thought it was not.

King John II, who ascended the throne in 1481, decided to put his money on the eastward route. Like Prince Henry, John was dedicated to the Asian enterprise. He was also one of the ablest, most vigorous, most ruthless rulers of his day, with none of Prince Henry's patience. Maritime exploring moved

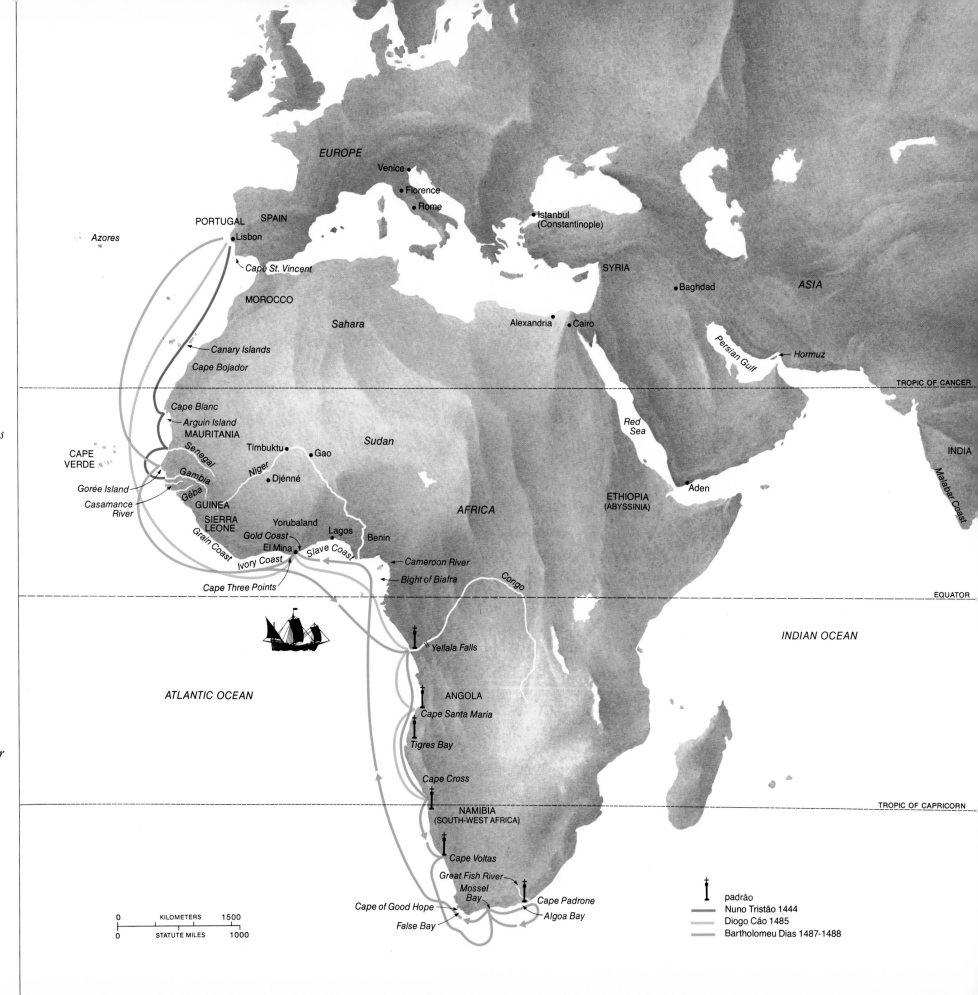

50   *Cape by cape, coastal waters fell under the bows of captains such as Nuno Tristão, one of Prince Henry's ablest. When John II became king in 1481, ships sailed past the Equator. Equipped to spread the flag and the faith, they carried* padrões, *carved stone columns topped by a cross, to erect on newly discovered points of land. Diogo Cão, in the middle 1480's planted markers at the mouth of the Congo, at Cape Santa Maria, and Cape Cross. Bartholomeu Dias, avoiding coastal hazards, swung into the open sea for a favoring wind. Storms later blew him beyond Africa's southern tip. He raised a pillar on a landfall to be called Cape Padrone. Several* padrões, *intact or in pieces, still survive. Acting on royal orders, explorers kept meticulous notes on distance and compass bearings from point to point. They recorded data on the prevailing winds, tides, anchorages, currents, hazards to navigation—compiling practical manuals of discovery for their countrymen to follow.*

EUROPE

Venice
Florence
Rome
Istanbul (Constantinople)

SYRIA

Baghdad
ASIA

PORTUGAL   SPAIN
Lisbon

Azores

Cape St. Vincent

MOROCCO

Sahara

Alexandria
Cairo

Canary Islands

Persian Gulf
Hormuz

Cape Bojador

TROPIC OF CANCER

Cape Blanc

Arguin Island

MAURITANIA

Red Sea

INDIA

Timbuktu
Gao

Sudan

CAPE VERDE

Senegal

Niger
Djénné

Gambia

Gorée Island

Géba

GUINEA

Casamance River

Aden

ETHIOPIA (ABYSSINIA)

SIERRA LEONE

Yorubaland

AFRICA

Malabar Coast

Gold Coast
Lagos
El Mina
Benin

Grain Coast

Slave Coast

Ivory Coast

Cameroon River

Cape Three Points

Bight of Biafra

Congo

EQUATOR

INDIAN OCEAN

Yellala Falls

ATLANTIC OCEAN

ANGOLA

Cape Santa Maria

Tigres Bay

Cape Cross

TROPIC OF CAPRICORN

NAMIBIA (SOUTH-WEST AFRICA)

Cape Voltas

Great Fish River

Mossel Bay

Cape of Good Hope

Cape Padrone

Algoa Bay

False Bay

| 0 | KILOMETERS | 1500 |
| 0 | STATUTE MILES | 1000 |

padrão
Nuno Tristão 1444
Diogo Cão 1485
Bartholomeu Dias 1487-1488

OVERLEAF: *Turning point of a continent, Africa's southern tip was first rounded in 1488, marking a breakthrough in sea discovery. Here where waters of the Atlantic and Indian oceans mingle, the Cape of Good Hope crooks a bony finger toward the spice-rich Indies.*

An ivory saltcellar of the early 1500's conveys an African's impression of a Portuguese ship captain. Side arms at the ready, he wears a sailing vessel complete with crow's nest atop his head. From Benin, part of present-day Nigeria, the statue measures nearly a foot high.

forward with explosive speed and new efficiency. He sent expeditions south of the Equator. The captains were professionals. The caravels, equipped for exploring, carried *padrões,* stone columns, to set up on newly discovered headlands.

On two voyages from 1482 to 1485 Diogo Cão set up his first padrão at the mouth of the Congo and his most distant on Cape Cross just north of Walvis Bay. He explored 1,450 miles of unknown tropical coast, sailing nearly to the Tropic of Capricorn.

The increasing length of the African voyages took explorers beyond known sources of provisions. Bartholomeu Dias on his expedition in 1487 began the practice of taking along a storeship. In a sheltered anchorage on the Angola coast he transferred provisions to his two caravels and left the storeship behind pending his return. With supplies renewed, the caravels pressed on southward, beating against wind and current until, about Cape Voltas, they stood out from the coast to seek a better wind. After many days, they picked up the prevailing westerly wind, which bore them toward the coast. They fell in with the land near Mossel Bay—the first Europeans to double the tip of Africa, but without seeing it.

Dias set up his farthest padrão east of Algoa Bay, on the headland later known as Cape Padrone. The surf rolling in to that exposed coast from the southeast must have made it difficult to land so heavy and awkward an object, but landed it was.

Here Dias's people—fighting wind, current, and surf along a coast that appeared endless—began demanding that the fleet turn back. This was not mutiny. Seamen of that day expected a voice in major decisions. Most captains did not belong to a so-

cial class bred to command, and they rarely ventured to override the majority will when far from home.

The ships turned at the mouth of the Great Fish River, from seaward an obvious gap in the coastline. After rains a wash of red mud streams away to the southwest, marking a forceful current. East of the river mouth the water is clear and the current warm. Dias must have realized he was on the doorstep of the Indian Ocean. Others would get the credit for his endeavor. He wept like a child, it was said, sailing back past that lonely pillar on Cape Padrone.

The southern tip of Africa with its bays, banks, headlands, and fierce currents is always dangerous to shipping. In the southern summer, the season when Dias was off the coast, winds blow from the southeast. A sailing ship coming from the west, if it rounds the Cape of Good Hope too close to shore, risks getting embayed in False Bay. Dias, by good luck, had stood far enough south to avoid the coastal dangers. He did not merely discover the Cape of Good Hope; he established a cardinal rule for sailing ships passing from the Atlantic to the Indian Ocean: Give the Cape of Good Hope a wide berth.

Returning, Dias first sighted the towering cliff at the end of the Cape Peninsula. The weather was so rough he called the place Cabo Tormentoso, Stormy Cape. After Dias's return, John II gave it the evocative and lasting name Cape of Good Hope.

For some nine years it would be a cape of hope deferred. Dias had disproved one of Ptolemy's tenets by finding a place where waters of the Atlantic and Indian oceans joined. But he had sailed 6,000 miles to reach it, a longer, harder struggle than the armchair geographers had dreamed of. To pioneer a sea

road across the Indian Ocean to India would require even greater feats of seamanship.

It would take, moreover, a commercial embassy, supplied with goods for trade and paraphernalia for ceremony, led by a man of public standing. It would take a bigger fleet of bigger ships—small caravels would not do—careful planning of routes and times, and heavy capital investment. Portugal was still a small, poor country; the king was ailing. In any event, the long-awaited fleet to India was dispatched not by John II but by his more flamboyant successor, Manuel the Fortunate. Its primary mission was to set up trading relations with rulers of the parts of India that exported spices.

In charge of the fleet was Vasco da Gama, a gentleman of the king's household. He sailed from Lisbon in July 1497. Da Gama had the training in arms and manners then customary for a courtier. Though not a professional seaman, he had somehow learned mathematics and navigation. He would prove an outstanding commander.

He also had a fierce temper and lacked tact and imagination in dealing with strangers. On occasion he could be savagely ruthless; for example, in "questioning" prisoners he loosened their tongues by dropping boiling oil on their bodies. In another instance he cut off the ears and hands of uncooperative captives. He made many mistakes ashore, but few at sea. The expedition, though not primarily for exploration, added much to nautical knowledge.

Manuel spared no trouble or expense in preparing the fleet. Two of the ships, *São Gabriel* and *São Rafael,* were built especially for the journey, under the guidance of Dias. They were square-rigged *naos,*

larger and stronger than caravels. Each of them carried about 20 small forged guns which fired stone balls weighing less than a pound. This armament was light, by the standards of European fighting ships of the time, and was suitable only for defense and ceremonial salutes; but in the Indian Ocean shipborne artillery was almost unknown. It proved formidable enough to be impressive.

The expedition also needed a caravel to maneuver close to shore when reconnaissance was needed. She was named *Berrio.* There was also a storeship whose name was not recorded. She carried the extra provisions and gear needed for so long a voyage, but was not brought back home. On the evidence of contemporaries, "all the supplies which seemed to be requisite were provided in great abundance"—presumably the best and most up-to-date available.

Men were selected as carefully. Of a complement between 140 and 170, the names of about 40 are known. Captains, pilots, and pursers were men of experience. Some had sailed with Bartholomeu Dias. Diogo Dias, his brother, was purser in the *São Gabriel.* Besides officers, tradesmen, and seamen, the fleet carried soldiers, musicians, priests, Arabic interpreters, and *degredados,* convicts. It was useful to have along a few expendable outcasts to be "adventured on land" in high-risk jobs such as spying. Some did survive, however. One, put ashore by da Gama in East Africa, made his way to India and eventually became commandant of the fort at Goa.

The fleet ran down the coast of Morocco and through the Canary Channel in company with Dias, who was taking a caravel to Elmina. They paused in the Cape Verde Islands for minor repairs and to top

up the provisions. Then away southeast. About a hundred miles off Sierra Leone, they parted company, with da Gama altering course to head west-southwest into the open sea.

The plan to sail south in the open Atlantic rather than struggle down the coast as Dias had done was the most important navigational decision of the voyage, and must have been worked out with Dias beforehand. Sierra Leone, at that time of year, was the last point at which da Gama could be confident of escaping into the open Atlantic. The long board to the southwest let him make the best use of the southeast trade wind in the central Atlantic, to cross the doldrums, the equatorial belt of calms, at its narrowest point. By luck and judgment, da Gama followed almost a textbook course, the one followed by hundreds of Indiamen in the next three centuries and still recommended for sailing ships today.

Da Gama, after crossing the Equator, began to feel the strong steady pressure of the southeast trade wind. He could then alter course to the southwest, sailing close to the wind. When they got within several hundred miles of Brazil, he would find the wind backing, so he could steer more directly south. At about 30° to 35°S he would pass beyond the trade wind and, with only a rough idea of how far east he had to sail, would probably try to steer due east along the latitude of the Cape of Good Hope.

He made land at Saint Helena Bay, about a hundred miles north of the cape, rounded the cape itself after a long board to seaward, and reached Mossel Bay in late November. His people had been continuously at sea for three months. Stores were redistributed and the storeship broken up.

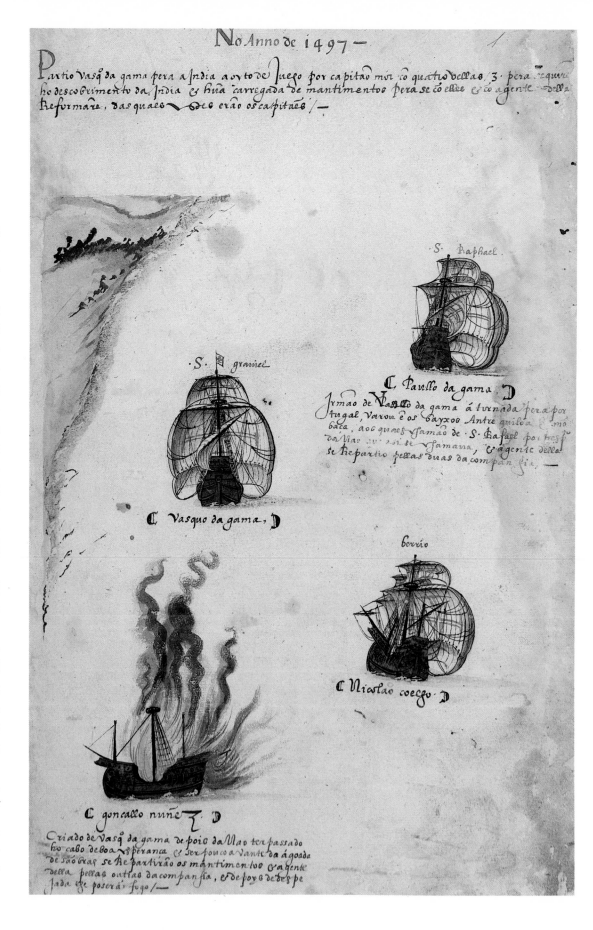

Two custom-made ships headed the fleet for Vasco da Gama's climactic expedition to India. Called naos, *they were stouter than the nimble caravels and had better quarters for the men. The flagship* São Gabriel *and the* São Rafael *are at upper left and upper right in this page from a rare manuscript.*

Flames engulf the unnamed supply ship, burned at Mossel Bay after she had served her purpose. The caravel Berrio, *used for reconnaissance work near shore, is incorrectly shown here as a square-rigger.*

In a two-year voyage, more than half of da Gama's company died, most of them from scurvy, the seaman's great scourge. From the São Rafael, *abandoned for lack of hands, da Gama saved the figurehead (opposite). It became a family heirloom and a memorial to Vasco's brother Paulo, who had captained that ship and died at the end of the voyage.*

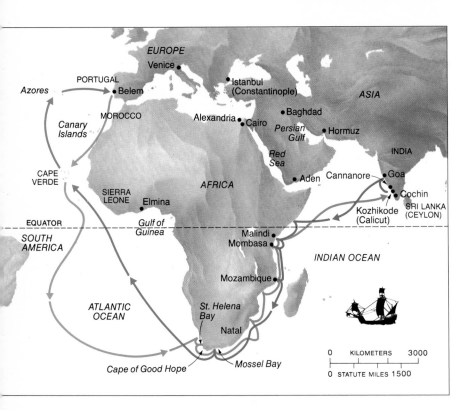

local ruler who welcomed an alliance. More immediately important, in Malindi they found a pilot—probably a Gujarati—to navigate them to Calicut in southwest India. Whoever the man was, he knew his business. Da Gama's rapid crossing of the Indian Ocean—2,300 miles in 27 days—was due mainly to his experience and skill. The chronicles allude to thunder and rainstorms. It seems likely that the southwest monsoon set in and pushed them along. Their real difficulties began in Calicut.

Da Gama's trade goods were unsuitable for India. He offered such presents as striped cloth and washbasins when the ruler wanted gold. The local king, though civil, did not wish to cross the resident Arab merchants by being overly helpful. Da Gama, at great trouble and expense, bought a small quantity of pepper and cinnamon and cleared for home.

The return crossing of the Indian Ocean, without a local pilot, was made at a bad time of year. There were storms, headwinds, sickness. The *São Rafael* had to be abandoned and burned for lack of hands. But once round the cape, da Gama was in more familiar waters and again made the best use of his winds. He arrived home in September 1499. In a two-year voyage, he had spent nearly 500 days at sea and lost more than half his men, chiefly from scurvy.

He was well rewarded for his accomplishment. In thanksgiving, King Manuel built the great church and monastery of the Jeronimos at Belem. Da Gama and his predecessors had blazed a sea road from Portugal to India. But merely to sail there was not enough. If the Portuguese meant to break into the spice trade of the Indian Ocean, since their goods were unwanted, they would have to use guns.

Christmas found the remaining ships off the coast in the agreeable country they named Natal. After weeks along the coast they reached Mozambique. They were no longer sailing an empty ocean, anchoring for wood and water in lonely bays, dealing with half-naked people who would barter oxen or ivory for glass beads. Instead, they now sailed up a busy coast, aided by local pilots—hired or kidnapped—putting into bustling harbors where merchants wore fine linen or silk clothes, spoke Arabic, used coined money, and traded in luxury goods. To most of these people the Portuguese were unwelcome as unbelievers and as commercial interlopers. Not until they got to Malindi, north of Mombasa, did they find a

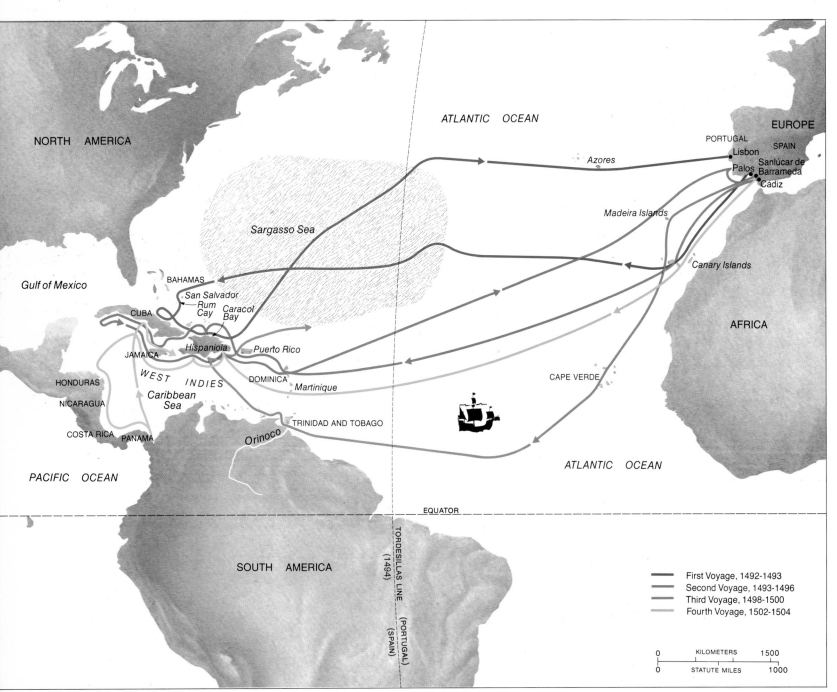

First Voyage, 1492-1493
Second Voyage, 1493-1496
Third Voyage, 1498-1500
Fourth Voyage, 1502-1504

May 12, 1492—"I left the city of Granada . . . and came to the town of Palos, which is a seaport; where I equipped three vessels . . . and departed from that port, well supplied with provisions and with many sailors, on the 3d day of August . . . taking the route to the islands of Canaria . . . that I might thence take my departure for navigating until I should arrive at the Indies."

* * * * *

The three vessels were the caravels *Niña* and *Pinta* and the ship *Santa María.* The voyager, Christopher Columbus. It was the sixth day of September when he took leave of the port of Gomera in the Canary Islands and shaped a course due west—for Asia. A week later sailors on the *Niña* reported seeing "a tern and a boatswain bird," and two days later, "many tufts of grass which were very green, and appeared to have been quite recently torn from the land."

Daily they scanned the horizon. Land must be imminent from the signs of it: floating grass and herbs, a clump of weeds with a live crab clinging to it, birds, drizzling rain without wind, a whale that keeps "near the shore." But no land.

The immense barrier of the American continents, spanning 122 degrees of latitude, was probably not suspected by Europeans in 1492, certainly not by Columbus. His voyage lacked any real precedent. His proposals were: to sail west to "discover and acquire . . . Islands and Mainland in the Ocean Sea." Exactly which ones we do not know. Antillia? Japan? China? the Golden Chersonese?

Columbus's geographical reasoning was based on a mishmash of cosmographical theory, travel literature, and inner conviction. In 1484, he had sought

Raising a cross on Hispaniola, Columbus takes possession for Ferdinand and Isabella of Spain "that your Highnesses hold this land for your own." As pictured by Theodore de Bry (below), Indians bring tribute. As recorded in Columbus's journal for December 12, 1492, they came upon a crowd of unclad natives, who fled. Sailors took chase, caught one lovely maid wearing only a gold nose plug, and took her aboard ship. They treated her courteously, gave her bells, beads, and finery, and freed her on the beach as a walking advertisement. After she had circulated among her friends, the sailors were made welcome.

Moonlit landfall: Pale cliffs of San Salvador spread a New World welcome mat. For weeks, homesick, anxious crews of the flagship Santa María, *the* Niña, *and* Pinta *watched the horizon of an unknown sea. Hopes rise with the gulfweed of the Sargasso Sea and the birds thought to portend land, fall when it fails to appear—until two hours past midnight on that jubilant October 12. Within weeks the newcomers have met "Indians" who sleep in suspended baglike nets of cotton—hammocks, to become standard sea beds for sailors. And who set fire to the end of a tight roll of dried weed leaves and inhale the smoke—tobacco.*

backing for his enterprise from Portugal's King John II. Rejected, he had spent the next seven years trying to interest one government after another in the project until at last he got the help of Spain's Ferdinand and Isabella. He was furnished the vessels that happened to be available. At the time a ship's size was usually reckoned by the number of tuns, or casks, of wine it could stow. By this ancient measure, the caravels were of about 60 tuns, the *Santa María,* perhaps around 100.

Columbus had a basic knowledge of hydrography and had sailed in Genoese and Portuguese ships, though not as commander. The voyage was to reveal him as a careful and practical navigator, but not up-to-date in his knowledge of instruments.

Apart from its terrifying distance out of sight of land, the outward passage was prosperous. Health was good. The trade winds are not always reliable so far north, and September is a season for hurricanes: Columbus was lucky to have fair winds.

To judge from his journal, Columbus expected to sight land earlier than he did and perhaps suspected that the fleet had missed its first objective. Mutinous mutterings arose and demands that they turn back. Just in time, 33 days out, they sighted San Salvador, among the outer cays of the Bahamas.

The island was inhabited. Two branches of humanity, separated for millennia, met that day by the bold and skillful use of the sea. The islanders were primitive, naked, "poor in everything," but they had canoes. After a fashion, they too made bold and skillful use of the sea. In his exploration Columbus—when he was able to interpret their signs—could get from the inhabitants of each island a course

for the next and an idea of what it held. Sometimes, even, a native pilot guided him.

Columbus thought his landfall was some Asian island near Japan which, by his calculations, lay 3,000 miles west of Europe. He apparently got this figure by mixing Marco Polo's overestimates of the breadth of Asia and Japan's distance from it with Ptolemy's underestimate of the girth of the globe.

He began to scout around for Japan. The expedition explored Santa María de la Concepción, which later and less pious sailors renamed Rum Cay; the northeast coast of Cuba; and part of the north coast of Hispaniola, modern Haiti and the Dominican Republic. Columbus had aboard a mariner's astrolabe, a Portuguese invention, but he knew nothing of sunsights. His polestar observations, made with a wooden quadrant, were sometimes wildly off.

On the night of November 2, 1492, off Cuba, he took a quadrant reading and recorded the latitude as 42°N, an error of some 21 degrees—or more than a thousand miles. Nineteen days later in a nearby area he took another reading: 42°N. He knew something was wrong. That was the latitude of northern Spain, and the climate here was far too balmy—like April in Andalusia—to lie in the same latitude. The quadrant must be defective. He put it back in the box, so to speak, until he could get it "repaired."

In cases of conflict with the instruments, he sensibly acted on his dead reckoning—which had an uncanny accuracy. He carried a compass rose in his head. He had been planning and preparing himself for many years for this enterprise of the Indies. As the introduction to his journal declared: "I resolved to describe each night what passed in the day. . . . to construct a new chart for navigating, on which I shall delineate all the sea and lands of the Ocean in their proper positions under their bearings. . . . I shall forget sleep, and shall work at the business of navigation, that so the service may be performed."

Faithfully he worked at carrying out the promises. But no one can forget sleep entirely. Late on Christmas Eve, off the coast of Hispaniola, fatigue overtook him, and he retired to his cabin. The sea was glassy calm. The man at the helm decided to nap. He turned the tiller over to a boy. The *Santa María* drifted onto a reef in Caracol Bay, and Columbus lost his flagship.

After the initial shock wore off, he told himself the hand of God was in the mishap: This was the place to start a settlement. From *Santa María's* timbers they erected a stockade. When Columbus sailed for home in the *Niña,* he left about 40 men behind with instructions to build houses and search for gold mines. None was to survive the year.

On arrival in Spain he found himself a national hero. Ferdinand and Isabella accepted his own estimation of his discoveries, conveyed in a letter, and honored all their promises. Their reply was addressed to: Don Cristóbal Colón, Admiral of the Ocean Sea, Viceroy and Governor of the Islands that he hath discovered in the Indies. In garments appropriate to his noble station, Don Cristóbal headed a festive cavalcade: one or two of his officers, some newly hired servants, Indians in their ornaments carrying bright parrots in cages. Across the plains of Andalusia, acclaimed at every village, he proceeded to Barcelona, where he was received by the sovereigns. He stayed at court several weeks.

Within six months the Admiral of the Ocean Sea was dispatched in command of a fleet of 17 ships. He was to establish a Spanish colony in Hispaniola and, using it as a base, to journey on to China and India.

The Spanish rulers moved quickly to secure the pope's backing for their title to Columbus's discoveries and to the westward route to Asia. A serious international quarrel might have developed. But Portugal's John II, geographically better informed, preferred to believe that Columbus had found just another group of Atlantic islands. John's chief concern was to make sure that Spanish expeditions would not trespass on his African preserves. The two sides agreed, in the Treaty of Tordesillas of 1494, on a line of demarcation running north and south through the Atlantic, the Portuguese having rights of exploration to the east, the Spaniards to the west.

Columbus on his second voyage spent almost three years exploring the West Indian islands. He found no Japan, no spices, no Cathay, no India. As a colonial governor he was a failure. When he returned to Spain in 1496 the colony was in tumult, with both the settlers and the natives in revolt.

Fitted out for a third voyage, he discovered the island of Trinidad and the western mouths of the Orinoco. But trouble flared anew in Hispaniola, and the king appointed another governor. The new man sent Columbus home in irons. Spain financed one more voyage. It revealed stretches of coast in Honduras, Costa Rica, Nicaragua, and Panama. But by this time Isabella was dead and Ferdinand was tired of pouring money into Columbus's ventures. He refused to trust him or use his services again. In 1506 the discoverer died, disgruntled but still wealthy.

Castled hills of a Moroccan port look down on the comings and goings of ships that supplied mainland Europe with goods from distant outposts of trade. Overcoming resistance of the local ruler, crews of high-castled trading galleons in this fanciful de Bry engraving managed to load a full cargo and return to Lisbon.

C: de Gel

What did Columbus add to knowledge of the sea? Chiefly, he set bounds to the Atlantic: as little as three weeks of sailing from one side to the other. Whether the ocean's western edge was the coast of a newfound continent or a remote and primitive back-side of Asia remained uncertain. Both theories had adherents; both appeared on contemporary maps. Clearly, to reach the spice- and silk-producing parts of Asia, ships would have to escape from the Atlantic. Dias had found a southeast passage, which da Gama used, and the Portuguese had raced to the spicery, armed and ready to do business.

The Spaniards had made no progress toward the spicery by the western route. They were hemmed in by the Tordesillas line, with Brazil bulging east of it, and by the continuous shore of the Caribbean.

In 1513 Vasco Núñez de Balboa had crossed the Isthmus of Panama and sighted the Pacific Ocean, then called the South Sea or the "Other Sea." The idea of the Americas as continents, with a vast ocean beyond, was far from being universally accepted. Balboa's Other Sea might plausibly be considered an eastern gulf of the Indian Ocean, with the spicery lying within a few weeks' sailing. This interpretation aroused lively interest in Spain.

How could they get ships into that new sea? One way was by building the ships on its coast. Another, more attractive way was suggested to the Spanish government by a Portuguese defector.

Ferdinand Magellan was a soldier of fortune who went out to India in 1505. In the East he had made it his business to gather information about the spice-rich Moluccas, including their latitude. Having tried and failed to make a satisfactory deal with his

64

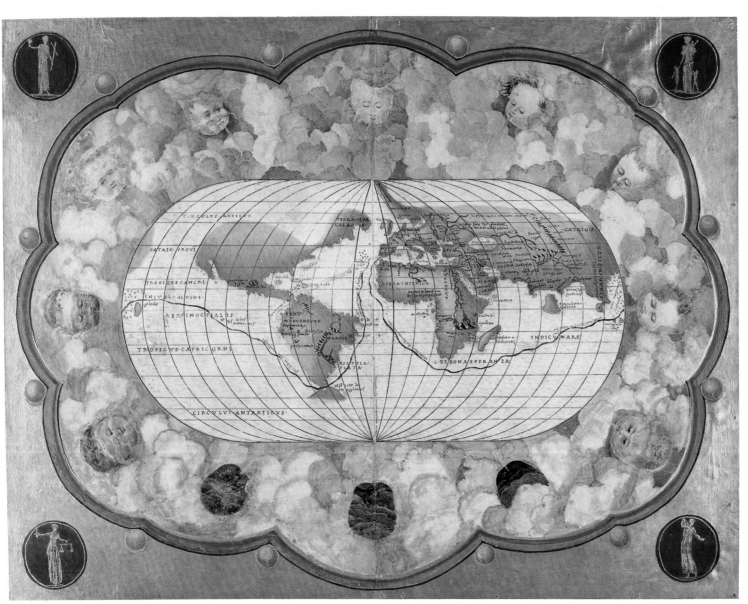

own government, he decided to offer his services and his valuable information to Spain. Luckily, he arrived in Seville just as Spain came under a new king, a hardheaded, glory-seeking youth, Charles I.

Magellan apparently offered to lead a Spanish fleet to the Moluccas or similar spice islands by a route wholly within the Spanish hemisphere of exploration. Maps kept in the Portuguese royal archives, he claimed, showed a strait linking the Atlantic with the South Sea. The passage lay south of the bulge of Brazil and west of the Tordesillas line. It would be a Spanish expedition, by an all-Spanish route. King Charles I's government was easily persuaded; the plan was agreed; angry protests by the Portuguese ambassador were rejected; and in 1519 the fleet was ready to set sail.

Magellan's five vessels, all merchantmen, were bought on the open market at Cadiz. We do not know their exact build, rig, or dimensions. The Portuguese consul reported to his royal master—wishfully, no doubt—that they were rotten and unsafe; but their performance would give him the lie.

The navigational equipment lacked new or experimental devices, but it included 23 charts, mostly of recent Portuguese origin. Heavy armament indicated that fighting was expected. It included 72 mounted guns and a generous supply of small arms, crossbows, pikes, and body armor. Trade goods also were amply provided. Items for primitive barter included red caps, brass bracelets, 1,000 mirrors, and 20,000 hawkbells. There were also articles intended for trade in the sophisticated East: bolts of silk, linen, and woolen cloth, and a ton of quicksilver. The company numbered about 270. Some of the officers,

Magellan's Globe-circling *Victoria*

"At last, when it pleased Heaven, on Saturday the 6th of September of the year 1522, we entered the bay of San Lucar. . . . the 8th of September, we cast anchor near the mole of Seville, and discharged all the artillery." Alone now, *Victoria* had reason for the celebration. She had sailed around the world—the first vessel in history to do so. Fourth in size of Magellan's five ships, *Victoria* had a capacity of about 85 tuns, or casks, that held wine or drinking water. Food for her company of 45 had crammed the hold: flour, ship's biscuit, beans, chick-peas, rice, dried fish and pork, vinegar, sugar, strings of garlic, dried fruit, nuts, cheeses. All this—and more—proved insufficient. Chandlers had cheated; the voyage took far longer than expected. Stowaway rats that had pilfered the stores from the hold became meat for famished crewmen. Cordwood fueled a portable galley used on deck, water bucket at hand. Navigating an uncharted sea with instruments stored in the binnacle, Magellan's captains missed habitable islands between South America's tip and Guam. Ships of discovery needed to be self-sufficient, carrying spare parts—spars, sail canvas, cordage—and tools and skilled men to use them. They had to foresee contingencies, stowing goods for peaceful trade, guns and hand weapons for unpeaceful encounters. The circumnavigation of the globe rounded out the most significant half century of sea discovery. But bankers who backed it preferred profits to new knowledge. Seaworn *Victoria,* patched up, was again pressed into service. She sank with all hands in mid-Atlantic.

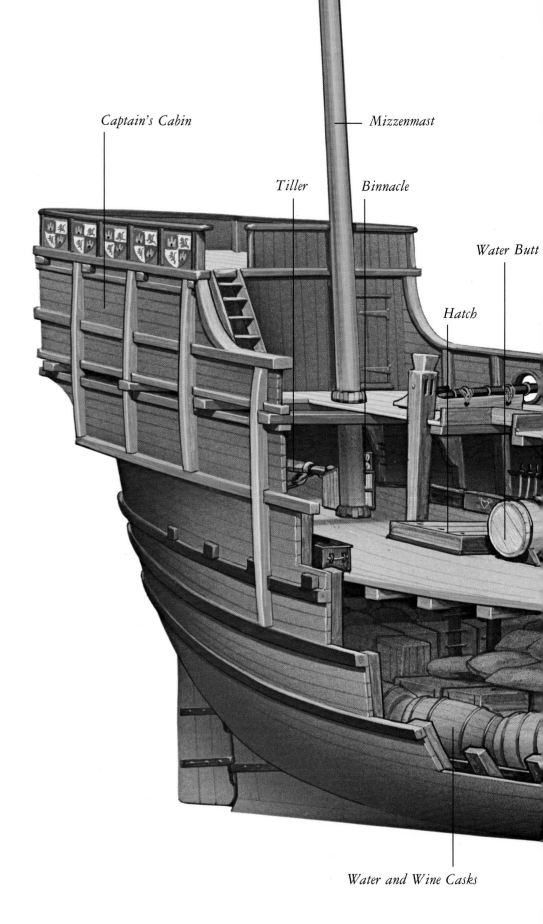

Captain's Cabin

Mizzenmast

Tiller

Binnacle

Water Butt

Hatch

Water and Wine Casks

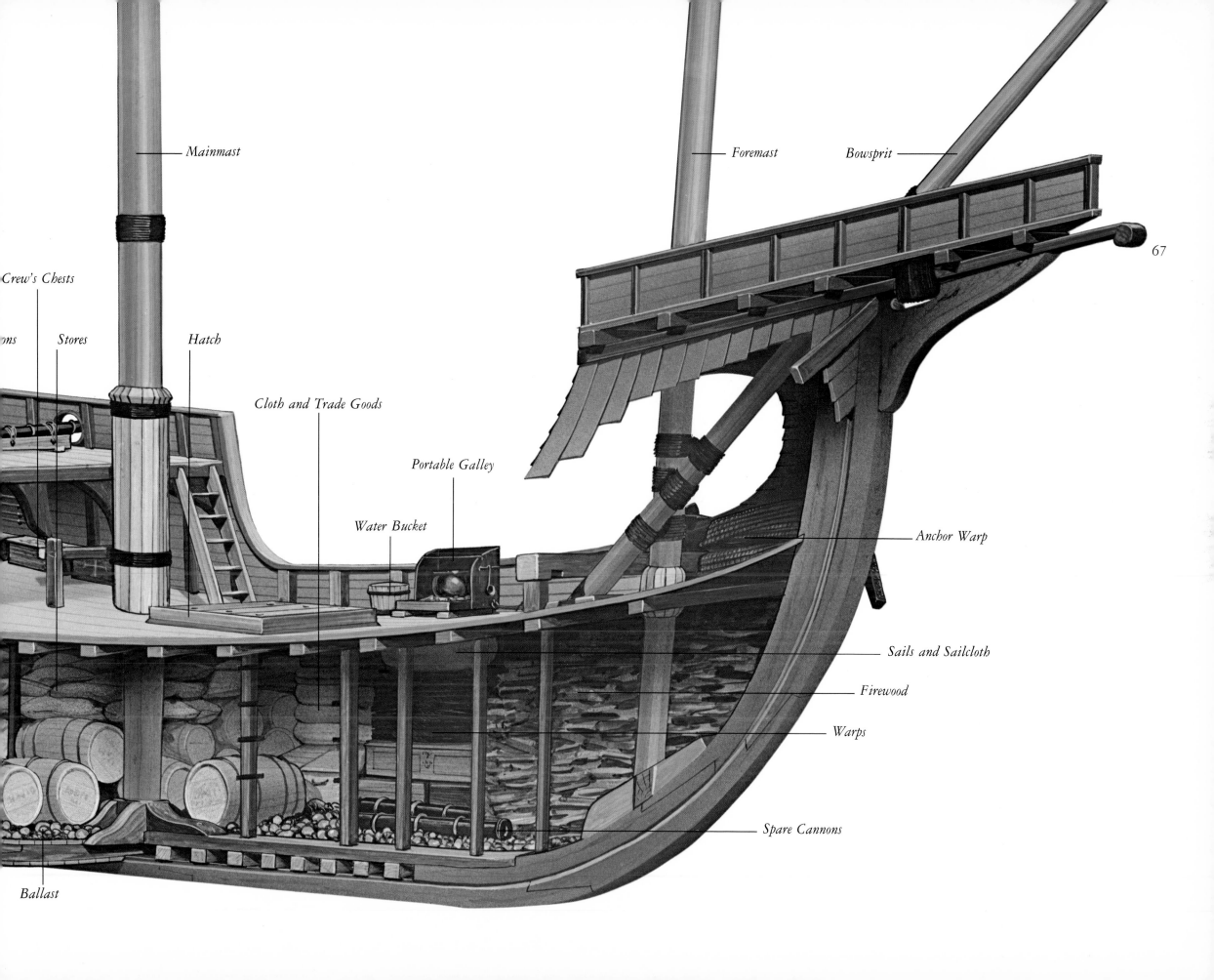

Mainmast

Foremast

Bowsprit

67

Crew's Chests

ons

Stores

Hatch

Cloth and Trade Goods

Portable Galley

Water Bucket

Anchor Warp

Sails and Sailcloth

Firewood

Warps

Spare Cannons

Ballast

Sailors,
Saints, and Demons
Of the Deep

Squalls and fierce head winds kept the fleet from advancing. Gargantuan waves washed over the bows. Magellan hung four lights on the poop of the *Trinidad:* Strike sail! Better to ride out the tempests than broach to and risk capsizing. These were shark-infested waters.

One black night during the storm, a fiery glow appeared at the top of the mainmast and lingered there. To the sailors, Saint Elmo's fire signaled a saint's protection. The light, said Pigafetta, "comforted us greatly, for we were in tears, only expecting the hour of perishing. . . . and as many times as that light . . . shows itself and descends upon a vessel which is in a storm at sea, that vessel never is lost. Immediately that this light had departed the sea grew calmer, and then, we saw divers sorts of birds."

Saint Elmo's fire, a crackling, sometimes moving, ball of light is a luminous discharge caused by ionization of positive and negative electrical particles. The phenomenon, which often occurs when storm fronts collide, has intrigued and awed mariners since the earliest times. Jason and the Argonauts, mythological Greek heroes, saw it as an omen of success. So did ancient Roman sailors. Both Greeks and Romans viewed the mysterious lights as a manifestation of the twin deities Castor and Pollux, who had powers over wind and wave.

Medieval mariners attributed it to Erasmus, patron saint of Mediterranean sailors, whose name survives as Saint Elmo. Bad luck usually followed if the fire descended from the masts, good luck if it rose, and better if multiple lights appeared, a sign that more than one saint was standing by.

A precarious and lonely life at best, seafaring through the ages has amassed much ritual, legend, myth, and superstition—

ways of dealing with the helplessness men felt when they confronted the awesome forces of the sea. Early mariners, only a plank from eternity, saw spirits at every turn—in the winds, clouds, moon, stars, the sea itself. Whirlpools, waterspouts, and wave-gouged rocks were seen as the abode of demons or dragons that had to be appeased if ships were to go their way unharmed.

Raising a wind when the sails went limp was a recurrent challenge. One method was to whistle—but not so vigorously as to stir up a gale. To assure a strong start for a journey, a captain could strike a bargain with a witch or sorcerer adept at the art of windraising. Friday was not an auspicious day to embark. Sunday was much luckier.

The vessel's contents and occupants could attract good luck or ill. Women on a ship were often thought to portend trouble. A corpse or a coffin at sea had a bad effect on the weather. Some animals were unlucky. Hares, linked to witches and devils, were not welcome aboard. Cats were often taken to sea but their antics were watched like a barometer. If a ship's cat sneezed, licked its paws, washed only one ear, frisked about the deck, drowned, or disappeared, it was an omen of storm—or worse.

In times of dire peril, seamen in the Great Age of Discovery usually turned to their religion for succor. They often vowed a pilgrimage upon safe return to land. Severe storms beset Columbus as he recrossed the Atlantic on his first New World voyage. He put beans in a cap, and all on board drew lots to decide who would undertake a pilgrimage if they survived. The storms continued. A second pilgrimage was promised, and lots drawn again. And yet a third. Columbus—luckier as a sailor than as a gambler—drew the marked bean two times out of three.

including all of the navigators, were Portuguese, presumably selected by Magellan; but Juan de Cartagena, second-in-command, and most of the seamen were Spaniards. Doubts about the exact chain of authority were to cause strife, especially since Magellan never fully revealed his intentions to his officers. It was usual on long, dangerous voyages to submit important decisions to a council of officers, sometimes to a whole ship's company. But Magellan—hard-boiled, taciturn, a foreigner in command of touchy Spaniards—did not confide, and the Spaniards tended from the outset to distrust him.

South of Brazil the fleet put in to the desolate harbor of San Julián to wait out the winter. The Patagonian coast was sparsely inhabited. The people made dwarfs of the wiry little Mediterranean sailors. Antonio Pigafetta, the Italian adventurer who chronicled the voyage, wrote that two Patagonian giants who came aboard ship ate an entire basketful of biscuits "and rats without skinning them, and they drank half a bucket of water at each time." Though not unfriendly, these naked nomads were of little help. They had no seagoing canoes, and no skill as guides to offer.

As winter closed in, hardships intensified, and Magellan was faced with a full-scale mutiny. Conspirators led by Cartagena gained control of three of the ships, planning to arrest Magellan and sail home. Magellan learned of the plot just in time and, by a combination of stratagem and force, regained control. Two of the mutinous captains were killed. One was stabbed to death by men Magellan sent aboard to retake the ship. Another ringleader "had his head cut off, and afterwards was cut into quar-

ters." Cartagena, who had royal connections, was marooned ashore and never heard of again. When weather permitted during that dismal winter, Magellan would send a ship south to scout the coast. On such a mission, the *Santiago* grounded and was lost. It was a chastened and unhappy fleet that weighed from San Julián Bay when winter broke, and sailed south to look for the strait.

The Strait of Magellan is difficult for all ships. For vessels driven entirely by the wind it is especially dangerous, a labyrinthine navigation complicated by shifting tidal currents and frequent bad weather. Approached from the east, it does not look threatening. The entrance is unobtrusive. From Cape Virgenes to Cape Froward, its banks are low and grassy, the country pleasant, as Pigafetta noted. But the western part is a fjord, "surrounded by very great and high mountains covered with snow" and hanging glaciers. The prevailing west wind sweeps through in savage, unpredictable gusts.

The 310-mile strait has few reliable anchorages. The bottom has sharp rock ridges that chafe through hempen anchor cables and set ships adrift. Safe passage of the narrows under sail requires a lucky combination of favoring spring tides with rare periods of easterly wind. The fastest passage in the 16th century was made by Francis Drake—16 days. But some navigators took three months or longer; some had to turn back in despair.

Magellan's fleet came close to giving up. The four ships arrived off Cape Virgenes already short of provisions. At least one of the surviving captains strongly advised Magellan, having found the strait, either to return home to report to the king, or else to

bear away for the Cape of Good Hope. Magellan was adamant, and his captains reluctantly obeyed. But inside the strait the biggest ship, the *San Antonio,* which had been under command of Cartagena, became separated from the rest. Her company mutinied, overpowered their Portuguese captain, and sailed the ship east toward Spain.

Giving her up for lost, the other ships stood on through the narrows, making fast to rocks at night and sending boats ahead to reconnoiter. Thirty-eight days from Cape Virgenes they entered open water, and fired a joyful salute to the Other Sea.

Pacific—at the time, at least—this great ocean covers one-third of the globe, an area exceeding all the landmasses of the world combined. Its dimensions came as a terrible surprise to Magellan's people. They probably expected a passage of a few weeks at most. In fact, they were at sea "three months and twenty days without taking in provisions . . . and we only ate old biscuit reduced to powder, and full of grubs. . . . the ox hides which were under the main-yard . . . also the sawdust of wood, and rats which cost half-a-crown each, moreover enough of them were not to be got." They suffered the torments of scurvy: "The upper and lower gums of most of our men grew so much that they could not eat . . . nineteen died." During the whole terrible passage from Cape Pilar their only sightings of land were two uninhabited islands. Eventually they came to Guam in the Marianas.

For the first time in months, they found themselves among seafarers, masters of single-outrigger

70 canoes "like dolphins bounding from wave to wave" under three-cornered sails of sewn palm leaves, in pursuit of flying fish. Magellan's men were less than enchanted with the magpie kleptomania of the Micronesians, who snatched every item of loose gear they could lay their hands on. The Europeans resented it and fights ensued. Dubbing the place Isles of Thieves, they sailed on west.

A week later, in the Philippines, the Spaniards touched the edge of a broad region of sophisticated sea commerce. The Chinese dominated it; many other peoples participated. Had Magellan so chosen, he might have enlisted navigators to guide him on to the Spice Islands. Instead, tragedy.

One of history's great sea commanders unwisely took up arms in a petty local war. Siding with the ruler of Cebu, a recent Christian convert, against rivals on the island of Mactan: "The captain decided to go himself with three boats. . . . We set out from Zubu at midnight. . . . we found the islanders fifteen hundred in number. . . . springing from one side to the other to avoid our shots . . . throwing arrows, javelins, spears hardened in fire, stones, and even mud, so that we could hardly defend ourselves. Some of them cast lances pointed with iron at the captain-general. . . . He died. . . ."

Besides Magellan, about 40 of his men were killed, including most of the senior officers. Those left on board weighed anchor and left the scene of tragedy. They had no pilots, no real idea of where they were, no set command. The *Concepción* had to be burned, for lack of men. The surviving two wandered about the islands for many weeks, men half starving, existing by petty piracies. Eventually, in

the Sulu Sea, they captured a local ship whose navigators guided them to Tidore in the Moluccas. Well-received by the ruler, who disliked the Portuguese, they exchanged their merchandise for cargoes of cloves and negotiated promises of future trade.

The ships left Tidore separately. The *Trinidad* set off across the Pacific for the Isthmus of Panama. She was forced back by head winds and was captured by the Portuguese, who set her crew to work building a fort at Ternate. Few of them saw Spain again.

The *Victoria* left Tidore at the end of 1521 under command of Juan Sebastián del Cano, to return to Spain by way of the Cape of Good Hope. Pigafetta deeply admired Magellan; he neither admired nor liked del Cano, and the journal does not mention him by name. Del Cano was a sailor of humble Basque origin, raised to command by an unknown method of acclamation. And he had been implicated in mutiny. He must have been a consummate seaman; perhaps less than perfect as a navigator.

In the Indian Ocean, with no local pilot to help, del Cano apparently took his ship too far south. Head winds forced them north again. With the ship leaking, the weather dismal, men sick, and their food running out, they beat around "that terrible cape"—Good Hope—in the wintry storms of May. Hunger and scurvy stalked them two more long months, to the Cape Verde Islands. To get rice they bartered spices, arousing suspicions of the Portuguese authorities, and had to weigh hurriedly to escape arrest, leaving 13 men behind.

At last, in September 1522, they crossed the bar at Sanlúcar de Barrameda. Eighteen enfeebled survivors staggered ashore at Seville, and the following

day those who could walk made a barefoot pilgrimage to the shrine of Santa María de la Victoria, to give thanks for their deliverance.

In human terms the first circumnavigation of the world had been a disaster, costing nearly two hundred lives and the loss of four ships from a fleet of five. Profits of the voyage were trifling. The few tons of cloves brought back barely covered expenses.

Yet the *Victoria* brought back a most important cargo: information. Some well-entrenched beliefs, mostly associated with Ptolemy, had been proven wrong and a more accurate picture of the earth had emerged. With its new continent and a new ocean terrifying in its dimensions, the world was far bigger than people thought. Some European optimists who had believed the riches of the Orient to be within their grasp had to think again.

But the world *had* been circumnavigated. This fact was no longer in dispute: The oceans of the world are one. Given skill, courage, and a reliable ship, a man could sail to any part of the world.

Searching For a Northern Passage

Attempting to find an ocean link between Europe and the riches of Asia, dozens of expeditions probed the inhospitable Arctic (map, opposite). Though all the early "passages" proved to be dead ends, impassable for the ships of the time, the unknown "mistie, melancholly, and snowie" world of the northern seas yielded many surprises. Crewmen of Englishman Martin Frobisher's expeditions (below) encounter fur-clad men who shoot "arrows and dartes" at the intruders and paddle through "ilands of ise" in skin boats. The explorers marveled at the adaptations of people and animals to their harsh environment. An Eskimo woman's sealskin dress protects her and her baby, peeking out from under the hood (opposite). John White, who accompanied one of Frobisher's three voyages, made the drawings.

Plowing through frigid northern seas, generations of explorers scoured a maze of islands and inlets for a passage linking the Atlantic and Pacific. Evidence for a passage in northern latitudes was flimsy, but hopes were high. It would provide a shorter way from Europe to Asia and also steer clear of routes claimed—and jealously guarded—by Spain and Portugal.

Explorers from England, Holland, and France came poorly prepared for the Arctic, where temperatures sink to minus 50°F and seas choke with pack ice. They discovered new lands, fishing grounds, and people, but the original goal—an easy northern passage from Europe to the Orient—remained elusive. The record of men who defied death and disappointment in the Arctic's forbidding environment is an epic of endurance.

In 1576, discovery of the Northwest Passage seemed to English Capt. Martin Frobisher "the onely thing of the worlde . . . yet undone, whereby a notable mind mighte be made famous and fortunate."

The captain met disaster early. His exploring party ventured to the raging northern seas in three clumsy vessels. One, a tiny pinnace, was swamped in a storm, drowning four men. Then men of his largest vessel, "mistrusting the matter," deserted and returned to England.

But Frobisher pushed on, threading icebergs until he reached the bay named for him. Here he saw what appeared to be 'some kinde of strange fishe; but coming nearer, he discovered them to be men in small boates made of leather." Their facial features convinced the captain that he had reached Cathay. Frobisher captured an Eskimo boater and took him to England; he paddled his kayak on the Avon River for a short time before dying—of a cold.

Even more of a sensation than Frobisher's "Asian" was a rock he had picked up on Baffin Island that was analyzed and said to contain gold. With the blessing of Queen Elizabeth, Frobisher later led 15 ships to mine the ore. He returned to bad news: The ore contained only worthless pyrite.

Frobisher was not the first to sail from England in vain search for the passage. In 1497 John Cabot had landed in Newfoundland or Nova Scotia, then tried to sail on to Asia, but found no opening in the ice.

Hugh Willoughby and Richard Chancellor led three ships to the northeast in 1553. A gale separated the ships early in the voyage. Chancellor "sailed so farre, that he came at last to the place where he found no night at all, and it pleased God to bring them into a certaine great Bay," the White Sea. At Archangel he met Russian traders, an event which led to the establishment of the Muscovy Company. Willoughby's ships got stuck in the ice. He and his crew were stranded on the coast. No one survived.

In 1587 John Davis discovered between Greenland and Canada the strait that now bears his name. Two decades later Henry Hudson, a tenacious passage-seeker, sailed the bluff-bowed *Discovery* to investigate some of the inlets.

The *Discovery* pitched and groaned as Hudson maneuvered her in to icy Hudson Strait. The crew were wary, but as land gave way, Hudson became confident that he had won the passage to Asia. Instead he had won Hudson Bay. The ship became locked in ice in November, and the crew, short of supplies, were reduced to eating moss and frogs to survive the winter. In June 1611 they mutinied, casting Hudson and his son adrift in a small shallop. The Hudsons were never seen again.

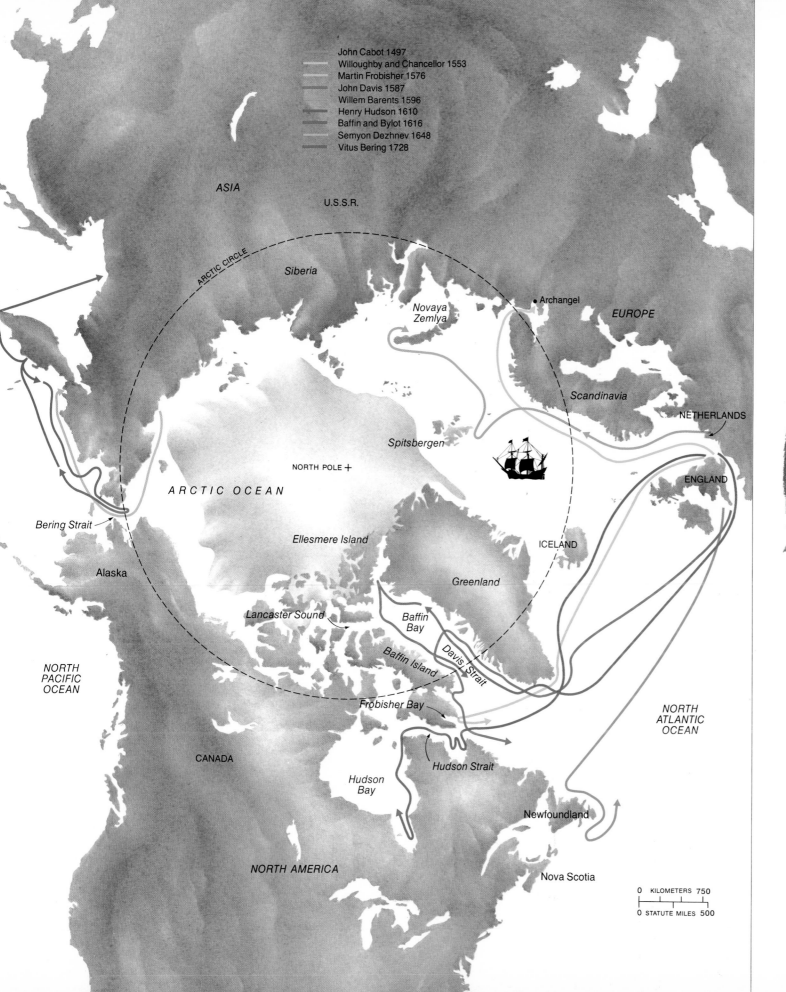

John Cabot 1497
Willoughby and Chancellor 1553
Martin Frobisher 1576
John Davis 1587
Willem Barents 1596
Henry Hudson 1610
Baffin and Bylot 1616
Semyon Dezhnev 1648
Vitus Bering 1728

ASIA

U.S.S.R.

ARCTIC CIRCLE

Siberia

Novaya Zemlya

• Archangel

EUROPE

Scandinavia

NETHERLANDS

Spitsbergen

NORTH POLE +

ARCTIC OCEAN

ENGLAND

Bering Strait

ICELAND

Alaska

Ellesmere Island

Greenland

NORTH PACIFIC OCEAN

Lancaster Sound

Baffin Bay

Davis Strait

Baffin Island

Frobisher Bay

NORTH ATLANTIC OCEAN

CANADA

Hudson Strait

Hudson Bay

Newfoundland

NORTH AMERICA

Nova Scotia

0 KILOMETERS 750

0 STATUTE MILES 500

In 1616 Robert Bylot and William Baffin explored Baffin Bay, the great arm of the sea from which the true Northwest Passage—Lancaster Sound—leads. The sound was frozen, the passage eluded them, and their discoveries were doubted. As late as 1818, maps did not show Baffin Bay.

Semyon Dezhnev first explored the strait between Alaska and Russia in 1648. The channel is named for Vitus Bering, the Danish captain who explored the area 80 years later for the Russian royal family.

After the ill-fated Willoughby exploration, Dutch expeditions under Willem Barents pressed the search for the Northeast Passage. In late August 1596, as Barents threaded the ice floes near Novaya Zemlya, the ice closed around his ship, trapping Barents and his crew 600 miles north of the Arctic Circle for the winter. Using wood hauled over the ice in sledges, they built a shelter in cold so bitter that when a man held a nail in his lips it froze "and made the blood follow."

On November 3 they saw the sun for the last time until January 24. The cold was deadly, the smoke in the cramped hut suffocating. When the ice thawed, the survivors began a 1,600-mile journey in small boats. Shortly after they began their awesome return voyage, Barents died. Before the ordeal was over, 5 of the 17 explorers had perished. For three centuries, Novaya Zemlya remained the limit of eastward navigation.

While the northern passage remained beyond the grasp of these explorers, their efforts changed world history. They aided colonization of the New World, shifted global trade patterns, and altered our view of the world in which we live.

Dutch explorers led by Willem Barents in the late 16th century had to fend off white bears of "most wonderfull strength." On his second voyage in 1595 men were digging for rock crystals (left) when "a great leane white beare came sodainly stealing out, and caught one . . . by the necke." Rescue efforts failed; two men were killed. The ships, their advance blocked by ice, returned home. The following year Barents resumed the quest for a Northeast Passage to Asia. On June 4 he "saw a strange sight . . . on each side of the sunne there was another sunne, and two rainebowes." Such a mock sun, or parhelion, occurs in frozen regions when light is refracted from ice particles in the atmosphere. In the engraving below, combining incidents a week apart, the explorers are so busy fighting a bear the wonder in the sky goes unseen.

These two ships later separated. Barents's vessel was trapped in the frozen seas at Novaya Zemlya. In a hut they built of driftwood and parts of the ship, crewmen endure the death-dealing cold of winter (right). The sick lie close to the fire, used also to melt snow and thaw frozen wine. On the spit the explorers roast a fox, which they compared in taste to rabbit. A lamp burns melted bear fat, providing dim light during the polar night. A large wine cask is used for bathing. The clock was a cherished companion until it stopped with the immense strength of the cold. A twelve-hour sandglass then served as timepiece. "It froze so sore within the house that the wals and roofe thereof were frozen two fingers thicke with ice." Ruins of the hut were found undisturbed in 1871.

Riding the Trade Winds

ealth had been the beacon for the voyages of discovery, and wealth flowed from almost every shore they touched. Within 17 years of Vasco da Gama's landing in India, Portugal had fortified trading posts from the southeast coast of Africa to southeast Asia. From the pepper of Malabar to the gold of Guinea, rich cargoes sailed for Lisbon. The Spaniards exploited their discoveries in Mexico, the Caribbean, and on the mainland of northern South America—the "Spanish Main"—where their ranches, plantations, and mines enslaved the New World to produce riches for the Old. Sugar and spices, borne on the winds, shaped modern history.

There are winds that blow "trade," that is, in a steady trade or track. Riding the northeast trades at the right time of the year, ships out of Lisbon or Seville rounded Africa or made an easy course to the West Indies. Of these two major ocean trading systems of the 16th century, the Spanish was far larger and more lucrative, though it served only a few hundred thousand settlers and Indians. Portuguese ships carried mainly money and passengers to man forts and factories, as the trading posts were called. But Spanish America was a good market for the ships from home.

Then the pattern changed. New World silver and gold made Spain rich. Tobacco and sugar began to flow eastward. The Dutch, French, and English greedily eyed the Iberian trade monopolies. At the end of the 17th century, Cadiz and Lisbon faded as Antwerp and London prospered. East Indiamen from many countries came home with spices, silks, porcelain, and tea. Lonely galleons labored across the Pacific from Mexico to Manila, exchanging Oriental luxuries for American silver. A web of trade spanned the world.

A fleet of early 17th-century Dutch East Indiamen loads spices and fragrant sandalwood at an Orient port.

One day in 1545 a Peruvian Indian on the hunt uprooted a small bush and laid open veins of silver richer than the world had ever known. The next year silver was found in Mexico. The Peruvian mines at Potosí boomed after the viceroy, Francisco de Toledo, saw how mercury helped to refine silver. Huancavelica, a mountain in Peru, held a great store of mercury, and Toledo arranged, he said, "the most important marriage in the world, between the mountain of Potosí and the mountain of Huancavelica."

From Zacatecas in Mexico and from the barren, blustery heights of Potosí, Columbus's Indies began to feed the treasuries of Spain, long starved for precious metals. By 1611 Potosí had grown to be one of the largest cities in the Western world. "The force of silver," observed the Spanish Jesuit, José de Acosta, "which drawes unto it the desire of all thinges, hath peopled this mountaine more then any other place in all these Kingdomes."

Spanish colonists demanded luxuries from home: clothes, paper, glass, utensils, books. They no longer needed shipments of bulky food. Their own wheat fields, orange groves, vineyards, and olive trees bore fruit. They exported hides; dyestuffs such as cochineal and indigo; tobacco and cacao, both catching on among fashionable Europeans; some gold; and silver, the product that mattered most.

In ingots, the silver was packed by mule train to port. From Zacatecas it went to Veracruz; from Potosí to Peruvian ports, then north by sea to Panama. It went across the isthmus to Nombre de Dios, but Drake's raid of 1572 and his attacks in 1585 and

1595 showed how vulnerable the place was. The terminus for the Peruvian treasure was moved to Portobelo, a harbor easier to defend. Goods from Europe destined for Lima, Cuzco, or Potosí were also packed across the isthmus, then coasted south.

A fat galleon in a shallow, open Caribbean harbor stood in danger of being blown ashore by a fierce three-day norther. Homeward bound, heavily armed and clumsy with its great load of treasure and hides, a ship had to negotiate the reefs of the Straits of Florida. A missed sailing date meant hurricane danger in the Caribbean. The open Atlantic always promised storms.

After eight or ten weeks, the fleet reached Spanish shores to face one of the infinite regulations governing New World trade. So that the king's officers could watch the treasure, most ships had to cross a shallow bar at Sanlúcar de Barrameda or transfer the silver to galleys for the 60 winding miles upriver to Seville. Conservative ship design produced vessels that taxed the handling skills of even the best masters. At Nombre de Dios in 1563, a hurricane drove seven ships aground. A norther broke up five others near Veracruz. In 1587 six wrecked on the bar at Sanlúcar. Three years later a norther caught 15 ships in Veracruz harbor, and another in 1601 destroyed 14 more. In 1591 storms claimed 16 homeward bound ships near the Azores.

The silver ships sailed well-known routes. In wartime (the usual state for Spain in those days) privateers haunted these lanes. A privateer was a civilian vessel commissioned by its government to prey on enemy ships—a "private" man-of-war. Spain and France were at war from 1521 to 1529. Hostilities

The marketplace at Goa in Portuguese India opens early, before the midday sun stifles trade. A lady of wealth rides in a closed litter (1) while servants carry parasols that shade gentlemen. From bulging sacks at right, women sell food.

The horse trader sets bells jingling to attract buyers (2). A wet nurse with an infant (3) passes by peddlers of drinking water (4). Money changers trade currencies (5), and a slave girl is sold by an auctioneer (6). South of this steamy port, on the coast of Malabar, people harvest the pepper that had

lured the Portuguese to India (left). They conquered Goa in 1510, killing 8,000 people.

The Jesuit, Francis Xavier, arrived here in 1542 to begin his great missionary work, fulfilling Vasco da Gama's claim that Portugal had come east for "Christians and spices."

HUDSON
Bay

Quebec

Acadia

NORTH AMERICA

New York
(New Amsterdam)

Roanoke
Jamestown

ATLANTIC OCEAN

Azores

MEXICO

San Juan de Ulúa

Zacatecas

Havana

JAMAICA

Veracruz

Acapulco

Hispaniola

Samaná Bay

Lesser Antilles

Caribbean Sea

Portobelo

Panama

Cartagena

Nombre de Dios

PACIFIC OCEAN

English

NETHERLANDS

Liverpool

ENGLAND

Plymouth

Amsterdam

London

Antwerp

Nantes

EUROPE

FRANCE

PORTUGAL

SPAIN

Lisbon

Seville

Cádiz

AFRICA

Red Sea

Gorée
Island

GUINEA

ASIA

JAPAN

Nagasaki

CHINA

Bandar 'Abbās

Hormuz

Calcutta

Amoy

Canton

Macao

Surat

Bombay

INDIA

Goa

Madras

Calicut

PACIFIC OCEAN

PHILIPPINES

Manila

Aden

SRI LANKA
(CEYLON)

Malacca

Singapore

Strait of Malacca

Bantam

Makassar

Spice Islands

Amboina

Jakarta
(Batavia)

Sunda Strait

Java

SOUTH AMERICA

PERU

BRAZIL

Callao

Lima

Cuzco

Pernambuco

Recife

Salvador
(Bahia)

Arica

BOLIVIA

Rio de
Janeiro

CHILE

Potosí

Spanish

PACIFIC OCEAN

St. Helena

Luanda

ANGOLA

Portuguese

MOZAMBIQUE

ATLANTIC
OCEAN

INDIAN OCEAN

AUSTRALIA

Buenos Aires

French

Cape of
Good Hope

Dutch

Major Sea Trade Routes

- Spanish
- English
- French
- Dutch
- Portuguese
- Atlantic slave trade

Wind, wealth, and continental barriers patterned sea trade routes of the 16th through the 19th centuries. Merchant ships rode the westerlies of the roaring forties latitudes and made speed with the reliable trade winds, a name derived not from commerce but from the steady track, or trade, of the wind direction. Portugal's Cabral discovered Brazil as he sailed westward on a favoring wind to the Cape of Good Hope. Da Gama's route around Africa made Portugal a leader in the spice trade. Silver mines and sugar plantations of the New World began the infamous triangle of the slave trade. In the West Indies, Indians at first worked the sugar mills (below). Trial and disease almost extinguished the native population, and African slaves replaced them. Ships foundered in storm-swept harbors of the West Indies, and in tricky seas off eastern Africa and northeastern Australia. Vessels of all nations, as they rounded the tip of Africa, made a victualing stop at the Dutch settlement on the Cape of Good Hope.

erupted again in 1542. French privateers ranged the Caribbean and the sea off the Azores. In 1555 a party of French corsairs sacked Havana, picked it clean, and startled the Spanish bureaucracy into action.

Don Pedro Menéndez de Avilés (better known for his later butchery of the French Huguenot "heretics" in Florida) set about securing the safety of Atlantic shipping. To meet the French challenge, the galleon had been developed as a specialized fighter. Heavily armed galleons chased privateers away from the Spanish coast and kept shipping lanes open. Menéndez then organized the convoy system.

Ships for the Indies left Spain in two groups, each headed for a silver port. One, the *flota*, set out from Sanlúcar in May and entered the Caribbean by the passage between Hispaniola and Puerto Rico, sailed through the Yucatan Channel and across the Gulf to Veracruz. The isthmus fleet, the *galeones*, left in August. Once in the Caribbean it sent word ahead by small boat and courier all the way to Potosí. Its destination was Portobelo, humid, insect and fever ridden—"the most evil and pitiful residence in the world," said the explorer Samuel de Champlain. Portobelo stirred to life only during the annual visit of the galeones. Settlers and merchants came to town to barter and sell produce and to buy goods from all over Europe which had filtered through Seville to end up halfway down the coast of South America.

Afterward, the precious silver and gold were tallied and loaded. The fleet wintered in the sheltered, fortified harbor of Cartagena. In March the galeones and the flota rendezvoused at Havana, took on food and water, and headed homeward. On the dependable flow of the Gulf Stream the two fleets sailed north, seeking a west wind for Spain. Aboard the armed escort—two to eight galleons—was the royal silver, revenue from many sources. There was a direct tax of one-fifth, the *quinto real,* weighed at the mines. There were duties, sales taxes, rents, charges levied on every colonial activity. In all, the crown exacted between a quarter and a third of every shipment of treasure.

The price was paid in human lives. Indians suffered in servitude on ranches which had taken their cropland. They labored in dark holes in the ground, mining silver and poisonous mercury. They died of measles and smallpox—European diseases to which they had no immunity. The first century of Spanish occupation of the New World wiped out 90 percent of the Indian population.

For the Spanish masters, a labor shortage was the result. Slave dealers stepped in to meet it. From the early 16th century, Portuguese traders had supplied African slaves to the sugar plantations of Spanish America. Then, in 1562, Englishman John Hawkins took a leaf from the Portuguese book. With three small ships he sailed to Sierra Leone where, by intimidation of the Portuguese dealers and outright kidnapping, he collected 300 slaves. In the Caribbean he found planters glad to trade sugar and hides for his cargo. At small harbors on the Main, Hawkins was resisted by officials who pretended to obey the law against dealing with foreigners. Hawkins used guns to force the Spanish to buy his slaves. The enterprise was so successful that Hawkins undertook a second voyage, this time backed by Queen Elizabeth I. Again he went home with a profit. In 1568, as Elizabeth maneuvered to keep peace between Spain

and England, Hawkins returned to the Caribbean with his kinsman Francis Drake. His ships, caught by bad weather, ran for shelter to San Juan de Ulúa, the harbor of Veracruz. Here he met no minor officials, easy to bribe and threaten, but the Spanish convoy under command of the viceroy himself. Hawkins's expedition was devastated, and he and Drake limped home in two small ships. Spain did not intend to share the New World.

Philip II of Spain ruled an empire that included the Low Countries. In 1560 there were scores of Spanish merchants in Antwerp. However, by 1568

Dutch East Indiaman: A Freighter Armed for Battle

It had to breast the open seas, yet slip through the shallows near land. It had to swallow copious cargoes half a world from home—twice as far afield as the earlier caravels had traded. It had to carry passengers in comfort, some even in luxury. It had to defend its treasures from pirates and warships. And it often dazzled the eye with ornamentation that told the world its proud owners prospered. Born of such diverse demands, the East Indiaman kept its basic design for two centuries.

The *Prins Willem,* shown here, was launched from her Netherlands shipyard in 1650. Rated at 1,200 tons, over 170 feet long, she was perhaps the largest square-sterned vessel built for the Dutch East India Company in the 17th century. She was outfitted as a warship to fight the English in 1652. We see her with the ports that were added to increase her armament to 40 guns. When she went back to merchant service after battle damage in the Channel, she kept the heavy artillery. Four times the *Prins Willem* came home with the silks, spices, and ivory of the Indies. In 1662, on her fifth return, she went down in a storm in the Indian Ocean.

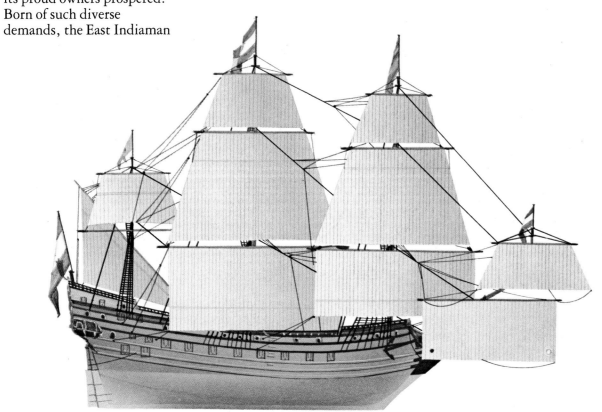

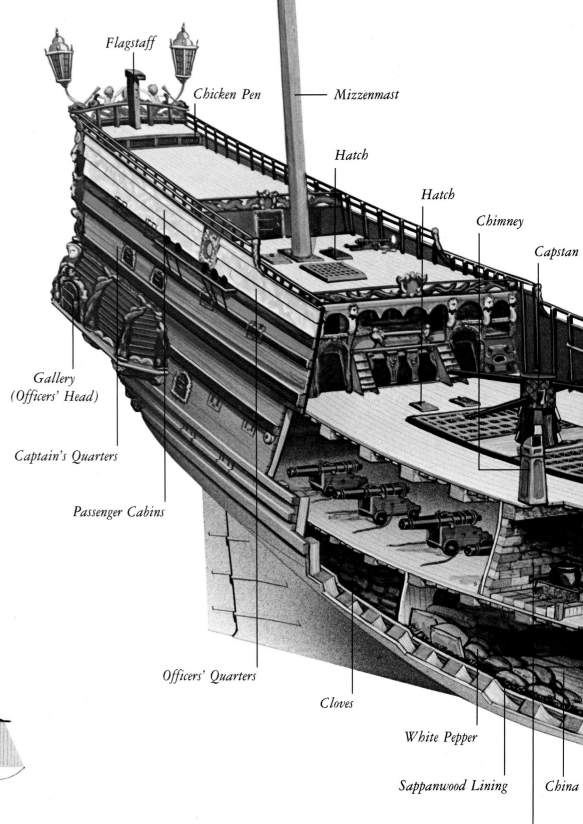

Flagstaff

Chicken Pen

Mizzenmast

Hatch

Hatch

Chimney

Capstan

Gallery (Officers' Head)

Captain's Quarters

Passenger Cabins

Officers' Quarters

Cloves

White Pepper

Sappanwood Lining

China

Galley

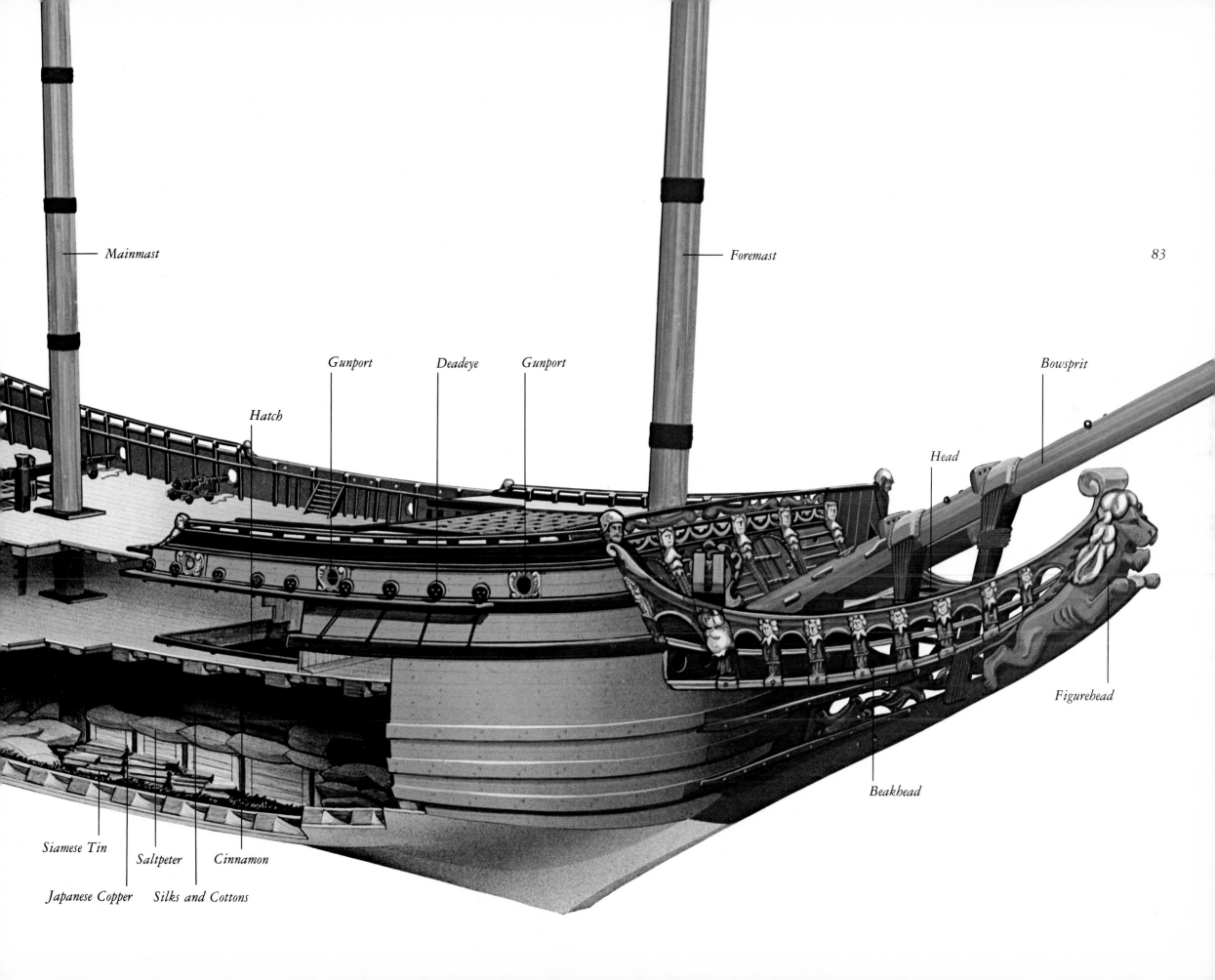

Mainmast

Foremast

Gunport

Deadeye

Gunport

Hatch

Bowsprit

Head

Beakhead

Figurehead

Siamese Tin

Saltpeter

Cinnamon

Japanese Copper

Silks and Cottons

Now rusty and silent, the guns of Portobelo once boomed at the enemies of Spain. This was one of three "castles" which guarded the harbor in the 17th century, pointing more than 60 guns toward the Caribbean. Mule trains packed Peruvian silver and gold across the Isthmus of Panama to Portobelo and the galleons which waited to carry it to Seville.

Captured Englishmen often were kept as slaves in Portobelo. When the buccaneer Henry Morgan took the garrison in 1668, he found in its dungeons "eleven English in chains who had been there two years."

Philip's persecution of Protestants had driven the Netherlands to revolt and to an uneasy friendship with England, a Protestant state. In 1578 the king of Portugal was killed. By military persuasion and Spanish silver, Philip asserted a hereditary claim to the Portuguese throne. Thus Spain and England— "papist" and "heretic," they called each other—pursued their commercial rivalry in a climate of violent religious hatred which took in allies and satellites in Europe, and colonies throughout the world.

Spain's annexation of Portugal in 1580 united the two halves of the world parceled out to the Iberian powers by Pope Alexander VI with the Treaty of Tordesillas in 1494. Portuguese Brazil, the trading posts on the African coast, the forts and factories in India, Ceylon, the East Indies, and the Spice Islands remained under Portuguese control. At the end of the 16th century, in spite of wars with England and with the Dutch, the Iberian powers still had the largest fleet in western Europe. They still sent fleets of 60 to 100 ships to the Indies each year. But their control of trade routes was precarious. The great ships were aging. And Dutch strength was growing, fired by success in both East and West.

The English, too, reached for bases from which to claim a share of the wealth. In 1583 Humphrey Gilbert landed in Newfoundland. Then the ill-fated Roanoke colonies were planted. In 1606 the Virginia Company was chartered to establish the Jamestown colony. Two years later, English Separatists began gathering in Holland, from where they eventually would find their way to Plymouth, Massachusetts. The French ventured onto the shores of northern North America in 1604 in Acadia and four years later at Quebec. In 1609 Henry Hudson established Dutch claim to the river that bears his name. In 1621 the Dutch West India Company was chartered as a commercial and military arm of the government. One of its first moves was to buy Manhattan Island from the Canarsie Indians.

Portugal turned to Brazil and sugar. During the Middle Ages, sugar had been as rare and precious as jewels. It made medicines palatable and gradually appeared as a sweetener on noble tables. By the late 16th century, sugar was a familiar sight, although still a luxury. One could find the hard, gray loaves in the shops of most large towns. More highly refined white sugar eventually became common. And most of it came from Brazil.

The cultivation and manufacture of sugar produced a plantation aristocracy whose size and wealth multiplied again and again. In 1576 there were only about 30 Brazilian sugar plantations. By 1584 there were 76, and by 1623 over 300. Sugar was as important to some Portuguese and Brazilians of that day as oil and gasoline are to the industrial nations of today. About 30 percent of the price of sugar in the 1620's was tax; some 40 percent of the total crown revenue came from sugar.

Cane was grown by small farmers or on the plantation by slaves and carried by oxcart to the mill, where it was crushed, boiled, and crystallized. The soil in Pernambuco and Bahia, the best sugar regions, was so fertile that Father Fernão Cardim, a Jesuit who traveled in Brazil, marveled in 1584: "They cannot keep up with the yield though they grind for three or four years; and each year there come to Pernambuco forty ships and they are unable

The Wind Seemed To Be Saying, "Death, Death"

In somber cadence an eyewitness narrative in the *História trágico-marítima* sets the stage for the impending shipwreck of the Portuguese merchantman *São Thomé* in 1589. "By now the sea was curdled with crates, spars, barrels, and every diversity of things which appear at the untimely hour of shipwreck. . . . It was a fearful thing to see, and it is a pitiable thing to tell."

The "untimely hour" tolled for many a proud and laden ship brought to grief in those days by the perils of the sea. Pirates. Rocks. Storms. Mutiny. Bad seamanship. And good ships worked until no longer worthy of the demanding sea.

Another of the hundreds brought to grief was the Spanish galleon *Conde de Tolosa*, pride of the Spanish fleet and bearer of a royal cargo as she and the smaller *Nuestra Señora de Guadalupe* set sail from Cadiz in 1724. The two were freighted with 400 tons of quicksilver—mercury—the strange liquid metal vital to the Spanish empire for extracting silver from ores at its mines in the New World. Leather bottles in the holds of the ships bore a year's supply. Gunports bristled with cannons, 144 in all; arsenals bulged with grenades, swivel guns, and flintlocks. And in quarters plain and fancy, some 1,200 passengers and crew carried hopes and possessions to the New World.

On the night of August 24 the two ships ran into a hurricane off the northeast coast of Hispaniola. Mountainous seas tore at masts and rigging and turned loose gear into lurching juggernauts. In Samaná Bay the *Guadalupe* crunched onto a sandbar; there her heavy cargo helped pin her upright, enabling 550 of her 650 souls to ride out the two-day storm and make it to shore.

Sea and storm were less merciful to the hapless *Tolosa*. Slammed from shoal to shoal, she finally wrecked on a coral reef, her mainmast thrusting out of the sea like a cross on a nameless grave. Somehow eight survivors clawed their way onto that precarious perch. And somehow seven of them survived until salvage ships plucked them off 32 days later.

Their tale must have been scant solace to the king, for salvors saved none of the precious quicksilver. Without it the mines would send back only a trickle of the silver which was the lifeblood of the empire for two centuries. And for centuries more, *Tolosa* and *Guadalupe* would guard their treasures and trinkets, yielding them at last to divers and scholars who would see in them the wreckage of hopes and dreams. Among the finds: a fine clock, hundreds of religious medals possibly destined for converts, and a poignant trove of wedding rings.

Peril often brought low the haughty aristocrat in the scramble for self-preservation. But not always; highborn ladies aboard one doomed Portuguese ship in the East Indies complained that the lifeboat, jerry-built of wreckage, had no staterooms for them. Even ashore, some nobles deserted by their litter-bearers preferred to await death rather than walk to civilization.

Such wrecks sprinkle the old sea-lanes that brought to Europe the riches of the New World and the Orient. Ten ships laden with silver were lost to a hurricane in 1715; another in 1733 wrecked twenty more. What riches must still strew the floor of the sea—as rich cargoes, thrown overboard in panic, must often have strewn the waves in a proud ship's final hour: "Waves," in one account, " . . . bannered with fine silk and scented with many spices. The silks were to become gravecloths and the spices embalming perfume in the fathomless tomb. . . ."

Marooned on the mainmast, survivors of the *Tolosa* ride out a month-long wait for rescue. A rag of a sail catches a little rainwater; flotsam affords a little food. Sharks and treacherous currents deter the men from trying to reach shore, though they can see the coast of Hispaniola only three miles away. There some 30 of their shipmates have managed to survive—but out here, sharks fatten on nearly 600 who have not.

Like giant treasure chests, the *Tolosa* and the Guadalupe yield their wares to divers. One pours a shimmering basin of mercury, remnant of a trove long since lost in sea and sand. Found-again finery includes a fragile wine decanter and ornaments of gold shown here awash in pearls—two of the pieces adorned with diamonds, another set with emeralds.

to carry away all the sugar." In the 1620's there were 130 ships carrying sugar from the Pernambuco plantations, 75 from Bahia, and 30 from Rio de Janeiro.

Dutch vessels took some of Brazil's sugar to Amsterdam, where it was refined again before being sold. Spain prohibited the traffic, but Dutch ships, with the connivance of the Portuguese, raised Portuguese flags and carried on as before. The Dutch reached beyond refining and shipping to distribution, credit, insurance, and marketing. Then, a brief truce with Spain ended, they turned to warfare.

A fleet of 26 Dutch ships with 3,300 men bombarded Bahia harbor and, in May 1624, took the town. Alarmed, with the Peruvian silver so close, Spain joined forces with Portugal and soon chased away the Dutch, who next turned guns on the Caribbean. In 1628 they captured the entire Mexican silver fleet, homeward bound off Cuba. Sale of the booty brought a 75 percent dividend to West India Company shareholders, backed further Caribbean raids, scuttled scores of Iberian ships in European waters, and mounted a new campaign against Portuguese holdings in northeastern Brazil. When the Dutch came back, they took the port of Recife, occupied Pernambuco, and fought for 24 years with the Portuguese sugar planters, who did not willingly work to enrich their former friends.

In 1640 Portugal, too, revolted and again established independence. Spain lost the Portuguese harbors and ships. Export trade to the Indies fell as Spanish America became almost self-sufficient, buying only goods manufactured in Northern Europe, seldom in Spain. Cargoes from the Indies were 80 percent silver and gold, and the crown's eager

Three tiny ships, like these replicas moored at Jamestown, Virginia, set out from London in the winter of 1606, bearing an English challenge to Spain's monopoly of the New World. Formed on the pattern of the English and Dutch ventures in the East Indies, the Virginia Company was directed to search for gold. Investors also hoped to profit when their Jamestown colony became a market for English goods and produced raw materials for the mother country. But the gentlemen-adventurers who shipped on the Susan Constant, *the* Godspeed, *and the* Discovery *(left to right) were unwilling farmers. And they found no gold in Virginia.*

appetite contributed to an inflation rate in Spain of 400 percent. By about 1625 the richest surface veins of American silver were played out. Seventeenth-century technology was hard put to cope with the rest. More and more silver stayed in the colonies to pay for administration and defense. From 1600 to 1650 silver imports fell by over 80 percent. By the mid-1600's seldom did more than 40 ships make the yearly crossing. Sometimes there would be fewer than 20, and more than half of these men-of-war.

No longer was the Caribbean Spain's ocean. The Dutch had seen to that, with their capture of Curaçao and Aruba and their promotion of English and French ventures in the Lesser Antilles: Barbados, Saint Kitts, Martinique, Guadeloupe. The final insult to Spain, in 1655, was England's capture of Jamaica, "lying in the very belly of all commerce."

Everywhere in the New World, sugar meant slavery. Slaves for Brazil came from Angola on the southwest African coast. A legend of the Pende, a tribe of Angola, tells of the Portuguese: "One day the white men arrived in ships with wings, which shone in the sun like knives. They fought hard battles with the Ngola and spat fire at him . . . the Whites brought us nothing but wars and miseries." Itinerant slave dealers went inland, carrying wine, cloth, cheap tobacco, guns, and the cowrie shells coveted as currency by Africans.

With these goods they bought the slaves, collected for them in tribal wars and raids, and marched the shackled gangs to slave barracoons on the coast. The town of Luanda was the busiest Angolan slave port.

From Luanda the slaver had an easy trade wind run to Bahia or Recife or Rio de Janeiro. After selling slaves, a ship's master bound for Portugal loaded gold, silver, sugar, hides, tobacco, and whale oil. A ship out of Lisbon for Angola or Guinea carried the textiles and other goods for the slave dealer. From Lisbon, headed directly for Brazil, the cargo was hardware and supplies for sugar processing, Chinese silks and porcelain, olive oil, and wine. From Angola the slavers carried their sad human freight to the Brazilian sugar ports and beyond. In the Azores they loaded livestock, cloth, and salt, sometimes paid for with silver smuggled from Potosí. And so the ships moved, in patterns dictated by the markets and by winds which the Portuguese had used long before other Europeans—the trades, equatorial calms, the westerlies of their own latitudes. To and fro, the ships endlessly crossed the Atlantic to satisfy Europe's demand for sugar.

The Dutch ruled 17th-century ocean trade. From a tiny homeland, beleaguered by the sea and the Spaniards, with a population of craftsmen in need of raw materials and markets, the Dutch became traders for the world. In their business methods there was none of the labyrinthian bureaucracy of old Spain. From Dutch shipwrights came new methods and improved designs. They introduced wind-driven saws to replace the backbreaking labor of the saw pit. They used blocks and pulleys instead of human muscle to handle simplified rigging. They combined the light construction and shallow draft of the coastal trader with the cargo capacity and handling ease of the seagoing ship, and they built ships to be manned by far fewer hands than in the past.

Tobacco leaves turned to gold for Jamestown. The first crops, sold in England, rescued the colony from collapse. Demand rose so high that in 1617 tobacco was planted in the fort and the streets. The "fine Virginea" praised by the British tobacconist's label (right) was used as money by colonists short of other forms of currency. Indentured servants, black and white, labored in the fields to sow, prune, weed, and worm. Planters worried about getting the crop cured and packed to meet the tobacco fleets each autumn. By 1639 the colony had established a single-crop economy and exported 1.5 million pounds of "their darling tobacco." Eventually it brought so much revenue to the crown that Londoners judged Virginia as important as "the Spanish Indies to Spain."

The *fluyt* was their most successful design. Cheap to build, with a cargo space made larger by a broad beam and a restricted cabin area, it was a safe sailer, although not a fast one. The first fluyt left the shipyard in 1595. By 1603 there were 80 under sail. The fluyt became the general cargo carrier in the middle of the 17th century, not only for the Dutch but for England, France, Germany, and Scandinavia.

To profit even more from their position in the New World, the Dutch fostered the infant settlements of France and England. Hollanders from Pernambuco carried cane cuttings to the West Indies and taught the French and English how to grow sugar. They supplied the planters with expensive rollers and kettles for their mills, on credit against the first crop. The Dutch freighted sugar from Barbados and tobacco from Virginia at cheaper rates than the English offered their own colonies.

When the American colonies began to turn a profit, England and France moved to protect their interests. Parliament enacted the first Navigation Acts in 1650 and 1651 to force out foreign middlemen, in particular the Dutch. (France passed similar laws.) The Navigation Acts required that all colonial trades be conducted in ships built, owned, and manned by Englishmen. Colonists could trade only with England. They were forbidden to import European goods except in English ships or in ships of the country where the products originated, and these needed a special license. Merchant shipping grew in England and in New England. The Dutch hold loosened. By the end of the century, Atlantic trade was in the hands of four or five European powers. Each guarded its own monopoly and poached on others.

DUM VIVO. FUMO.

Edw.ᵈ Halford's fine Virginea.
The best in Holbeach, for a Guinea.

Backers of the first New England ventures had looked to the fur trade for profit. But as the spread of settlement drove animals away, New England diminished as a source of fur. The French, on the Saint Lawrence River, and the Dutch, with New Amsterdam at the mouth of the Hudson, controlled water routes to the forests of the Great Lakes with their beaver, mink, fox, and otter. When England seized New Amsterdam in 1664, the Netherlands lost an important hold on North American commerce. Wildest and most productive of fur, however, was the area surrounding *(Continued on page 96)*

Slavers: Ships of Misery And Profit

"Going into the middle among them all, they chose the smallest of them, because they could get more of these into their boat, of whom they took fourteen. . . . And for this good booty, and all the grace that God had shown them in those days, they rendered Him much praise. . . ."

Those so rapt in thanksgiving were Portuguese mariners on a voyage of discovery and conquest to Guinea. When their laden caravels returned home, the African captives were placed in a field. Some had "faces bathed in tears . . . others stood groaning . . . others struck their faces with the palms of their hands. . . . then it was needful to part fathers from sons, husbands from wives, brothers from brothers." So goes a chronicle of one of those 15th-century voyages that probed down the western coast of Africa, pioneering the way for the climactic sea discoveries of da Gama, Columbus, and Magellan. The African voyages also pioneered Europe's descent into the slave trade. The Atlantic trade ended some four centuries later, but its costs did not.

Between 1451 and 1870 some ten million slaves were landed alive in Europe and the Americas. These were the survivors of brutal shipboard conditions and disease. Many more had set out. Some historians estimate that one out of every five slaves died in passage from Africa to the New World.

The impetus for trading in human cargoes—as with pepper, silks, or silver—was profit. The plantation economies that arose in Latin America and what eventually became the southeastern United States sorely needed labor. Mainland native populations could not supply it, and the Indians of the major Caribbean islands were annihilated within a century of the discoveries.

Crewmen pass buckets of food through the fence that segregates the human cargo by sex. Through another opening in the barrier a ship's gun, withdrawn from its port, is aimed at the males. Above the crowded deck a shackled piece of merchandise raises an arm to fend off a flogging.

Belowdecks, in slime and filth, slaves were wedged like logs. The plan of one hold of the 300-ton Liverpool slaver Brook, *frigate-built in 1781, displays the space allotted—for each man a grave-size rectangle some $1\frac{1}{2}$ by 6 feet, less for women and children. At times the occupants slept on their sides, "fitted together spoon fashion." Design capacity supposedly limited the* Brook *to fewer than 500 slaves, yet she was found packing in more than 600. When the*

vessels of misery reached the New World, slaves who survived the crossing were "refreshed"— washed up, perhaps fed with fresh food ashore, and doctored in various ways to improve their health and appearance on the auction block.

Most slaves went to British, French, and Dutch possessions in the islands, Spanish territories in Central and South America, and Portuguese-held Brazil. Over the four centuries, a total of only half a million went to North America, though the black population increased to some 4.5 million by the end of the Civil War.

In the Virginia colony, democratic elections and the first captive blacks on record arrived within a month of each other. In July 1619 Jamestown convened the New World's first representative legislature; in August "came in a dutch man of warre that sold us twenty Negars." Some historians believe that these early arrivals were regarded as indentured servants. In time, colonists, if not the servants, came to appreciate the benefits of "perpetual servitude," but not until the 1660's did the Virginia statutes recognize slavery.

The great triangle track of the slave ships began in Europe. From Liverpool, Nantes, Amsterdam, or Lisbon, they sailed for Africa with firearms, metals, woolens, trinkets, casks of liquor. Trading these for slaves, the ships embarked on the second leg, the notorious "Middle Passage" to the New World. There the live cargoes departed, to be replaced by the dead weight of sugar, tobacco, rice, rum, ginger, cotton, or coffee for sale at home. Thus a tidy profit was turned on each leg of the triangle. The circuit took about a year.

The long journey into slavery usually began with a raid by Africans upon Africans—though Portuguese mestizos and Arab traders were also involved in gathering and selling African people. All in chains and shackles, the males additionally yoked in pairs, the prisoners began the trek to the shore, often a march of hundreds of miles.

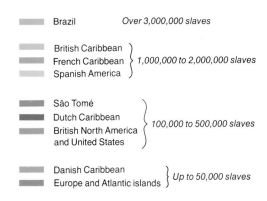

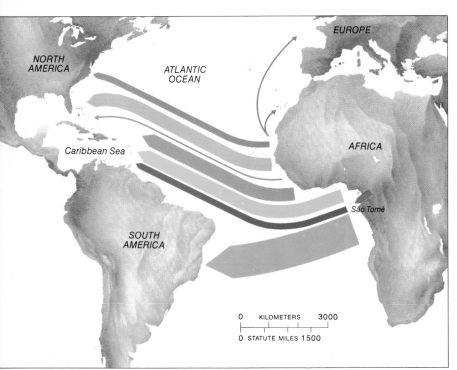

EUROPE

NORTH AMERICA

ATLANTIC OCEAN

Caribbean Sea

AFRICA

São Tomé

SOUTH AMERICA

```
0    KILOMETERS    3000
0  STATUTE MILES  1500
```

Between 1451 and 1870, the tide of human chattels flowed mostly to the American tropics— some 75 percent to the plantations of the Caribbean and Brazil. A sizable fraction supplied the slave marts of Spanish America. To the tobacco, rice, sugar, and cotton fields of North America came only four percent of the total in the four centuries of the transatlantic slave trade. It yielded high

On the coast the slaves were driven into sweltering way stations such as Senegal's infamous Gorée Island. When a slaver arrived, the haggling commenced; the men's muscles were checked, the women's breasts measured, the children's teeth examined. A healthy male, 12 to 35 years old, brought the best price. Next came children, then older men, and finally women up to the age of 25. A deal made, the ship unloaded its exchange cargo for the local trader, and the slaves were rowed out to the vessel.

Aboard ship the unbranded slaves were branded, then all were stowed in the upper hold, a space 5½ to 6 feet high just below the main deck. A partition segregated the sexes—men fore, women aft. Often, to maximize profit, shelving was added to increase capacity—crowding each captive into less than a coffin-size space for a journey of about two months. At times the tightness left no room to lie down; slaves slept sitting up or leaning against one another.

Mutiny among the slaves was a constant threat; crews checked belowdecks for knives or other weapons. Death was often the result of such a desperate bid for freedom. Suicides were common; slaves jumped overboard or simply refused to eat.

As prudent men in trade, ships' crews and owners understood that the most profit lay in keeping as many slaves as possible alive—and healthy. They were brought up on deck in fair weather and were made to exercise, on pain of flogging, by jumping up and down in their chains. Twice a day they were fed, usually Guinea corn, yams, cassava, or beans. Typically ten slaves, each with a wooden spoon, ate out of a single tub. Half a coconut shell of water might supplement the meal. The slave hold was regularly swabbed with vinegar. Hot irons

dipped in water made steam to drive out the foul air. Under fair skies, scuttles and hatches stayed open to freshen the hold. Such precautions sought to counter the effects of hundreds of excreting, vomiting, sick, and dying human beings crowded together for several weeks, at times in extreme heat or cold. Little wonder that slave decks were lousy, the slaves tortured with seasickness, diarrhea, mouthrot, boils; and scurvy was always a problem.

If measles or smallpox struck, it could take as savage a toll among the crew as among the slaves. In such an outbreak, insurance rules might make it advantageous to fling slaves who were unlikely to survive the epidemic overboard along with the dead. In the famous case of the *Zong,* a Liverpool slaver that ran short of water in 1783, the captain thus killed 132 slaves who were "sick or weak, or not like to live." Insurance against "perils of the sea" covered such a loss; it would not have if the victims had died on board. A jury held that the insurers must pay, for under the existing law "the case of slaves was the same as if horses had been thrown overboard." But an appellate court ruled that a "higher law" governed in this "shocking case." For the first time a court judged that slaves should no longer be considered only as merchandise.

There had been voices of protest from the very first, denunciations in the 16th century as fierce as those that in the 19th helped exorcise the curse. Moral revulsion against the slave traffic gathered strength, leading to its abolition in Europe and most of Latin America by 1850. But in Brazil, Cuba, and the United States, it continued. Then came the upheaval of civil war in the United States. And finally, abolition came to Cuba and Brazil in the 1880's.

Shipwrights flesh out a skeleton at Amsterdam in the 1600's, the golden century of Dutch commercial power. At the East India Company yards, men lay a deck athwart beams; others shape the hull with "skin planking" around riblike frames that curve up from the keel. Natural growth, steam baths, hot water, or flames on wet wood put curves in timber.

Design helped to produce profit. Dutch ships, noted Walter Raleigh, "hold great bulk . . . and . . . sail with few men." They held twice as much cargo as English ships of the same length and beam.

A Chinese porcelain plate (left) bears the VOC mark, which shows that it was made especially for the Dutch East India Company.

96

Hudson Bay. The Hudson's Bay Company, chartered in London in 1670, flourished from the first, with its own fleet, harbors, forts, and factories on the shores of the vast inland sea.

Tobacco profits astonished everyone. Cultivated by Spaniards on the Main and by Portuguese in Brazil, tobacco had a small market in Europe in the 16th century. Later, the smoking craze sped around the world. Some colonies grew almost nothing for export but tobacco: Barbados and Saint Kitts until sugar took its place in the 1640's; Virginia and Maryland, where sugar would not grow.

In 1660 the British Parliament passed a Navigation Act which stipulated that several products which were the heart of colonial economy must be carried to English ports—such things as sugar, tobacco, and dyestuffs used in the English woolen industry. But some trade between colonies and foreign ports was legal. New England bought salt from Portugal and sent its salt fish to Jamaica as food for slaves. The West Indian islands had to import food from France and Ireland as well as from North America. From North America also came the hoops and staves for barrels to pack sugar and tobacco. Trade between North America and the West Indies was largely in Yankee hands. Returning ships carried sugar, perhaps to be smuggled to Europe; molasses, to be made into New England rum; and other products including gold and silver.

Sugar and tobacco sent to Europe paid for the tools, textiles, and other manufactured goods used in the American colonies. They were not bulky cargoes. Passengers made up the difference in space on the return trip. All the settlements needed people to clear the forest, break the ground, and grow the crops which furnished both food and trade. Some settlers emigrated at their own expense, but for others the indenture system offered a passage which had to be repaid by years of labor. Multitudes seized the chance to leave war-torn, plague-ridden Europe. Some indentured servants went into bondage on West Indian plantations. Some went farther north. Perhaps 75 percent of all the immigrants to Virginia came under indenture. As the demand for labor exceeded the flow of immigration, English planters turned, as the Portugese and Spanish had before them, to that reservoir of humanity, West Africa.

By the Peace of Utrecht in 1713, which finally broke the European dominance by Spain and France, England gained the *asiento,* the sole legal right to the Spanish slave trade. Slaves had long been traded by a system in which the Spanish crown licensed contractors to sell slaves in Spanish ports. Portuguese had held the asiento until 1640. Then the Dutch had a turn, while England and France contended for the prize by simply ignoring the law and carrying slaves in unlicensed ships to eager colonial buyers. This contraband dealing absorbed an enormous quantity of New World silver. Throughout the 17th century, as much as a quarter of the silver from Potosí found its way through Brazil into Portuguese pockets.

From Jamaica, England traded manufactured goods and slaves for silver. Much of this business used Spanish ships, in defiance of the Navigation Acts, and was so successful that Spanish silver flooded through English markets, including the North American colonies. England formed the South Sea Company in 1711 especially for the asiento trade and used it as a cover to smuggle goods into Spanish colonies. As Spanish merchants were crowded out, the fairs at Portobelo and Veracruz began to ring with the accents of London and Plymouth. By 1800 the Jamaican trade was bringing to the English East India Company as much as half of the silver bullion it exported to the East.

Throughout the 16th century, sea trade around Africa to Asia was a Portuguese monopoly. Every year two or three ships left Lisbon for Goa in western India, where they loaded pepper and cotton cloth. Goa, then the major European foothold in Asia, was captured in 1510 by a fleet of 20 ships under Affonso de Albuquerque. At first Goa was less a colony than

a garrison, defended by mercenaries from the slums and prisons of Lisbon. It prospered and in its heyday was "Golden Goa." The Portuguese ruled the sea route around the Cape of Good Hope. For a hundred years they had no European competitors there. They had seized and fortified bases at Hormuz and Malacca from which they controlled the major spice routes. The Portuguese attacked Muslims and other native shipmasters who had not bought safe conduct documents from the Portuguese forts.

Few European goods found a market in the sophisticated East but silver opened every door. By coastal trade in the Indies the Portuguese earned the money to pay for the Oriental products they took back to Lisbon. In 17th-century China the Ming emperors had forbidden trade with Japan; Portugal stepped in and dealt with both. Portuguese ships took horses from Mesopotamia and Arabian copper to India, Indian hawks, peacocks, an occasional tiger to China. They carried slaves, whether African laborers or little girls for Cantonese brothels.

Carracks sailed from Goa, bringing European manufactured goods and Indian pepper to Macao. At Macao the carracks loaded Cantonese silk and porcelain, which went to Nagasaki where it was sold for silver. The silver could then be taken back to Macao and traded, at a profit, for gold. Sometimes silk traveled to Makassar to be exchanged for spices and sandalwood, and sometimes to Manila, the great way station in the Philippines where traders of the East, come halfway around the world, met traders of the West. Spain had established a settlement in the Philippines in 1565. For the next two and a half centuries a shipping route linked Manila and Acapulco.

Silk, porcelain, tea—exotic, elegant wares from "the most remarkable of all countries yet known." They came from China, where the secret of silkmaking lay hidden for 3,000 years. They spread over the world in junks and carracks, galleons and clippers. In the Middle Ages the women below were shown ironing a piece of newly woven silk. By then Europeans knew how to make it.

Porcelain, too, had its secrets. "Flesh" of kaolin, a china clay; "bones" of petuntse, a feldspar; thin glaze "skin"— these made washable, lustrous ware that mystified Western potters and alchemists until Meissen, Germany, matched it in 1708. China had exported millions of pieces such as those coming out of the domed kilns (left)—dinnerware, bowls, chamber pots, tea services. The West also craved tea. European traders sample China's "liquid jade" as porters pile it for export (left, below).

OVERLEAF: Dutch East Indiamen jam the roadstead of Saint Helena under the shelter of volcanic crags. The Portuguese discovered the South Atlantic island in 1502 and made it a secret victualing station for their trading fleets. Other nations found it; the English and the Dutch took it and retook it from each other.

and could not easily make port. In summer the wind blew from the southwest. Ships had to fight to leave Goa's harbor. Out of Lisbon the India fleets met a tight timetable, or they met delay and danger. Raiders prowled the north Atlantic, and after 1580 Portuguese ships were fair game to the enemies of Spain. The voyage lasted up to nine months each way. Distances were great between victualing stops: Brazil or Mozambique if outward bound; Saint Helena, Luanda, or the Azores if bound for Lisbon.

These Portuguese fleets were smaller than the great Spanish silver fleets. Sometimes only one or two ships sailed, seldom more than five or six. They were heavily armed galleons, or carracks which carried fewer guns and were prized for size and endurance rather than speed. Many were built of teak in Indian shipyards. For their time they were very large. One of the monsters, the *Madre de Deus*, was captured in 1592 by Englishman William Borough. Brought to Plymouth, she amazed all who saw her. "Farre beyond the mould of the biggest shipping used among us," said the chronicler Richard Hakluyt.

The great trade empire stretched Portugal's human resources, creating a chronic shortage of trained seamen. The India fleets lost scores of men to scurvy and disease on every voyage and replaced them for the homeward trip with untrained Indian recruits. From 1550 to 1600, one out of six India sailings met disaster. Warring Spanish troops sacked Antwerp in 1576 and again in 1585, destroying one of Europe's great trade centers and the ultimate destination of most Portuguese spice routes. Europe's other center for spices, Venice, was also in difficulty. Each year, spices grew scarcer and more expensive. In England

Mexican silver went out in the holds of the Manila galleons. Return cargoes included spices, drugs such as musk and camphor, and everything desirable the East had to offer: silk, brocade, velvet, embroideries, fine Indian cotton, stockings, ornate vestments, Oriental rugs, gems, trinkets of ivory and jade, exotic animals, gilt furniture, porcelain, slaves. A great share of this wealth found its way to Peru, where the Spanish population enjoyed boom times. "All wear silk," the viceroy boasted to King Philip III in 1602. "The gala dresses and clothes of the women are so many and so excessive that in no other kingdom of the world are found such."

The crucial link in the *carreira da India*—the route from India—was the connection between India and Portugal. It was also one of the weakest. On the west coast of India the monsoon governed sailing schedules. Monsoons are winds that seasonally reverse direction. For three months every winter, ships approaching Goa faced a northeast monsoon

Squeezed by Saint Helena's hills, Jamestown flows down its valley to the harbor that gave it life and fame. The English East India Company seized the lonely island for the second time in 1673. Eventually more than 1,400 ships called here in a single year. Capt. Robert Jenkins, minus an ear, cut off, he said, by Spanish seamen,

arrived in 1740 to govern Saint Helena just after British warships sacked Portobelo in the War of Jenkins' Ear. In 1815, eager to isolate Napoleon once and for all, England ordered him here, 1,200 miles from the African coast. Passengers of visiting Indiamen eagerly anticipated

an interview with the former emperor. With steam and the Suez Canal, this rest stop on the trade wind run between Cape Town and Africa's bulge lost its strategic purpose. Saint Helena became once again, in the words of an old sailor, a "meer wart in the ocean."

and northern Europe, especially in the Netherlands, investors were tempted. They judged the time ripe to defy the Portuguese monopoly.

Three ships left Plymouth, England, in the spring of 1591. By the time the expedition reached the Cape of Good Hope in July, so many men were so ill with scurvy that one of the ships turned back with the sick. "A mighty storme and extreme gusts of wind" vanquished a second ship. The last, the *Edward Bonaventure,* was struck by lightning, suffered such hardship that her crew nearly mutinied, and was eventually pirated by a small force left aboard when the commander, James Lancaster, landed at a Caribbean island to find food. Lancaster and a few of his men made their way home after three years.

Such haphazard voyages clearly did not satisfy Queen Elizabeth's determination to "enter her people directly upon a commerce to East-India." In 1600 she chartered the East India Company, giving this merchant group a 15-year monopoly on Eastern trade. The next year the first fleet set out with Lancaster in command. He had been especially chosen by the prosperous merchants who backed the venture because he was not a "gentleman," but a professional seaman. The expedition carried letters from the queen to Indian kings and costly presents such as looking glasses and silver cups.

In the Strait of Malacca, Lancaster captured a Portuguese carrack loaded with calico. At Bantam, a Javanese trade center, he exchanged the cloth for pepper and left behind a group of men with permission to establish an English factory. On his return to England, he was knighted.

But the New World had captured the English

imagination. Ten shillings for a hundred acres in Virginia seemed a better proposition than twelve pounds for one share of East India stock. The company cautiously awaited the return of one fleet before launching the next until 1608, when it began to send out ships every year. Still, during the 17th century England remained content with a fairly small commerce in the East.

Not so the Dutch. In their precarious independence, they brought a purpose and vigor to seagoing. Many Dutchmen piloted Portuguese ships. Others served the Portuguese as seamen or clerks. In September 1592 Jan Huyghen van Linschoten came home to the Netherlands after thirteen years in the East, five as clerk to the archbishop of Goa. A few years later Linschoten published books which, more than any of the popular Eastern accounts of the time, encouraged his countrymen. The decadent Portuguese, said Linschoten, would be easy game.

In April 1596 four Dutch ships left Holland for the East Indies. In spite of fever and scurvy, the crews loaded a cargo of spices at Bantam and Bali. So trying was the two-year voyage that only 89 of the original 284 men lived to see Holland again. But seamen's lives were cheap. The investors, the Far Lands Company, sent another fleet to Indonesia. It returned with a cargo of spices and a 400 percent profit. Three years later five different groups sent ships to trade for spices in the East Indies. In 1602 these competitors organized into the Dutch East India Company—the VOC in its Dutch abbreviation—and laid siege to the Portuguese monopoly. By 1621 twice as many Dutch ships as Portuguese were loading spices, silk, and porcelain for Europe.

Linschoten had described Java, a market abounding with cloves, nutmeg, and the best pepper, frankincense, and diamonds, as a place where "men might very well traffique, without any impeachment, for that the Portingales come not thether." By company instructions, VOC shipmasters at first avoided Goa and Malacca. In Linschoten's book they had read, "South Southeast right over against the last point of the Ile of Sumatra, on the south side of the Equinoctiall lyeth the Iland called Java . . . where there is a straight or narrow passage betweene Sumatra and Java, called the straight of Sunda." Dutch skippers soon discovered the value of these directions. The Sunda Strait lies south of the monsoons, in the path of the southeast trades. From the south, ships can easily enter the strait. Dutch ships turned eastward at 30° or 40°S latitude where westerlies of gale force blow for weeks at a time the year round—a dangerous course that demanded seaworthy ships. In its wild career before the roaring forties, a ship might find itself too far east, wrecked on the coast of Australia. But "running the easting down" with care became the standard technique of navigators in the south Indian Ocean.

The Dutch discovered, as the Portuguese had, that Asians did not want many European goods. The Dutch exported European silver to buy Oriental products. They captured Portuguese factories and took over the country trade, coasting from port to port. They used guns to drive away competition and compel trade on Dutch terms. They encouraged disputes among local rulers to Dutch advantage. The small principalities of Java were constantly at war. The VOC chose for themselves the good harbor and

Calicut, proclaimed in this 16th-century print "Most Celebrated Emporium of India," faces a harbor bustling with trade ships (below). Portuguese, British, French, and Danish merchants built posts here on the west coast of India.

Calicut gave its name to the Indian cotton called calico. Europe prized "painted Calicuts" like this wall hanging in which flowers frame Indian women taking their ease (opposite). By the 1660's, calico clothes had swept the world of fashion. Weavers rioted against the imports. England banned some of them until the

Industrial Revolution made local cloth competitive. Indian cotton was traded for elephants in Ceylon. It paid for slaves in West Africa, and coarse calico clothed them in the Americas.

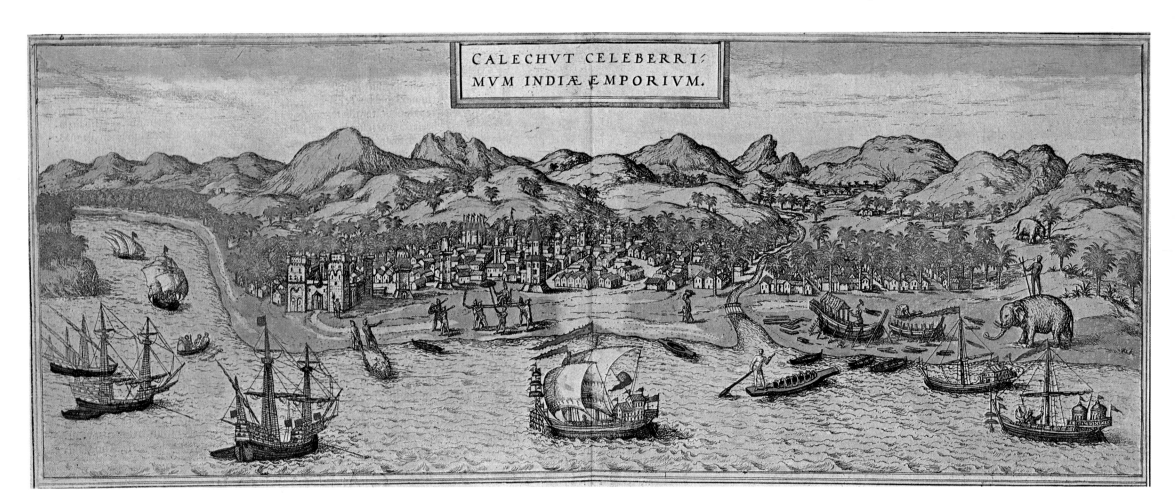

CALECHVT CELEBERRI: MVM INDIÆ EMPORIVM.

strategic location of Jakarta. They attacked the town and occupied it, renaming it Batavia, an ancient poetic term for the Netherlands. Under the governor, Jan Pieterszoon Coen, who boasted that "all the kings of these lands know full well what the planting of our colony at Jakarta signifies," they devastated the Spice Islands; 15,000 people were killed and many islanders sold into slavery. To secure their monopoly, they destroyed by the thousands clove trees

they did not need. Malacca withstood a blockade for years, but in 1641 it fell to the Dutch, who then left it to decay and diverted its trade to Batavia. In southern India and Ceylon, Portuguese factories became fortified Dutch towns, complete with canals and treelined streets.

Golden Goa was a little Lisbon, with a cathedral, a palace, monasteries, and market squares. It suffered a Dutch blockade which lasted from 1637 to

1645 and broke its power. Throughout the 18th century, as Portuguese middlemen sustained local trade, Goa endured, a relic of 16th-century audacity.

The English East India Company had helped the Dutch war against the Portuguese. In 1622 an English fleet enabled Shah Abbas of Persia to expel the Portuguese from Hormuz, the island of which Linschoten had said, "It hath neyther greene leafe nor hearbe in it, nor any sweete water, but onley rockes

of salte stones . . . and great traffique." The Dutch drove the English from most of their trading stations on the Indonesian islands. England then concentrated on the mainland of India. The English factors at Surat ran a profitable business, shipping cotton fabrics, indigo, and saltpeter to England, and paying for them in silver. Company ships policed the Muslim pilgrim route across the Arabian Sea and privateered against the Dutch and Portuguese.

English control in India grew slowly, while in the islands the Dutch contended with a multitude of minor princes and squeezed out competing native trade. By the end of the 17th century much of Java was Dutch. The Javanese survived by growing crops for their only customer, the Dutch East India Company. With the capital and methods of a trading company, the VOC was trying to run an empire.

And the world no longer needed a great spice trade. Europeans had learned to grow winter fodder for their cattle, and fresh meat became common. Fashions changed. Women discovered muslin and calico (named for Mosul and Calicut, the Eastern cities from where they first came). The English and French East India companies, with their factories in India, had the advantage.

England was also in the right place when it came to the biggest money-maker of all in 18th-century trade—tea from China. Ming China had been closed to foreign traders for 200 years. But in 1684 during the reign of K'ang-hsi in the Manchu dynasty, south China ports were opened to commerce. The Dutch later grew coffee in Java, but they failed at first to see

A *Dutch ship defies English sovereignty in the Channel and hoists a red battle flag. The British vice admiral's striped ensign flying at her stern, the* Vanguard *replies with a broadside.*

the rewards in a tea trade. The English leaped to enter the door that the Chinese had set ajar.

In 1685 the *China Merchant* made the first English visit to Amoy in southeast China. The French and other nations followed, but England held the lead. By 1715 the English East India Company had loaded 43 tea ships at Chinese ports. England traded raw cotton and opium from India. But most tea was paid for with American silver. Silver and tea kept the English East India Company in business in China long after its rivals had gone, and long after its Indian trade had strayed into politics.

The most powerful ruler in India by 1800 was the English East India Company. No longer did its chief employees work in commerce. They were soldiers or civil servants. Company ships carried passengers and supplies, not trade goods. Behind the shop front, the company brandished a sword.

Tea profits gave the East India Company the most impressive sailing fleet ever controlled by a private corporation. But it did not own the ships. The owners, "ships' husbands," were shareholders and often directors. East Indiamen were built to company specifications and inspected at every stage of construction. In the late 18th century, about a hundred Indiamen were in service, stout, capacious ships, often country-built of teak instead of English oak, as warships were. By then, the Indiaman had a vertical side in place of the archaic "tumble-home" and a flush upper deck instead of the deep waist, once meant to thwart boarding parties. It had iron spindles and pawls on the capstans and iron knees to brace the decks in place of weaker, bulky wooden knees. The ships were designed for their leisurely

trade and the comfort of passengers, but the apple-cheeked Indiaman could put on a turn of speed when it had to. Yankee shipping had entered the Eastern trade and in 1817, to outrun the American competition, the entire East India China fleet—13 ships stuffed with tea—raced from Canton to England in 109 days, about 40 days less than their usual time.

Indiamen were merchantmen outfitted to look like warships. Most were pierced for 30 to 40 guns, although some of the gunports were painted dummies and many of the real ports often were empty. On occasion, the Indiaman's masquerade worked. During the Napoleonic Wars, in 1804, a squadron of French warships sighted the homebound China fleet off the east coast of Malaya. There were five large Indiamen with an escort of country ships. The French admiral thought he had blundered upon

British seamen and the tools of their trade decorate a 1693 pamphlet: "England's Safety: Or, a Bridle to the French King" (left). Designed to recruit a strong navy, the broadside promised aid to the wounded, education for the male children of fatalities, and the chance to plunder enemy ships.

English sea power triumphed around the globe. The splendid deepwater harbor of Singapore (opposite) became an East India Company trading post in 1819, when Sir Stamford Raffles saw it as a key link in the China trade. He turned the jungle island at the tip of Malaya into the emporium of the Eastern seas. In spite of Dutch power, Raffles made Singapore a free port, open to all nations.

IN THESE LYE THE STRENGTH AND GLORY OF ENGLAND

This Encouraged, *England* muſt Flouriſh.

ships of the line and turned tail. The English commodore hoisted a signal to his fleet, the "general chase," and the merchantmen pursued the squadron until nightfall.

Officers of the East India Company served in magnificent uniforms. The captain wore a blue coat that had black velvet cuffs, each with four gold embroidered buttonholes and crested, gilt buttons; black velvet lapels with ten buttonholes; and a velvet cape lined with buff silk serge. The chief mate's velvet cuffs bore only one button apiece. On dress occasions the captain buckled on a sword. When he stepped ashore in India, he rated a 13-gun salute.

All company posts depended on patronage. Owners appointed the ship's officers. The captain was usually named as soon as a keel was laid. While his vessel rose in the shipyard, the captain could supervise. But if his ship was already in service, and if this was to be his first command, he might go to sea on another, earning the money to buy the captain's berth from his predecessor and the ship's owner.

The captain of an Indiaman collected passage money from company servants, army officers, and others bound to or from India, and he engaged in private trade. Officers and seamen took English goods out: beer, wine, a miscellany of manufactured items from cutlery to carriages. Tea and silk were company business on the coveted China run, but everything else was stowed in the "privilege" space allotted to every man on the ship. The captain got the lion's share, at least five times as much as his chief mate, who had more than the other mates, the midshipmen, the carpenter, the sailmaker, and so on, down to the deckhands. After a few tours with

the company, a captain could usually retire in ease.

Passengers got only cabin space for their money and had to bring their own furniture and bedding. Baggage allowances were governed by social rank. Certain gentlemen could carry two chests of wine, but colonels only one. Ladies were allowed to include musical instruments. Three-course meals, with fresh meat, dessert, and formidable quantities of beer, ale, and wine, were served to first-class passengers, who dined at the captain's table but could not dally. When the captain left the table, everyone left. Shipboard guests enjoyed dances and plays.

The ordinary seaman's lot was not so happy. He may well have come into company service at the hands of a crimp, the civilian version of the navy's infamous press-gang. If so, he would have been accosted in the streets, enticed by rum and bribes, and locked up until the sailing date of the ship whose commander had set the crimps after him. Seamen preferred Indiamen to warships. The salt-horse-and-hardtack diet was much the same, discipline less brutal, the ship not so crowded. And even a common seaman could profit from his voyage on an Indiaman if he used his privilege space with care.

The silver fleets, the tobacco packets, the sugar ships, and the slavers crossed the Atlantic year by year. Indiamen plied the Indian Ocean and China Sea. But only Spain sent ships regularly across the Pacific. The Manila galleons carried some of the most valuable cargoes ever to sail. For more than 200 years, they followed routes that never sighted land. They never stopped at Japan. They never saw the Hawaiian Islands. To the north and the south of their path rolled a broad, mysterious sea.

Quest in the "Other Sea"

The captains of the Great Age of Discovery—Dias, Columbus, da Gama, Magellan—had presented Europe with an earth a great deal bigger than most people had supposed. The Ocean Sea of the ancients was now finite, bounded on the west by a vast continent whose existence had not been expected. Beyond that continent was another ocean, Balboa's "Other Sea," of unknown size. The great oceans were all connected, at least in the Southern Hemisphere, by navigable passages. Ships, therefore, could sail all the way around the earth.

This was a momentous discovery, and understanding its geographical and commercial implications would occupy Europeans for generations. But 16th-century explorers had left a great geographical question still unanswered: How many continents remained to be discovered? The most likely place to look was in the far south, where Ptolemy had theorized that the earth needed a great landmass to balance Eurasia. Yet no land had actually been sighted in the southern oceans, other than cold, windy, inhospitable Tierra del Fuego on the south shore of the Strait of Magellan. Were the southern oceans unbroken water? Or might there be a continent in that vast, mysterious expanse? A Terra Australis Incognita—an Unknown Southern Land?

Although doomed to failure, the quest for this great imagined landmass was to prompt a new round of expeditions—the Second Age of Discovery. It would culminate in the three great voyages of England's James Cook from 1768 to 1779. Cook's was a stupendous achievement; in effect he mapped half a planet. But that success came only after two centuries of European exploration oriented more to making profits than to solving geographical riddles.

Gunshots to repel menacing natives mark Capt. Samuel Wallis's 1767 visit at Tahiti—and Europe's push into the Pacific.

Reaching the Juan Fernández Islands in 1709, English privateers found "a man clothed in goatskins, who looked wilder than the first owners of them." Alexander Selkirk had deliberately marooned himself over four years earlier, after quarreling with the captain of the Cinque Ports. *Selkirk spent the time dancing with the goats he had tamed—he also ate 500—and praying and singing psalms. "He said he was a better Christian . . . than ever he was before or than, he was afraid, he should ever be again." His story inspired a 1719 best-seller, Daniel Defoe's* Robinson Crusoe.

Amid shouts of "Vive le Roi," Louis Antoine de Bougainville hoists his ship's colors on a rock in the Strait of Magellan. On this first French voyage around the world, Bougainville claimed Tahiti in 1768, unaware that Wallis had beaten him to it by nearly ten months.

In the late 16th century, those who accepted Terra Australis as a possibility rarely showed much eagerness to go looking for it. One who did was the religiously zealous Álvaro de Mendaña de Neyra, commander of an expedition to the southwest Pacific in 1567-68. His stated destination was biblical: Ophir, the Isles of Solomon. (The viceroy of Peru, who supported his voyage, may have remembered that Ophir was where Solomon had procured gold.)

The expedition actually found some of what are now the Solomon Islands, but failed to fix their position. On a second expedition, in 1595-96, Mendaña could not find them again. He died of fever while trying to found a colony in the Santa Cruz Islands. Pedro Fernandes de Quirós, the chief navigator, conducted what was left of the expedition to its mutinous, disease-racked end at Manila.

Quirós dreamed of becoming the Columbus of the Pacific. On a voyage in 1606, he found what he called Australia del Espíritu Santo—actually the large island in the New Hebrides still called Espíritu Santo. But hunger and skirmishes with the islanders nearly led to mutiny, and Quirós sailed back to Mexico. As with Mendaña, there had been an air of heroic madness about his undertakings.

Quirós had left part of his expedition in the New Hebrides under the command of Luis Vaez de Torres, a capable seaman with no trace of heroic madness. Torres found his way to Manila by following the south coast of New Guinea, through the strait that now bears his name, and so proved New Guinea to be a very large island, part of no continent. This important discovery went unannounced.

The last thing Spanish authorities wanted known was a passage through which Dutchmen or Englishmen might sail from the East Indies to Peru. Torres's report went into limbo in the Manila archives.

Meanwhile, an English expedition had dealt another blow to the Terra Australis theory. In 1577 Francis Drake set out on his most famous voyage, probably intended as an armed reconnaissance of southern South America. After passing westward through the Strait of Magellan, he ran into a gale that drove him far south of Cape Pilar. He found no evidence there of another continent—nothing but a waste of wild water. The Atlantic and Pacific met "in a most large and free scope." Ships could now, he thought, sail from one ocean to the other through open water and avoid the treacherous currents, narrow limits, and sudden squalls of the strait.

But Anglo-Spanish relations were tense. Queen Elizabeth saw no reason to trumpet abroad the details of a voyage that had given offense to Spain. The untested notion of the Drake Passage, like the discovery of the Torres Strait, received little notice.

In 1616 the Dutchman Willem Schouten confirmed Drake's inference. Schouten's backer wanted to find a route to the East Indies that would not infringe on the monopoly the Dutch East India Company held in Holland. The new route would have to avoid both the Cape of Good Hope and the Strait of Magellan. Schouten therefore sailed down the east coast of Tierra del Fuego and, finding open water, rounded a small island—the southernmost point of the Americas. He named its precipitous headland Cape Hoorn, after his hometown in Holland. Drake and Schouten between them lopped Tierra del Fuego

off the "Great Southern Continent," but they did not sink Terra Australis. On his port side as he neared Cape Horn, Schouten had seen the mountain peaks of an island. Or was it a peninsula of a continent? Most geographers assumed the latter, and Terra Australis received a new lease on life.

Halfway around the world, meanwhile, in the Indian Ocean, the captains of Dutch Indiamen were sighting the coast of a place that their company decided to call New Holland. Some ships foundered there. It was an inhospitable shore—rocky, arid, the tepid waters of its bays and inlets alive with repellent poisonous creatures. This was in fact Australia's northwestern coast, but Dutch captains thought it too desolate to be the giant, lush Terra Australis.

An unusually enterprising and imaginative governor-general of the Dutch East Indies, Anton Van Diemen, decided to mount an expedition in 1642 to solve the New Holland riddle. The commanding

officer was Abel Tasman, a young captain who, though somewhat of a plodder and lacking the curiosity of the true explorer, was a first-class seaman.

The plan was for a one-year search: southwest into the Indian Ocean, east in the southern latitudes until even with the presumed longitude of the Solomons, then straight north. Tasman's instructions led him to sail around Australia without ever seeing it. He was the first European to sight what he named Van Diemen's Land—later called Tasmania—but he did not recognize it as an island. Cook would make the same mistake more than a century later.

By sailing too far east, Tasman made his most important discovery, New Zealand. He sailed up the west coast of both islands without realizing their nature. To him the towering mountains of South Island suggested a continent.

The 120 years or so following Tasman's trip added little of significance to knowledge of the great

blank areas on the chart of the world: the Pacific, the southern oceans, and the regions about the Poles. If any seafarers visited these areas, they were usually merchants or buccaneers, not explorers.

The buccaneers did, however, help maintain public interest in geographical questions. Some of them were articulate rascals who, on returning from a cruise, would write up their journals, occasionally with the aid of "ghosts." (The idea of rounding off a life of crime by publishing memoirs of it is not new.)

The most influential adventurer of all needed no ghostwriter. A talented and successful author, Englishman William Dampier said he became a buccaneer "more to indulge my curiosity than to get wealth." He was also an excellent navigator—he analyzed the wind system of the tropics—and a naturalist with a keen eye for exotic flora and fauna. Dampier circumnavigated the globe three times. The journal of his first trip, A New Voyage Round the World, published in 1697, enthralled England and persuaded the Admiralty to grant him a commission to explore Australia. A rotting hull and a mutinous crew prevented him from seeing more than the northwest coast, but no one else would even attempt the exploration until Cook came along 71 years later. Narratives by Dampier and other buccaneers, along with a variety of scholarly books, helped prepare the public mind both in England and in France for the Second Age of Discovery.

New technology also facilitated the explorers' task by improving the handling qualities of ships. Not until early in the 18th century was a method devised to harness a ship's tiller to a wheel mounted on the quarterdeck. The wheel enabled the helmsman

"*I presume that this voyage will be found as compleat as any before made,*" wrote James Cook in one of the greatest understatements in exploration history. In three years (1768-71) aboard the Endeavour, he charted Tahiti and other Society Islands, as well as New Zealand and Australia's long east coast. Two voyages and a decade later, Cook had filled in most of the Pacific map from the Antarctic to Alaska.

His dour portrait to the contrary, Cook was humane, recognized even in his time as "*the ablest and most renowned Navigator this or any country hath produced.*"

114

Cook's first voyage 1768-1771
Cook's second voyage 1772-1775
Cook's third voyage 1776-1779
Voyage after Cook's death 1779-1780

KILOMETERS 2500
STATUTE MILES 1500
Scale at the Equator

ARCTIC CIRCLE

Bering Strait
Alaska

ASIA

Aleutian Islands

NORTH PACIFIC OCEAN

Nootka Sound
Vancouver Island
NORTH AMERICA

1779

JAPAN

1778

NORTH ATLANTIC OCEAN

TROPIC OF CANCER

Macao

Hawaiian Islands (Sandwich Islands)

MEXICO

Manila
Kauai

PHILIPPINES

New Ireland

Christmas Island

EQUATOR

Jakarta (Batavia)
INDONESIA (Dutch East Indies)
New Guinea

SOLOMON ISLANDS

Galapagos Islands

SOUTH AMERICA

Marquesas Islands

Society Islands

Tuamotu Archipelago

PERU

Santa Cruz Islands
Louisiade Archipelago

Cook

Torres Strait

Great Barrier Reef

VANUATU (New Hebrides)
FIJI
Samoa Islands

Islands

Tahiti

MARCH 1774

TROPIC OF CAPRICORN

1774

New Caledonia

TONGA
1773

Pitcairn Island

Easter Island

Queensland

AUSTRALIA (New Holland)

New South Wales

1769

Juan Fernández Islands

New Zealand

Tasman Sea

1770

NEW ZEALAND
North Island

1777

INDIAN OCEAN

South Island

JULY 1773

Strait of Magellan

Tasmania (Van Diemen's Land)

Cape Pilar

SOUTH PACIFIC OCEAN

NOV. 1774

Cape Horn

Tierra del Fuego

Drake Passage

ANTARCTIC CIRCLE

DEC. 1773

ANTARCTICA

ANTARCTICA

Ross Sea

to watch the sails and to make far more sensitive use of the wind. It could be used in all types of weather, and even in a heavy following sea it could be managed by far fewer men than the number needed to hold a big ship's tiller steady.

As important as the wheel was the introduction of fore-and-aft sails, long known in barges and small boats, especially in the Netherlands, but not introduced in big ships until early in the 18th century. The sails, like the wheel, saved labor. They also made ships nimbler and quicker and greatly improved their performance in beating against the wind—including emergencies such as clawing off a lee shore. The sails were crucially important to ships entering the Pacific Ocean from the east, whether by threading the Strait of Magellan or, increasingly, by rounding Cape Horn.

More crucial still, from the explorer's point of view, were improvements in the technique of navigation. To appreciate their importance, we have to imagine the master of a small vessel afloat on the trackless deep. He could use ancient means to reckon how far north or south he was, but he could only surmise how far east or west. That was what the problem of longitude was all about. To a captain far from any landmark, fixing a position could make the difference between life and death. Also, it did little good to discover a group of islands if the discoverer did not know where he was; the islands might be lost for generations, as the Solomons were.

Fortunately, it was an age of exuberant scientific inquiry. Every science strode boldly forward, accompanied by earnest perfectionism in manufacture. The octant, the sextant, the reflecting and achromatic telescopes, and micrometers were admired for the integrity that made them good servants of the most demanding navigators.

For all the marvels of these instruments, however, the problem of longitude at sea, which had frustrated explorers for centuries, remained unsolved. Old maps, drawn from known latitudes and estimated longitudes, displayed gross east-west errors.

In 1598 Philip III of Spain offered a reward for solving the longitude dilemma; no one won it. In 1714 British captains and merchants petitioned "That the Discovery of the Longitude is of such Consequence . . . that, for want thereof, many Ships have been retarded in their Voyages, and many lost." They said that "due Encouragement"—meaning prize money—could lead to a breakthrough. The British Parliament soon formed a Board of Longitude empowered to award £20,000 for the discovery of a method of determining longitude to an accuracy of one-half of a degree.

The key to capturing the longitude prize was *time*. The earth revolves exactly 15 degrees every hour. To state it roughly, if a navigator had a chronometer—a highly accurate timepiece—that told him the time back at his home port, he could subtract his own time, figured astronomically, and multiply the difference in hours by 15 to find his longitude in degrees.

John Harrison, a young man when he heard of the prize, set to work on a marine timepiece and kept at it for decades. The Board delayed the award until his chronometers could be tested, and he was in his seventies before he saw much of his prize money.

But his chronometer and authorized copies of it were amazing precision instruments, and they led

115

The chronometer that helped chart the course of an epic journey rests on one of Cook's journals. Larcum Kendall's "K.1," a copy of John Harrison's "H.4," was one of the first timekeepers to be proved reliable at sea. Cook, considered the most exacting navigator of his age, returned from a three-year, around-the-world voyage in 1775 and reported that the instrument had been steadfast through heat, cold, and storm.

A new age of navigation was under way. Never before had mariners been able to calculate their longitudes—how far east or west they were—with such speed. Any navigator who knew the time at some fixed point, such as the Greenwich meridian, and his own local time could pinpoint his longitude on the vast expanse of ocean. Now once-discovered lands could easily be found again, and fearful hazards avoided.

Cook's *Endeavour*: Pathfinder Of the Pacific

Built for the sooty business of hauling coal, this North Sea bark was refitted for a royal mission. New cabins built in the hold accommodated scientists and artists on Cook's first Pacific voyage; ordinary seamen had to sling hammocks above the stores. Workers sheathed the lower hull with extra planking and armored it with nailheads against shipworms. Twelve swivel guns and ten carriage guns were added for defense. Even with a face-lift and a new name, however, the stubby, tugboat-size *Endeavour* looked so homely that the Portuguese viceroy at Rio de Janeiro refused to recognize her as a king's vessel, prompting Cook to stay on board in protest.

But she proved ideal otherwise. The slow, broad-bowed, and flat-bottomed vessels of *Endeavour*'s class could sail safely in shallow water, an advantage for a ship in unfamiliar territory. Also important, according to the Navy Board that chose the vessel, was a collier's capacity for cargo: "Their kind are roomly and will afford the advantage of stowing and carrying a large quantity of provisions."

Large enough, in fact, for a voyage around the world. The *Endeavour* was packed solid with stores, among them over 9,000 pounds of flour; 3,032 gallons of Madeira; barrels of lemon syrup, malt, and oatmeal; with enough room left over for two dogs, a goat, and 94 men. On deck, gallows held the ship's boat, along with spare planks and spars. Red knightheads, one of the few concessions to art on this workhorse, ornamented the windlass. She was sturdy and reliable—traits that prompted a practical Cook to request only colliers for his remaining voyages.

Gunport

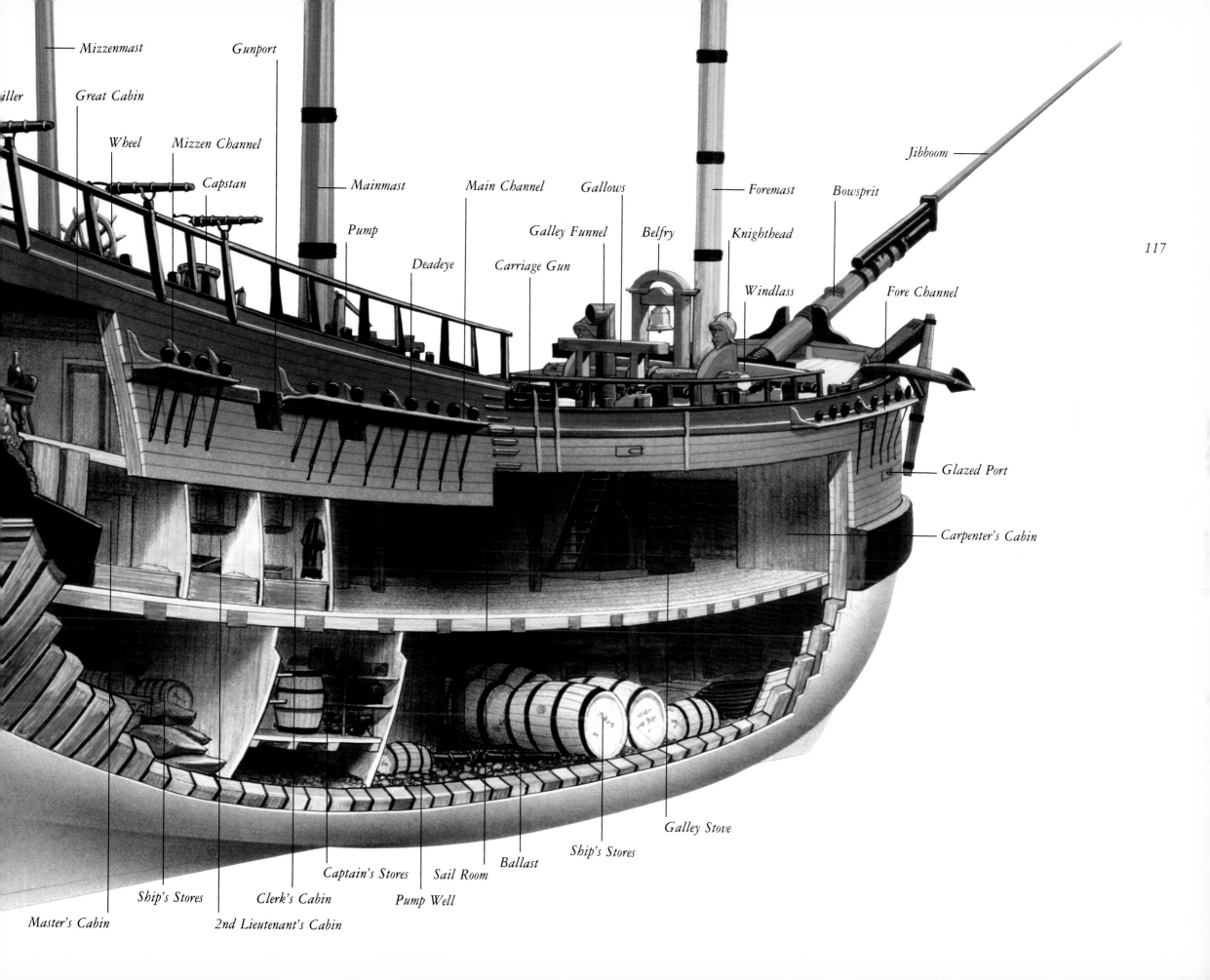

Mizzenmast

Gunport

Tiller

Great Cabin

Wheel

Mizzen Channel

Capstan

Mainmast

Pump

Deadeye

Main Channel

Carriage Gun

Galley Funnel

Gallows

Belfry

Knighthead

Windlass

Foremast

Bowsprit

Jibboom

Fore Channel

117

Glazed Port

Carpenter's Cabin

Master's Cabin

Ship's Stores

2nd Lieutenant's Cabin

Clerk's Cabin

Captain's Stores

Pump Well

Sail Room

Ballast

Ship's Stores

Galley Stove

explorers into a new age of certainty about where they were sailing. Cook, who had taken a copy made by Larcum Kendall on his second and third voyages, praised its accuracy and ease of use.

The device perfected by Harrison, the patient stay-at-home watchmaker, soon became standard equipment on far-flung British explorations. Now a place once discovered would stay discovered. The explorer could sail great distances in confidence, far from known landmarks.

The systematic exploration of the Pacific marked a new kind of international rivalry, less damaging to Europe than war. Ocean exploration became an affair of governments and learned societies, of naval officers and scientists. The profit motive ceased to be all-powerful.

A great series of Pacific voyages was under way in 1766, when the *Dolphin,* the first copper-sheathed ship to have undertaken a long ocean passage, was sent out under England's Samuel Wallis. He had demanding instructions: to search for "Land or Islands of Great extent"—the Great Southern Continent—"between Cape Horn and New Zeeland."

Wallis crossed the Pacific slightly farther south than most of his predecessors. He sailed through the Tuamotus, their cliffs teeming with birdlife, and eventually came in sight of the peak of a large island. At sunset some crewmen spotted in the south what appeared to be range upon range of high mountains: "We now suposed we saw the long wishd for Southern Continent, which has been often talkd of, but neaver before seen by any Europeans." What they had actually sighted was undoubtedly hazy ranks of clouds, which can take on the appearance of distant land during tropical sunsets. Wallis made for the "northernmost land in sight," the island Tahiti.

The *Dolphin* inched her way through the surf into Matavai Bay, where she lay for more than a month. The men provisioned the ship, recovered their health, and with some difficulty established good relations with the amiable inhabitants. Possibly too amiable: In exchange for their affections, the attractive young women of the island began to demand payment in iron nails. The sailors responded by surreptitiously extracting vital hardware from the ship's woodwork. Inflation set in as asking prices rose from 20- or 30-penny to 40-penny nails, then to large spikes. Wallis finally had to discipline the men to keep his ship from falling apart.

Wallis explored no farther to the south, and returned home in 1768 by way of the East Indies and the Cape of Good Hope. In England he learned that Cook's *Endeavour* expedition was fitting out and that a rival French expedition under Louis Antoine de Bougainville was already at sea.

Bougainville had a frigate and a storeship. He was the first explorer-commander to take along a scientific team: Pierre-Antoine Véron, an astronomer, and Philibert Commerson, a botanist. It was not easy to fit civilian specialists into the daily life of a warship. Commerson, for example, had brought along a young "valet" who was discovered, partway through the voyage, to be a woman. But Bougainville handled people as ably as he did his frigate, the *Boudeuse,* and the voyage proceeded without mishap. Like Wallis, whose track he roughly followed,

After escaping Australia's reefs, Endeavour *crept north. She left behind some 50 tons of jetsam: oil jars, decayed stores, stone and iron ballast—and six cannons, which lay on the reef 199 years before they were salvaged (left). Cook beached his damaged vessel on the coast of what is now Queensland (above). The crew unloaded anchors and cargo to lighten her, then tilted her over for repairs. During the weeks-long job the mariners ate kangaroo, turtle, and wild plantain.*

Bougainville found Tahiti and "took possession." This was a mere formality; the French did not occupy the island until 1843. Nevertheless, it is Bougainville's name, not Wallis's, that is intimately associated with Tahiti. Bougainville's bust adorns a quay on the Papeete waterfront. The Frenchman understood the significance of the lovely and exotic island, a place that would, more than two centuries later, remain a symbol of faraway peace and beauty.

Yet his stay there lasted only two weeks. He sailed on westward through the Samoan group and the New Hebrides, and on, farther west than anyone had gone in that latitude, until the sound of surf on Australia's Great Barrier Reef warned him to turn. Then he sailed northeast, through the Louisiades and Solomons, along the coast of New Ireland, and on to Batavia and back to France, reaching home in March 1769. He arrived not knowing how close he had been to the great prize—Australia, still unrecognized as an island continent.

Each expedition of the middle 1760's crossed the Pacific from southeast to northwest, in latitudes with good prevailing winds. The expanse to the south remained unknown. To Cook's *Endeavour* fell the challenge of pushing into the latitudes where adverse winds had repelled earlier explorers.

The *Endeavour* was as different from Bougainville's *Boudeuse* as her commanding officer was from Bougainville. Cook's vessel was not even a warship, except by courtesy. She was a North Sea collier, a very strongly built ship with a flat bottom and a capacious hold to carry coal. Though neither elegant nor fast, she was weatherly, dependable, and tough. The Navy Board, realizing the need for a roomy ship

Fierce New Zealand Maoris greeted the Endeavour *in 1769 by brandishing weapons. They were not bluffing; Maoris of that day would eat enemies with "peculiar satisfaction," according to the ship's surgeon. But their tattoos (far left) and carvings, this one from a war canoe, bespeak skillful artistry.*

"The whole made a grand and Noble appearence such as was never seen before in this Sea," wrote Cook on viewing Tahiti's war fleet in 1774. More than 300 canoes, with upturned bows and sterns, carried warriors and provisions. A towering white-feathered hat and colored robes adorned a chief (center, front boat). Though impressive, the dress seemed to Cook "ill calculated for the day of Battle." Cook's four visits to Tahiti won him the islanders' affection and respect, and their title, Arii Tute—Cook, the chief.

to carry provisions for a long voyage, had authorized her purchase for the expedition. The navy had refitted her and mounted a few guns, but she retained the good qualities of her origin.

The first—and public—purpose of the expedition was to convey astronomers to a good place for observing a transit of the planet Venus across the disk of the sun. This rare event offered an opportunity to calculate the distance of the sun from the earth. While plans were being discussed, Wallis arrived with his reports of Tahiti. He described it as a fine site for the Venus observation and a suitable base for exploration of the landmass south of Tahiti that his men claimed to have seen. The search for land between Tahiti and New Zealand became the second—and secret—object of the expedition.

The Admiralty appointed James Cook to command the *Endeavour*. Cook had volunteered for the Royal Navy as an able seaman in 1755, on the eve of the Seven Years' War among the major European powers, when anyone could see that war was coming. Such action was unusual, eccentric even, in a merchant seaman, and the recruiting lieutenant at Wapping, accustomed to dragging recruits from dockside taverns, must have been surprised and gratified to see Cook.

He was voluntarily entering a service notorious for harsh discipline, poor pay, worse food, and an appalling record of health, to say nothing of the hazards of battle. To be sure, there was the possibility of a career as an officer. Eighteenth-century naval officers usually came from a higher social class than Cook's, but they were not members of a closed caste. Some officers came in "through the hawsepipe"—up

from the ranks—but Cook could not have counted on promotion by that uncertain channel.

In 1755 he was a mate on a collier based in Whitby—the very port where the *Endeavour*'s keel was to be laid. He had been promised a skipper's berth. If he had simply been bored with the coal trade and had wanted more distant voyages, he could easily have shipped on an Indiaman with better pay, an easier life, and the prospect of modest affluence through private trade. Why the navy?

It may have been patriotism. Cook, though certainly not simple, was unselfconscious about ideas such as love of country. He may have joined the navy on the eve of war because he thought it was his duty.

We may never know, for Cook was a reticent man. He was not taciturn—he talked engagingly of his experiences—but he was literal, matter-of-fact, precise. His surviving personal correspondence is courteous and formal. (His wife, after his death, destroyed the revealing letters he had written to her.) His journals are voluminous, for he had much to describe. But he stuck to observed facts and did not waste words. Only rarely, after some major crisis, did he reveal a glimpse of his inner thoughts.

Except for flashes of temper, Cook had none of the theatricality that often forms part of a hero's equipment. He was tolerant and courteous, as little given to moral judgments as to petty quarrels. But in

"The discovery of a Southern Continent is the object . . . in view," wrote Cook in 1773. That January he became the first explorer to sail across the Antarctic Circle. He logged 12,000 miles in the Antarctic seas, dodging "Ice Islands" and floes until pack ice made it impossible to go "one Inch farther South," yet failed to find the rich southern land he sought. His naturalists saw petrels, seals, whales, and penguins (left), but found little else surviving the cold. Cook later concluded that "no man will ever venture farther than I." He did not anticipate how enticing his reports of seals and whales would sound to hunters.

seamanship he set himself the most exacting standards of conduct and competence. His stern professionalism is probably the most important clue to his character. The man was inseparable from the seaman. Although fair, he was a hard taskmaster. Men who had sailed with Cook knew their business.

"Of course I had a *heiva* of the old boy," wrote Midshipman James Trevenen after Cook had raged at him for carelessness. "Heiva" was Polynesian for dances "which bore so great a resemblance to the violent motions and stampings on the Deck of Captain Cook in the paroxysms of passion."

Like any naval officer, Cook was a strict disciplinarian, but he was surprisingly lax about drinking. The quantity of spirits consumed on Cook's ship must have been substantial. On Christmas Day 1768 "all hands get abominably drunk so that at night there was scarce a sober man in the ship." One wonders who took the wheel. Perhaps Cook thought that in so arduous a service occasional excess, accompanied by loyal toasts, was good for morale.

By 18th-century standards, Cook was relatively mild in meting out punishment. Fear was not the basis of his superb power of command. He was trusted and respected as few commanding officers have ever been. He was even loved, in a distant fashion, by the officers who knew him best.

Cook's achievements, the three great voyages that made him famous, had one characteristic in common: Each provided a host of unexpected discoveries, yet on each journey the major questions Cook had been told to resolve turned out negatively. Optical discrepancies rendered the Venus observations at Tahiti inconclusive. Then, between Tahiti and

"Take to the boats!" Cook shouted, beset on this 14th day of February 1779 by a mob of Hawaiians, who had revered him just weeks before. Perhaps they had tired of feeding his crew. Now a dispute had developed over a stolen boat, and Cook could see the danger. He waved for reinforcements

too late. "A chief gave him a stab in the Neck or Shoulder, with an Iron spike, by which he fell, with his face in the Water." Other natives joined in the fray. In seconds the great explorer lay dead, his voyages finally done.

Canoeists paddle through the chop near the green-cloaked volcanic crags of the Kauai coast. The Hawaiians' boat-handling impressed the explorers of Cook's day: "So perfectly masters of themselves in the Water, that it appears their natural Element."

New Zealand he found no landmass. He proved New Zealand to be two islands, not the peninsula of any vast continent. On the second voyage Cook explored the icy Antarctic seas so extensively that maps began to omit the "southern continent." And the third trip established that the Northwest Passage, if it existed, was not for sailing ships.

The unexpected benefits from Cook's first voyage included a survey of New Zealand's coasts and a self-assigned exploration of eastern Australia. History is unclear as to which European first saw Australia, but the Dutch had already reconnoitered the northern and western shores in the early 17th century. Thus Cook did not "discover" Australia. He did establish that it was not entirely desert, that the coastal lands on the east were habitable, agreeable even (though the convicts who were the first settlers may not have found them so). Probably the most important discovery of this voyage was the rich land that would become the Australian state of New South Wales. The Great Barrier Reef was an important scientific find, which also provided some of the most harrowing moments of Cook's career. At least twice he almost lost his ship there. Had Bougainville, two years earlier, braved the reef as Cook now did, Australia might have become French, not British.

In the course of the triumphant circumnavigation of his second voyage, Cook made the first probes south of the Antarctic Circle and his first crossing of the Pacific from west to east. Aided by the newly perfected chronometer, he collected precise navigational information. He left the relatively familiar islands of Polynesia for the largely unexplored region of Melanesia, where he surveyed the New Hebrides.

Bounty, Breadfruit, And a Mutiny Of Never-dying Fame

"I'll Pawn my Honor, I'll Give My Bond, Mr. Christian, never to think of this if youll desist." Fletcher Christian, however, had had enough. "No, Captain Bligh. . . . 'Tis too late, I have been in Hell for this Fortnight passd and am determined to bear it no longer." In one of history's best-known mutinies, the captain and 18 loyal men were set adrift in the *Bounty*'s 23-foot launch.

Sixteen months before that fateful day in April 1789, the *Bounty* had set sail from Spithead, England. In command was William Bligh, formerly master on Captain Cook's *Resolution,* now sent out to transplant breadfruit trees from Tahiti to the British West Indies as food for slaves.

A sparing lash, fresh food, "a strict regard to cleanliness," "chearfullness with exercise, and a sufficiency of rest" were among Bligh's prescriptions for his men. Results were good: hardly "a symptom of either Scurvy, Flux or Fever." But Bligh had flashes of bad temper and could be abusive:

"Scoundrels, damned rascals, hounds, hellhounds, beasts, and infamous wretches," as he was wont to characterize the crew.

After ten months at sea, the *Bounty* reached Tahiti. On this "Paradise of the World" discipline weakened. "Such . . . worthless petty Officers . . . never was in a Ship as are in this," the captain wrote. More than five months went by before the ship, now filled with plants, resumed its voyage.

But life ashore with "most . . . affectionate" women had spoiled the crew for sea. Railed at by Bligh, Fletcher Christian, the captain's erstwhile favorite, shot back, "Sir . . . I have been [in] hell for weeks with you." Bligh's accusations about missing coconuts humiliated Christian in front of the crew. He decided to escape, but a midshipman intervened: "There's no need to swim. The people are ripe for anything!"

The next Bligh knew, Christian and three others "came into my Cabbin . . . and seizing me tyed my hands with a Cord . . . and threatned me with instant death if I

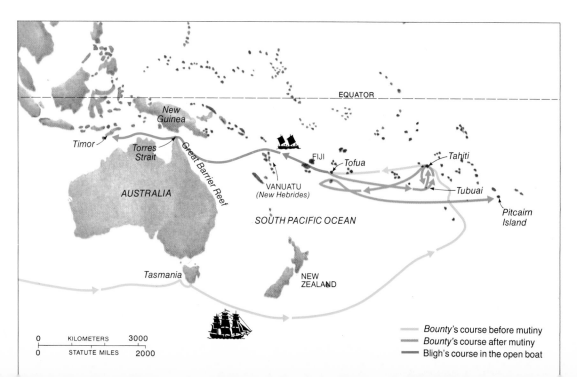

"Loaves of Bread, or . . . a most excellent substitute growes here," wrote Cook about South Pacific breadfruit (below). Why not introduce it to the colonies? Mutineers diverted Bounty from the task, but Captain Bligh persisted. In 1793 he reached Jamaica in the breadfruit-laden Providence, but slaves there refused to eat the fruit. It fed only pigs until humans developed a taste for it many years later.

spoke." Bligh was cast off near the island of Tofua in an overloaded boat with five days' supply of food, a compass, a quadrant, the ship's log, and four cutlasses. In 47 days the half-starved men reached the island of Timor—3,600 nautical miles away. A year later in England a court-martial acquitted Bligh of loss of the *Bounty*.

After trying to settle on the island of Tubuai, 16 of the mutineers voted to return to Tahiti. A British frigate eventually found 14 of them; 10 made it home for trial. The whereabouts of Christian and the others remained a mystery for 19 years.

In 1808 a ship from Boston stopped at lonely Pitcairn Island. There among some 30 women and children lived a solitary Englishman. He told of the *Bounty's* 7,800-mile odyssey in search of a home: west to the Fijis, then east to Pitcairn. He told of debauchery, revenge, and thievery—of how suicide, drunkenness, disease, and murder took their toll. Of Christian's little band of nine, only one had survived to tell the tale.

"It was such cases as that of the Galápagos . . . which chiefly led me to study the origin of species," wrote Charles Darwin after his five-year voyage on the Beagle. These islands sheltered strange creatures. The giant tortoises were so large it took

"six or eight men to lift them." For centuries buccaneers, sealers, whalers, and explorers had carried off these beasts, for they made excellent eating and could live for months aboard ship without food or water.

The Beagle *left England in 1831 on a routine mission—to chart South America's coasts and take longitude readings—*

but Darwin's presence wrote her trip into science history. This young naturalist of "enlarged curiosity" made fossil, plant, and animal observations which led him to a stunning theory: that species evolve from other species by means of natural selection.

Everywhere Cook went, he either dashed into oblivion the casually recorded "discoveries" of a dozen earlier voyages or established them as true islands and mainlands, accurately charted at last.

Although he found no South Sea continent, one item of evidence persuaded him to suggest the existence of a land of hostile clime: "I firmly beleive that there is a tract of land near the Pole, which is the Source of most of the ice which is spread over this vast Southern Ocean."

This place lay remote and uninhabitable, beyond the roving ramparts of ice. As Cook surmised, "Thick fogs, Snow storms, Intense Cold and every other thing that can render Navigation dangerous one has to encounter and these difficulties are greatly heightned by the enexpressable horrid aspect of the Country, a Country doomed by Nature never once to feel the warmth of the Suns rays, but to lie for ever buried under everlasting snow and ice."

The third voyage provided still more discoveries. After stops in the South Pacific, Cook struck boldly north, his mission to seek the Northwest Passage from the Pacific side. In January 1778 he came upon Kauai. The first European to visit the Hawaiian chain, he named it in honor of his friend and patron, the Earl of Sandwich. Cook and his men found the natives "very fearful of giving offence, asking if they should sit down, or spit on the decks."

From Hawaii he saw only empty sea until reaching the coast of present-day Oregon. The *Resolution* badly needed repairs. He sailed north along the shore, looking for a good harbor, and found one on the west coast of what is now Vancouver Island. His entrance amazed the local Indians who, mistaking

the ships' masts for bare trees, assumed that their visitors had arrived on floating islands. Cook's party leaped to conclusions as well: When the Indians called out the word *nutka,* the newcomers decided it must be the local place-name. In fact they were hearing directions to "go around the harbor." Thus came into being the name Nootka Sound. The Indians warmed to the newcomers, and would often put on ceremonial masks and serenade the crew. (One time, a maskless Indian improvised by appropriating a ship's kettle to wear on his head.) The month needed for repairs passed in relative quiet.

The visit was to be one of Cook's last happy encounters with the peoples he discovered. After an arduous survey of the North American coastline and a futile attempt to penetrate the ice beyond the Bering Strait, he headed south, planning to winter in the newfound Sandwich Islands. But his warm welcome on the big island of Hawaii soon turned sour. One

dispute let to another. At last, in a confused stabbing incident on a Hawaiian beach, Captain Cook met his end, at the hands of the Polynesians he had studied for so long.

Cook's tragic death did not lessen the contribution he made to geography, anthropology, and science. On his first voyage, he was better off than Bougainville in his choice of scientific companions: Joseph Banks, the rich young amateur in botany and zoology, and Daniel Solander, the learned Swedish botanist. The Admiralty was delighted to accommodate a scientist who would pay his own way and Solander's too. These gentlemen and the accompanying retinue—Banks took along two artists, a secretary, four servants, and two dogs—did not easily fit into a ship the size of the *Endeavour.* Cook had to share his day quarters in the Great Cabin with them. He bore no grudge.

Although Banks could be petulant and Solander careless, both were scholars of distinction, and Cook found his daily talks with them enlightening. He acquired in considerable measure the scientists' habits and methods of inquiry.

Banks ungraciously refused to go on the second voyage, because the Admiralty prohibited the *Resolution* from sailing top-heavy to suit his requirements (which this time included two horn players). His replacement, Johann Reinhold Forster, sorely tried Cook's patience with his complaints and paranoia. Banks did send David Nelson, a quiet but attentive botanical collector, on the third voyage, but Cook made many observations himself. He was sharply attentive, particularly in anthropological matters. His precise and shrewd comments place all

Gripped by ice and then frozen fast, H.M.S. Terror *founders in the Arctic seas south of Baffin Island. Capt. George Back had sailed her north on a surveying mission in 1836. In summer the ice released its hold, having imprisoned the ship for over nine months. "Crazy, broken, and leaky," she limped home for repairs.*

In 1840 James Clark Ross sailed the Terror *and the* Erebus *to Antarctica, where he made countless discoveries, including the ice shelf and sea that now bear his name.*

130 students of Pacific peoples and customs in his debt.

Cook is also known for his application of science to a practical purpose—health at sea. It is difficult today for us to grasp the terrifying dimensions of this problem. Of the 170,000 or so men in the Royal Navy during the American Revolution, 1,200 were killed in action, 42,000 deserted, and 18,000 died of disease. Diseases were many; but on long voyages, scurvy was probably the worst and most dreaded. After suffering gross disfigurement, its weakened victims would often die of infection. Yet Cook brought a ship's company through the three-year first and second voyages without losing a single man from scurvy.

Scurvy is caused by a deficiency of vitamin C, which is found in many fresh fruits and vegetables. No one in Cook's day had heard of vitamin C, but many had observed that men who ate fresh food did not get scurvy. Cook tried everything; neither he nor his surgeons knew what contributed most to his success. He kept his ships scrubbed, ventilated, and fumigated; his men wore warm, clean clothing. If nothing else, this policy kept the crew healthier than usual on such voyages.

Cook took along foods that he thought might prevent scurvy: sauerkraut, carrot juice, and a "portable soup." This last was brown meat broth evaporated into gelatinous sheets that looked like slabs of glue. The stuff was boiled up with oatmeal or whole-grain wheat for breakfast. One slab, which went around the world with Cook, is on display at Britain's National Maritime Museum.

Probably the most important elements in Cook's success were his deliberate policy of short passages where possible, his energy and persistence in procuring fresh food wherever he went, and his strictness in making men eat it. This was not always easy. He once had two men, unaccustomed to fresh meat, flogged for refusing their rations of beef.

Cook's views on scurvy prevention overrated malt and undervalued lemon juice, the best of defenses. But his example carried weight, and the Admiralty waited until 1795 before ordering a daily issue of juice to all hands. By 1800 the fleet was virtually free of scurvy. The lemon- or lime-juice drinking earned British ships the appellation "lime-juicers," which in turn yielded a nickname for the sailors and for the English in general: "limeys."

The Second Age of Discovery reached its zenith with the return of Cook's ships in 1780. His achievements left no vast, unknown areas in the world's oceans, except near the Poles. At the end of the century, navigators like George Vancouver had only to fill small gaps in the Pacific picture Cook and his predecessors had painted.

Few explorers in Cook's time showed much interest either in trade or in dominion. Officers and crewmen in Cook's and Vancouver's ships conducted some private trade, particularly in furs, but surely neither captain would have turned aside from the Northwest Passage, as Martin Frobisher did, to chase a tale of gold. Their job was to explore and describe matters of interest. Cook's reward, he wrote, was "the pleasure which Naturly results to a Man from being the first discoverer, even was it nothing more than sand and Shoals."

Past Barriers
Of Ice
To the Poles

To some explorers, the bitter winds of the polar seas sang a siren's song, offering the promise of a northern passage between the Atlantic and Pacific oceans and the chance to conquer a frozen frontier.

In 1818 the British Parliament, by offering rewards for Arctic missions, inspired an era of exploration that would put men at the Poles within the century.

The 375-ton British bark *Hecla* almost made it through the Northwest Passage in 1820 before she met an ice barrier. The *Erebus* expedition led by Sir John Franklin in 1845 sought the same elusive goal. The renowned explorer and his crew starved to death, but the 40 search parties sent to look for them virtually completed the map of the Canadian Arctic. It was a Norwegian, Roald Amundsen, who in 1906 finally navigated the passage in a six-man converted herring boat, *Gjöa*.

Other expeditions sought the North Pole. In 1881 the American steam yacht *Jeannette* was crushed by ice while trying to reach the Pole from the Bering Strait. Although 30 sailors met frigid death trying to escape, the tragedy provided an important lesson when, only a year or two later, pieces of the ship turned up far across the Arctic Ocean, on Greenland's shore. The wreckage proved that polar ice drifted long distances.

Fridtjof Nansen of Norway thought he could ride this drifting ice to the North Pole. He built the *Fram* with a round hull and smooth sides so "instead of nipping the ship, the ice should raise it up out of the water." *Fram* failed to reach the Pole, but she survived three years in the pack ice.

April 1909: "The Pole at last," Robert E. Peary wrote. "The prize of three centuries." The American naval officer had rammed his

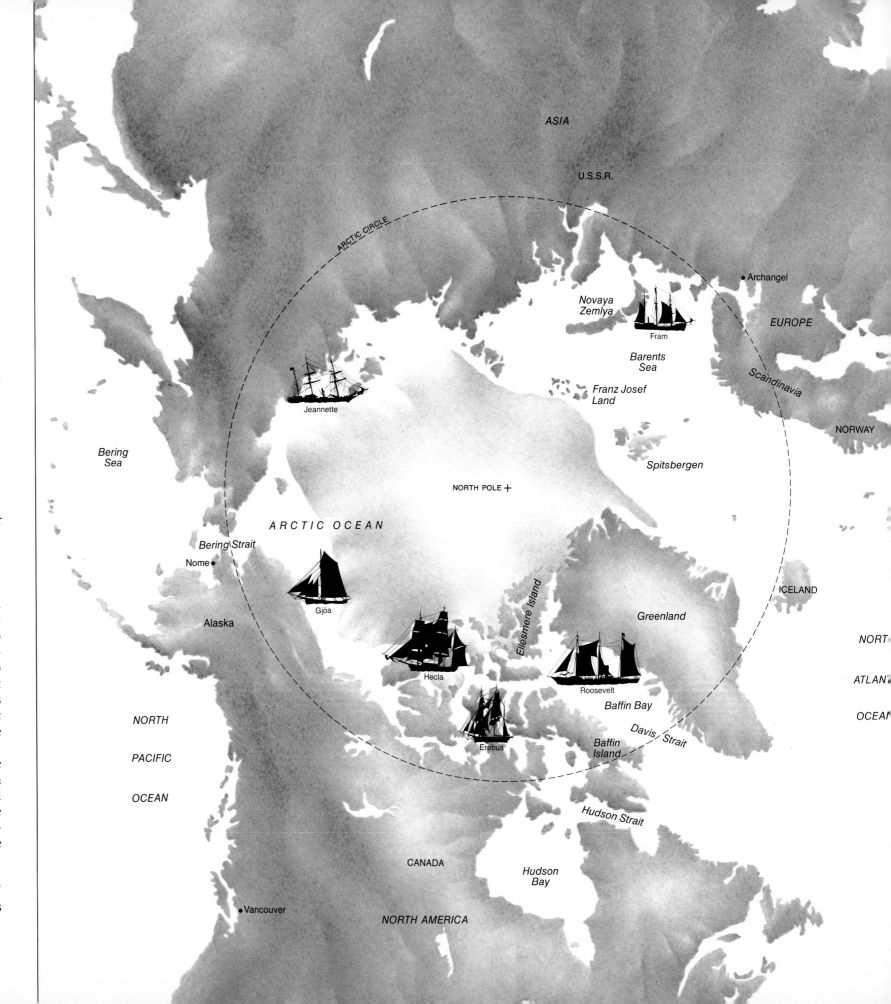

schooner *Roosevelt* into the Arctic Ocean until he could go no farther, and then trekked 420 miles over ice to be the first man at the northernmost point on the planet.

News of an American flag at the North Pole hit Roald Amundsen with gale force. He had planned to sail Nansen's old *Fram* north, but now decided to shift his aim southward, to Antarctica.

Ever since Captain Cook found seals in the Antarctic, hunters had been making discoveries in this region. The U. S. sealer *Hero* found what is now the Antarctic Peninsula in 1820, and the British sealer *Jane* penetrated the Weddell Sea in 1823. By 1840 a U. S. expedition on the sloop *Vincennes* established Antarctica as a continent.

Now, in 1910, Amundsen was determined to be the first man to reach the only Pole left to discover. The British explorer Robert F. Scott, in the whaler *Terra Nova,* was en route to the same goal. The two men battled ice floes, scurvy, and cold as they fought an undeclared race. Amundsen's expedition went like clockwork, and in December 1911 he stood at the South Pole— 34 days ahead of the British. Scott, too, made it, but he and his party died on the return trek, defeated by hunger and storm.

Sir Ernest Shackleton's crew faced a comparable threat in 1915, when the *Endurance* crumpled in the ice of the Weddell Sea. For 16 months, including more than 100 days camped on an ice floe, they battled the elements. All were finally rescued.

The barkentine *Bear of Oakland* carried supplies on one of five expeditions Richard E. Byrd made to Antarctica between 1928 and 1955. Known as "Admiral of the Ends of the Earth," Byrd explored more than 100,000 square miles of the continent and was the first to fly over both Poles.

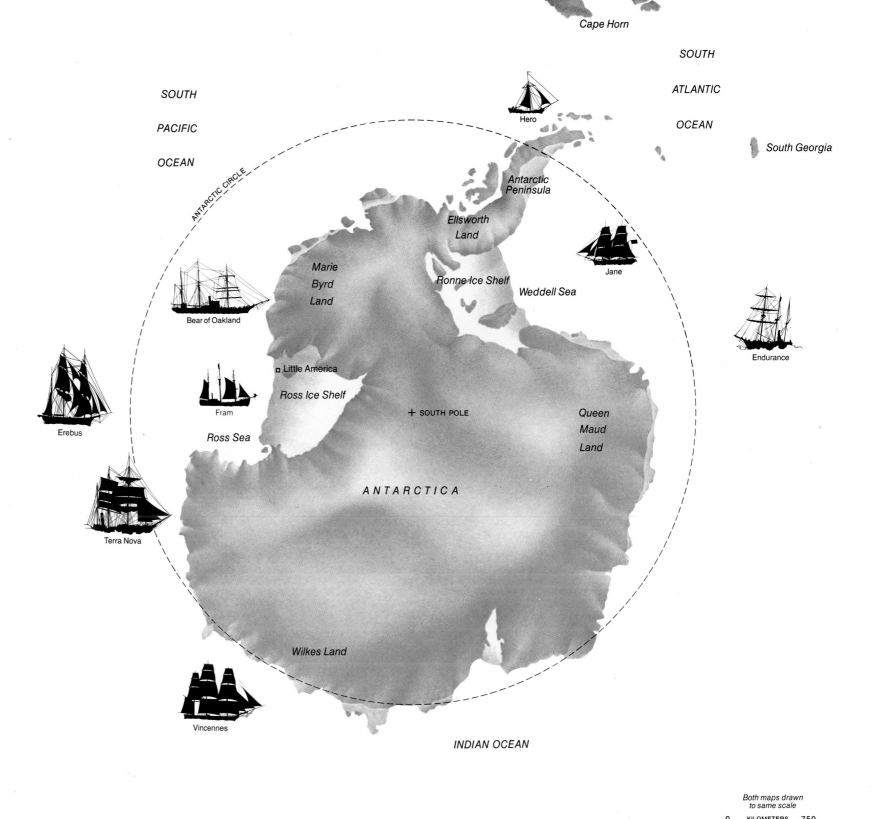

SOUTH AMERICA

Cape Horn

SOUTH ATLANTIC OCEAN

SOUTH PACIFIC OCEAN

South Georgia

ANTARCTIC CIRCLE

Hero

Antarctic Peninsula

Ellsworth Land

Marie Byrd Land

Ronne Ice Shelf

Weddell Sea

Jane

Bear of Oakland

Endurance

□ Little America

Erebus

Fram

Ross Ice Shelf

+ SOUTH POLE

Queen Maud Land

Ross Sea

A N T A R C T I C A

Terra Nova

Wilkes Land

Vincennes

INDIAN OCEAN

Both maps drawn to same scale

0   KILOMETERS   750

0   STATUTE MILES   500

Wolves and Shepherds

Buccaneer, sea wolf, swashbuckler, the pirate of fiction—golden earrings, pistols in belt—sails a black ship with the Jolly Roger at the main peak. He swaggers through adventures too lurid to be true. And yet . . . pirates in 1720 captured a heavily armed Indiaman that had put into a lonely bay near Madagascar. Most of the captives joined the pirate crew. The captain and his loyal crewmen were about to have their throats slit when a black-bearded giant with a wooden leg thumped forward and stopped the murders. He said he had once served with the good captain and found him decent. A century later Robert Louis Stevenson came across the story, and from that real one-legged pirate emerged the immortal Long John Silver.

Since Phoenician times outlaws have preyed on peaceful trade and travelers. Pirates seized Julius Caesar and Miguel de Cervantes, giving both fuel for their literary imaginations. Pirates sailed the sea-lanes as marauders and at times as merchants. Chaucer's 14th-century Shipman—"of nyce conscience took he no keep"—occasionally engaged in piracy. There was little law on the high seas. Most deep-water merchantmen went armed for protection and, if a likely victim happened in range, for plunder.

In the 16th and 17th centuries, however, piracy ceased to be a free-for-all. The pirate became a professional. Maritime powers, lacking regular navies, increasingly employed pirates as sea fighters. The beys of the Barbary States in North Africa were the most notorious sponsors of pirates-for-hire. But, from the middle of the 16th century, European governments grew weary of dependence on treacherous mercenaries and began to launch their own navies. The best men for the new navies were often former pirates.

A Dutch man-of-war splinters a Spanish galley in 1602, dooming chained oarsmen and—by such triumphs of sail—galley warfare itself.

Even at the height of his fame, people in England who disliked Sir Francis Drake called him the "master-thief of the unknown world." For he had been a slaver, a smuggler, a privateer, and, with or without royal backing, a pirate on the Spanish Main. But Queen Elizabeth made him a knight after he had become the first Englishman to sail—and plunder—around the world. And Drake would become a distinguished officer in the navy that the queen launched with the loot and skill that he and her other predatory sea dogs provided.

Drake did most of his early raiding and acquired most of his loot in the New World. For a hundred years and more after his time the Spanish Main—the northeast coast of South America and nearby waters—remained the classic haunt of pirates. The Caribbean, an important source of plunder, lay outside the ordinary range of European navies. Spanish warships escorted silver shipments across the Atlantic, but the ships were rarely effective in the Caribbean itself. The other colonial governments—English, French, and Dutch, mutual rivals as well as enemies of Spain—had to rely either on ineffectual planter militias or on gangs of buccaneers. Mercenary desperadoes paid by plunder, buccaneers were human flotsam washed up on the Antillean beaches by the tides of settlement and war.

The French word *boucan* means the process of curing strips of meat by smoking it over a slow fire. The original *boucaniers* were men who lived by hunting and by selling hides and smoked meat to passing ships. All the islands of the Greater Antilles supported great herds of feral pigs and cattle, the

descendants of animals that escaped from Spanish farms and ranches onto the virgin savannas. The pursuit of these ownerless beasts provided a rough living for masterless men—marooned or ship-wrecked sailors, deserters, escaped felons, runaway indentured servants, and all who disliked organized society. They soon graduated from hunting to robbery, and thence to piracy, in ships taken by force from some of their customers.

They moved from the inland forests to the harbors, where they established their own settlements: Tortuga, off the northwest coast of Hispaniola, and Port Royal at the entrance to Kingston harbor in Jamaica. By the middle of the 17th century they had formed vicious outlaw bands, well armed and, when it suited their selfish goals, well led. They became a formidable menace to the shipping of all nations and to small harbors throughout the Caribbean.

No armed force in the area was strong enough to suppress buccaneering. National governments were rarely willing to spare warships. Colonial governors dealt gingerly with the buccaneers, for they never knew when they might have to call on their violent services. Whenever war broke out, French and English governors promptly issued letters of marque to buccaneer leaders, converting them by a stroke of the pen from pirates to privateers, legalizing their plundering and directing it against the enemy. When a war ended, the buccaneers simply went from public employment back to private enterprise, from privateering to piracy. They disposed of their voluminous loot—sugar, hides, cacao beans, Spanish silver—in North American ports. The good people of Providence, Boston, and New York made

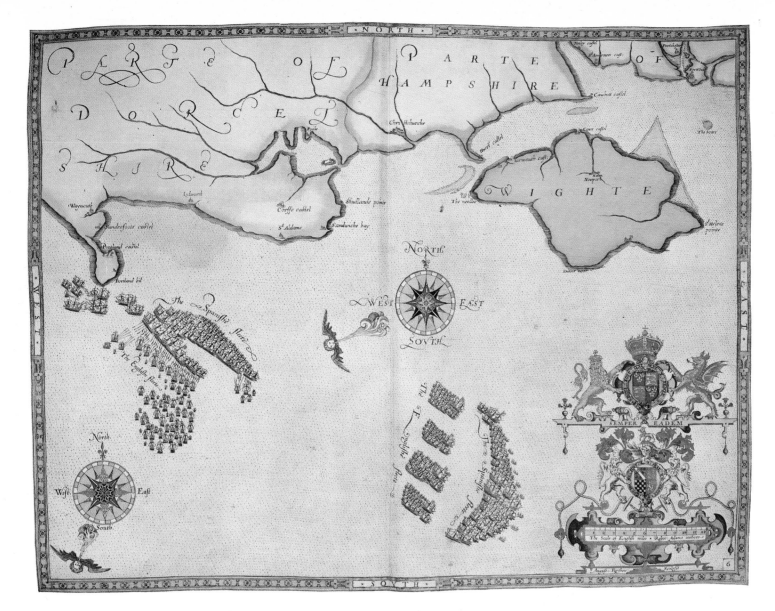

In 1670 the governor of Jamaica commissioned Morgan to raise a fleet for defense against a possible invasion from Cuba. He collected 36 vessels, manned by about 1,500 English and French buccaneers. Not content to "defend," he marched his men across the Isthmus of Panama and sacked Panama City. For this exploit—carried out when England and Spain were at peace and negotiating a treaty of friendship—Morgan received a slap on the wrist. He was arrested and shipped to England, as was the governor, who was lodged briefly in the Tower for appearance's sake. After a decent interval, Morgan was released, knighted, and appointed lieutenant-governor of Jamaica, with a special commission for suppressing buccaneers.

Some buccaneers—expendable rogues—he arrested and hanged. Others, perhaps for a consideration, he countenanced. He led no more piratical expeditions, but he reportedly invested in them. The government wearied of his prevarications and removed him from office in 1684. Morgan died four years later from an excess of rum and bad living.

Morgan's principal base, old Port Royal—wicked, opulent, and shabby—did not long survive him. It paid the price of its sins, so the pious believed, and disappeared beneath the sea in the great earthquake of 1692. The port's pirates scattered to less conspicuous bases in the Bahamas.

In the second half of the 18th century, pirates ceased menacing shipping, except in a dwindling number of places where governments protected them, or in areas such as the China seas and Malay archipelago that were too remote from naval bases to be controlled. This increasing safety on the seas—at

no puritanical inquiries about the source of these cheap imports.

Many buccaneers died in battle or by the rope. Those who came to "swing and sun-dry at Execution Dock," however, were mostly small fry. They had found in the grog shops and whorehouses of Port Royal reward enough for the hardships and dangers of their trade. The more intelligent leaders set out to make their fortunes by piracy but at the same time tried, by mercenary services, to remain friends with the colonial authorities. They hoped eventually to make a deal for a pardon, to buy their way into respectable official employment, and to die rich in their beds. Some attained all of these hopes.

Henry Morgan was perhaps the most celebrated. The young Welshman sailed out to the Caribbean about 1655 and eventually joined the Port Royal buccaneers. Morgan saved up enough loot to buy his own vessel. He soon became known as a bold and lucky captain, the leader of a large and well-armed gang. He carried out many profitable raids on Spanish shipping and harbors. At Portobelo, Morgan acquired an unparalleled reputation for pillage and torture of prisoners. At Maracaibo, chased by three Spanish warships, he lured them into shoal water, then sent a fire ship alongside. One Spanish ship was set ablaze, another grounded to be looted and destroyed later, and the third captured.

The Deep Sleep
Of Royal Warship
Vasa

Stockholm is a maritime city, but her archipelago is long, and captains must be patient as they thread the rocky channels to the sea. In the 17th century, families of crew members could go along as far as the last headland; then they were put ashore, and the fearsome Swedish fleet sped forth to fight for control of the Baltic Sea.

And so it was that on a quiet Sunday afternoon in August 1628, more than 200 men, women, and children boarded the royal ship *Vasa* for her maiden voyage. She was beautiful and big—the richly ornamented conveyance of her country's culture and ambition. A soft breeze carried the sound of vesper bells. The crew warped the ship along until they reached a wider part of the harbor. Then they raised four sails and the

Vasa set forth. She was gaining speed when a gust of wind suddenly blasted down from high harbor cliffs. She listed sharply. Water surged through the open gunports of the lower deck, the ship rolled over on her port side, and the passengers and crew began sliding across the decks.

Only 1,500 yards away, witnesses on shore scarcely had time to grasp what was happening. In a moment there could be no doubt: Scores of survivors were swimming, but the *Vasa* had disappeared.

Over the centuries, the dark harbor mud embraced her ever more tightly, and the *Vasa,* lost, became a legend.

Then, one day in 1956 . . . "Can't see a thing," the diver reported from 110 feet down. "Shall I come up?"

"You might as well," said Anders Fran-

zén, the amateur archaeologist who had searched for the *Vasa* for years.

"Wait a minute!" cried the diver. "I just reached out and touched something solid . . . it feels like a wall of wood! It's a big ship, all right! Now I'm climbing the wall . . . here are some square openings . . . must be gunports!"

Confirmation that the *Vasa* was really there inspired a salvage effort that had to go beyond known technology. No fully identified wooden warship near the *Vasa*'s size (200 feet long) and so nearly intact had ever been found. Her oak had survived because the Baltic is not salty enough for ship-worms, which have devoured untold numbers of wooden hulls in other waters. Divers with special hoses tunneled beneath *Vasa*'s hull so they could lay six lifting cables.

When she broke the surface in 1961, Swedes felt they had recaptured their Renaissance past. Her 700 sculptures, still showing traces of colorful paint, proclaimed Swedish might, and 24,000 artifacts were a cross section of 17th-century life.

Today, visitors at the Vasa Museum can gaze at the imposing three-master, with her 65-foot-high aftercastle, and marvel at wooden carvings of gods, beasts, angels, and emperors. Above, a crowned lion snarls from the *Vasa*'s stern. Gun carriages stand at open ports as they did on that fateful day. A pewter tankard and bottle, a clay pipe, and a leather slipper typify sailors' possessions. And so the *Vasa,* built for war, sunk before she fought, has risen at last to her ironic triumph: peaceful Sweden's most cherished maritime treasure.

least in peacetime—resulted from increases in the size, efficiency, and range of professional navies, especially those of Europe's principal maritime powers. In the Caribbean and other traditional hunting areas of European predators, the age of the buccaneers was followed by the age of the admirals.

Navies are not designed primarily as maritime police forces. They are intended as instruments of war, and in most parts of the world, until relatively modern times, they existed only in times of war. Before the introduction of effective shipborne artillery, sea battles were almost always fought by boarding and entering.

The attacking ship would range alongside an enemy ship and fasten to it with grappling hooks and lines so that fighting men could jump from one gunwale to the other and fight the enemy hand-to-hand. Pirates always fought this way, because their object was to capture and loot the ship, not destroy it. Until the 16th century, fighting ships normally used this method, for they had no way of crippling or sinking an enemy before capture, except by sending a blazing fire ship toward the enemy ship, shooting fire arrows, or slinging wads of flaming tow. But these devices were often as dangerous to the attacker as to the attacked.

A warship in the days of Chaucer's Shipman merely transported fighting men. When a maritime state went to war, its government promptly commandeered enough merchant ships—preferably the biggest and most stoutly built—to form a temporary navy. Crowded with fighting men-at-arms in addition to their normal crew of sailors, the merchant ships sailed off as warships for the duration.

"Cast loose the guns!" comes the first order, and the crew of a muzzle-loader begins its complex and dangerous job. The loaded gun, lashed down between actions, is rigged so that ropes will restrain recoil. The gun is leveled, the wooden muzzle plugs (tampions) are removed, all by precise orders, then, "Run out your guns!" The muzzles poke through the gunports. "Prime!" Powder is put in a vent near the breech. "Point your guns!" Men elevate and train the gun as the gun captain directs. "Fire!" A slow match or, later, a flintlock ignites the primer. The gun recoils. "Worm and sponge!" The barrel is swabbed to remove unignited powder. Within two minutes, powder and shot are rammed home, the gun is run out, and once more the orders build to "Fire!"

142

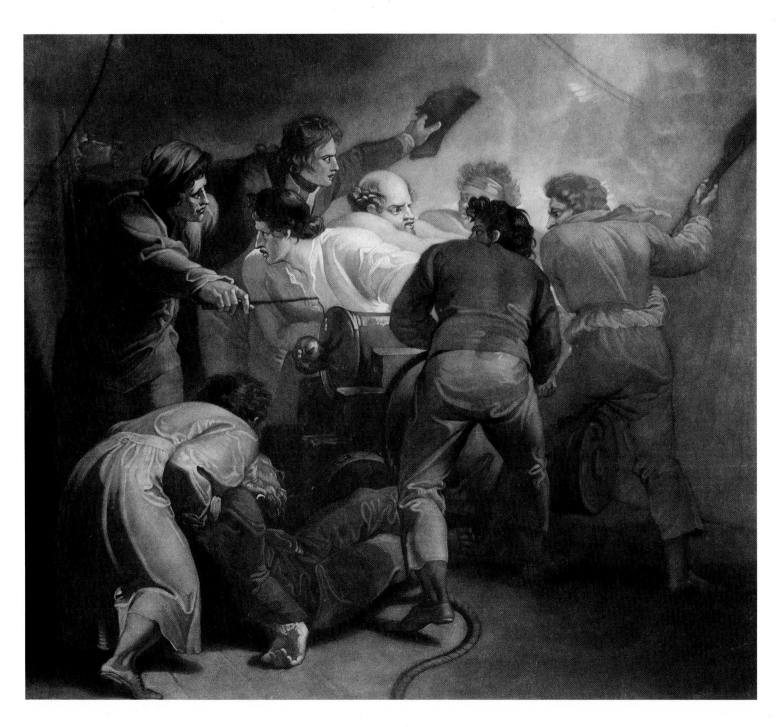

In the Middle Ages such ships were often fitted at each end with castle structures, temporary wooden towers in which archers got the advantage of height during combat. This was all the adaptation the ships needed. When the war was over, the castles might be dismantled. But by the late 15th century they had proved so useful for other purposes—for conning the ship and for cabin accommodation—that they came to be part of the permanent structure. That is why the forward superstructure of a ship is called the fo'c'sle—forecastle—to this day.

Professional or semiprofessional navies appeared in the Mediterranean several centuries before they did elsewhere in Europe. The Venetians and the Genoese rowed their vessels, as had the Greeks and Romans. Galleys generally used sail on peaceful passage. In battle, they employed oarsmen and had a major advantage—independence of the wind. Their big crews were another advantage in an age when sea fighting was hand-to-hand, because the oarsmen could also be armed for fighting. For this reason, the Venetians hired volunteer oarsmen, when they could get them, rather than slaves.

Galleys usually attacked in line abreast, each vessel guarding the vulnerable flank of its neighbor. They would try, with a burst of speed before the moment of contact, to catch the enemy broadside on.

Galleys never became major weapons of naval war in the Atlantic. Long, low, and lightly built, they were too vulnerable to Atlantic weather. And their operating range was short because of big crews and small storage capacity.

Guns had been used at sea in European waters since the 14th century. For 150 or 200 years they

A

B

C

D

E

Naval guns at first were stuck on, not built in. The swivel gun (A) of the 15th century was mounted on the gunwale. The low-slung lombard (B), its barrel of welded iron rods reinforced with hoops, had breeching tackle to check its recoil. Columbus *carried versions that could hurl a stone ball 1,000 yards. The 17th-century saker (C) slammed a 9-pound ball 1,500 yards. The carronade (D), made in Carron, Scotland, could smash hulls at close range. The 24-pounder (E) armed the* Constitution *and remained standard until the advent of armor plate.*

143

were small, wrought-iron pieces that fired stone shot. The guns were used as a supplement to crossbows and primitive hand firearms. In galleys, they were mounted to fire ahead from the fighting platform in the bow. In the smaller sailing ships they were mounted on swivels along the rails, or wales (from which we get the name "gunwales"). In bigger ships they were also fired from the "castles."

Not until the 16th century were ways found to cast guns light enough to be mounted in a ship, yet powerful enough to pound and perhaps sink an enemy. The best of them, made not of iron but of more elastic brass or bronze, could fire stone or iron shot weighing from 5 to as much as 60 pounds. The guns were heavy, awkward pieces, from 5 to 12 feet long. The larger ones among them weighed several tons.

Guns were used in the Gulf of Patras, off the coast of Greece, during the Battle of Lepanto in 1571. "The sky could not be seen for the arrows and shot," an eyewitness reported. "It was . . . dark from the smoke . . . of many fire projectiles which were inextinguishable even in the water."

More than 400 Turkish and Christian ships fought in that last great clash of galleys—the only major maritime defeat the Christians ever managed to inflict on the Turks. The Christian galleys carried "great guns" on forward fighting platforms, where the earlier, lighter guns had been mounted. Five guns at most could be mounted there. This limitation, more than anything else, caused the gradual disappearance of fighting galleys.

In sailing ships, the weight and recoil of great guns made it impractical to mount them in flimsy superstructures high above the water. The 16th-

century solution was simple and revolutionary: Mount the guns along the ship's sides, the smaller ones firing through embrasures in the gunwales, the larger ones between decks, firing through holes or gunports cut in the sides. The price was partial loss of the ship's cargo space.

The great gun gained recognition slowly, and so did the specialized ship that carried it. The English fleet that fought the Spanish Armada in 1588 still consisted largely of armed merchantmen commandeered for the battle. About 195 English ships took part in the action, but most of them were very small. Even among the hundred ships mustered at Plymouth, only about 25 were real warships.

The men who sailed in them were a mixed lot, too. The commander-in-chief, the Lord High Admiral of England, Lord Howard of Effingham, though he understood the principles of sea fighting, was not a professional seaman. Few of his captains were truly naval officers in the modern sense. Many were masters of armed merchantmen operating as privateers and many were part-time pirates. The line was hard to draw.

The Armada was the most serious threat England had faced in 500 years. It was a powerful fleet of some 130 sail, but, like the English fleet, it did not wholly consist of proper warships. The Armada's commander-in-chief, the Duke of Medina Sidonia, like Lord Howard, was an experienced naval administrator but not a professional seaman.

Medina Sidonia was to join the Duke of Parma, in command of Spanish forces in the Netherlands,

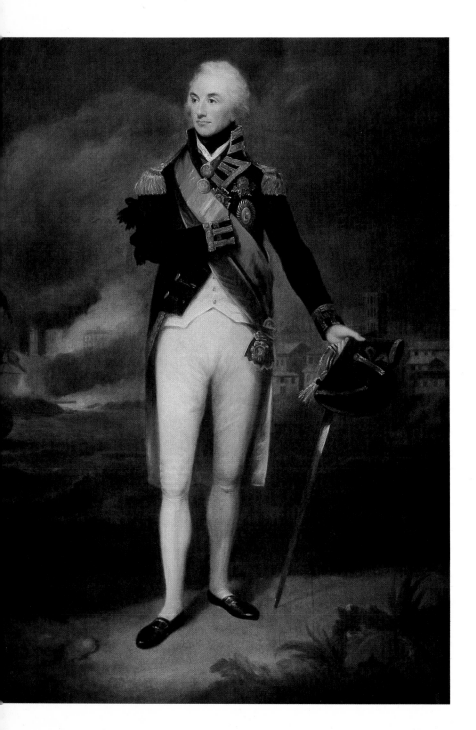

Horatio Nelson, England's greatest naval hero, earned honor with his brains and blood. His secretary said he could "think more in a minute than most men will do in an hour." Long years of war with France cost him an arm and the sight of an eye.

A brilliant and innovative tactician and a charismatic leader, he took command of the Mediterranean Fleet, and "the Nelson touch" shaped that fleet into an invincible fighting force. On October 21, 1805, the British devastated the combined French and Spanish fleet off Cape Trafalgar

(right). Struck down by a French sharpshooter, Nelson died to the sound of cannon, knowing he had given England a victory—one that would assure her of supremacy on the seas for the next hundred years.

secure at least temporary control of the Channel crossing, and convoy Parma's army across for the invasion of England. If the Spaniards landed, the English military would not be able to repel them. England's fate rested on the sea battle.

Medina Sidonia, committed to a combined operation with Parma's army, was hampered by transports and supply ships that had to be protected. He brought his fleet up the Channel in a close crescent formation, warships leading in the horns of the crescent, the transports massed in the center out of harm's way. The formation had defensive strength but it was inflexible. If Medina Sidonia could have moved faster on a wider front, he might have kept Howard's fleet bottled up in Plymouth—and he might have won. But Medina Sidonia remained the captive of his rigid instructions and ponderous war machine.

Howard worked most of his ships out of Plymouth Sound with the ebb tide and against the southwest wind. He threaded his way between the Armada and the coast and "seized the weather gauge"—got to windward of the Spanish. This was the first English success.

Then followed the long running battle up the Channel. The fleets were about equal in number and firepower, though the Spaniards had more big ships and more fighting men. They were superior in short-range, heavy-shotted guns, the English in the lighter, longer-range pieces called culverins.

English guns were admired throughout Europe, and some of the best guns in the Spanish fleet had been secretly purchased in England. Neither the English nor the Spanish had *(Continued on page 153)*

Victory Won, Nelson's Flagship Lives On

She was a long time in the making. Her keel of elm was laid in 1759. Shipwrights completed her hull in 1765. She finally put out to sea and went into battle in 1778, her target the French. Her name was *Victory,* and from her first battle until 1797 she served her nation valiantly. But in that year England pulled her off the line as a flagship and moored her on the Medway River as a prison hulk and hospital ship.

Old, proud, and dying, the *Victory* languished for two years. Then she got another chance at life. She was refitted, altered, and recommissioned in 1803, when England was at war against Napoleon. She became the flagship of Lord Nelson, who would sail her to his destiny at Trafalgar.

From *Victory*'s masthead on that day of glory flew the flags of a new signal system that carried Nelson's stirring message to his fleet: "England expects that every man will do his duty."

In that navy, a man could serve who was not yet a teenager. Nelson himself had become a midshipman at 12. In the *Victory*'s crew was a boy of 10. Of the 703 on the ship's rolls, 100 were under 20. Legend makes one of the crew a woman.

Aboard another ship in the British fleet was an 11-year-old boy who wrote his mother and father a letter: "We live on beef which has been ten or eleven years in corn and on biscuit which quite makes your throat cold in eating it owing to the maggots which are very cold when you eat them, like calves-foot jelly. . . . We drink water of the colour of the bark of a pear-tree with plenty of little maggots and weavils in it and wine which is exactly like bullock's blood and sawdust mixed together. I hope I shall not learn to swear. . . ."

A figurehead of Nelson stands watch over his last flagship, Victory, still officially a commissioned warship. In her dry dock at Portsmouth, she survives as he knew her in 1805. With 104 guns, she was a first-rate ship of the line. (A ship of the second rate carried 90 or 98 guns, a third-rate usually 74.) Each of Victory's three gun decks bristles with a different size of cannon, dubbed for the weight of shot fired. On her lower gun deck she had thirty 32-pounders; on her middle deck, twenty-eight 24-pounders; on her upper deck, thirty 12-pounders. She had a dozen 12-pounders on her quarterdeck and two more on her forecastle, along with two 68-pounder carronades. Nelson ordered the yellow stripes to be painted on all his ships.

OVERLEAF: The lower gun deck stands still today, as it never would at sea. Sailors made the deck their crowded home—and battle, with its blood and fire, made it their hell.

On the ship of Nelson's final days lives the memory of his great love, Emma, Lady Hamilton, wife of a diplomat. Her affair with Nelson, whose child she bore, scandalized England. Her portrait hangs in his dining cabin (right). Emma begged to visit him, but Nelson refused her entreaties, adding, "Am I, that have given orders to carry no women to sea in the Victory, to be the first to break them?"

The boy assured his parents that, despite all the hardships, he did like his life at sea. That life ended when he fell from the rigging at the age of 14.

The *Victory's* crew was divided into three sections: the starboard and port watches, totaling some 540 men, and the "idlers"— meaning the officers, marines, boy servants, and skilled men such as sailmakers, caulkers, and armorers.

When the *Victory* sailed into battle, a drumroll and a trumpet call sent every man to an action station. Decks were sanded so that bare feet would not slip on blood. The furniture of the officers' cabins went into the hold. The stern windows were removed to make way for the guns. Tackles creaked as black muzzles were run out through the ports. Gunners stripped to the waist and wound neckerchiefs around their foreheads to keep the sweat from running into their eyes. . . .

The drumroll summoned *Victory* to her last great battle at Trafalgar, off the coast of Spain, on October 21, 1805. She fought courageously. But when that day ended, she was severely crippled. Barely able to raise sail on her ravaged masts, she limped via Gibraltar to England, victorious against the foe but vanquished by deaths: 57 officers and crewmen, including Nelson, slain. She bore his body home in a cask of brandy.

The ship soon was threatened with demolition, but a patriotic outcry saved her, and she was made the flagship of the Naval Home Command. She has survived the ravages of dry rot, timber-eating deathwatch beetles, and a World War II air raid. Lovingly preserved at historic Portsmouth, in southern England, she remains as a midshipman once described her: a "gallant and noble ship" of "beautiful fabric."

A Harsh Life
Under the Threat
Of the Lash

One. Two. Three. . . . The cat-o'-nine-tails stripes the seaman's bared back, the weighted tails slicing into his flesh. *Four. Five. Six.* . . . The boatswain's mate flails harder; his orders say the lashes must be "laid on with a will." *Seven. Eight. Nine.* . . . Officers and crew, mustered as witnesses, count silently. *Ten. Eleven. Twelve.* . . .

A member of the crew, naval gunner William H. Meyers, painted the scene around 1842, the twilight of an age when sailors lived under the constant threat of the lash. Meyers witnessed this flogging aboard the U.S.S. *Cyane,* an 18-gun sloop of war that saw action in the Mexican War.

The man's crime? He may have been last one up the shrouds when the crew was ordered aloft. Or he may have been "doubling the tub"—slipping into the mess line for seconds. His punishment? In 1799 Congress had passed a law that limited a flogging to 12 lashes. But a captain could charge a sailor with several offenses and decree a dozen lashes for each. Seven or eight dozen lashes would usually kill a man. But a flogging was for punishment and for displaying authority, not for getting rid of sailors, who were always in short supply.

The U. S. Navy evolved from the Royal Navy, which traced its harsh code of corporal punishment to Richard the Lion-Hearted. He was said to have learned of Mediterranean maritime law while on the Crusades. His law prescribed that anyone who "shall kill another on board ship shall be tied to the dead body and cast into the sea with it." An errant navigator could lose his head to the crew. A sailor who drew a knife in anger would have his right hand cut off, and a thief was shaved and crowned with tar and feathers.

On land the cruelty of the Middle Ages gave way to enlightenment and a crude sense of justice. But on the sea the medieval code prevailed. Officers and many sailors believed that only the harshest punishment could preserve discipline. A handful of officers, living a life of comparative ease, ruled a band of desperate men. Usually dragged aboard, fed maggot-infested food, confined in port lest they desert, crewmen during wartime were prisoners. Their keepers believed that only the fear of pain and death could maintain discipline and prevent the ultimate crime, mutiny.

Some captains went beyond discipline. Men were keelhauled: hoisted aloft, dropped into the sea, then hauled under the keel and up to a yardarm. Many were yanked up dead. Sick men were flogged before being turned over to the ship's surgeon, who was often incompetent. Men were hanged for desertion, but this worsened the manpower shortage. So flogging became the punishment for desertion, and, as the number of authorized lashes grew to the hundreds, this too became impractical because it killed. For years some officers had tried to rid the U. S. Navy of the lash. Fi-

nally, in 1848, Congress asked for a report. The Navy admitted to widespread use of the "cat" and the "kitten" or "colt," a single-strand whip for use on boys. One ship, the frigate *United States,* averaged more than five floggings a week. One man got 12 lashes for "seditious conduct in cursing the ship when ordered to go in a boat." A teenager got six lashes with the colt for "dropping slush bucket from aloft."

The *United States* had the most savage record of flogging, and one of her seamen was a young whaleman and writer named Herman Melville. As the anti-lash sentiment crested in Congress in 1850, Melville's *White-Jacket,* based on life aboard the frigate, was published. His vivid eyewitness account of 163 floggings dramatically supplemented the Navy's official report. Congress that year finally voted to abolish flogging aboard U. S. warships and merchantmen. The Royal Navy "suspended" the punishment in the 1870's, but never officially outlawed it.

Commodore Matthew C. Perry, though a relatively merciful officer, had opposed the drive to stop flogging. "I would not care to go to sea under the present state of discipline of the Navy," he wrote to a friend in 1851. But go to sea he did (see page 172), and his prediction that the Navy "will go to the devil" did not come true.

Corporal punishment lingered on. With steam engines came the "sweatbox" cell, set up next to the boilers. At least one man died before it was outlawed. Men still were clapped in irons or hung by their manacled wrists. Men still were crippled by punishment. The victims became the patients of ships' surgeons, and it would be these officers who would lead the final campaign to end legal cruelty at sea.

Recruiting with club and sword, an 18th-century press-gang plucks two new Royal Navy seamen from a London street. The gang's captain sizes up a short third. In ports, gangs were made up of sailors; inland, landlubbers did the pressing, with the promise they would not themselves be pressed. Gangs once got a shilling for each recruit. But quality fell off, and bounties were given only for collaring deserters.

Impressment, an ancient practice during time of war, survived the Magna Carta and other guarantees of freedom. By the early 19th century, when England needed some 75,000 seamen, well more than half of a typical crew had been impressed. The gangs seized men of other nations, including the United States. Her outrage over impressment triggered the War of 1812.

as yet acquired much experience with these weapons in a major battle.

The English, having windward advantage and nimbler ships, chose to fight beyond the range of Spanish heavy shot. But at that range the English fleet's own shot, if it hit the target at all, usually failed to penetrate. So both sides expended huge amounts of powder and shot without inflicting much damage.

The captains of Lord Howard's irregular navy were more interested in prize money than in following orders. They eagerly broke formation to chase stragglers in quest of riches. Drake himself left his position at the head of his squadron, at night without warning anyone, to pick up the damaged galleon *Rosario*. She was a big prize, for she carried the pay chest for much of the Spanish fleet. Nobody seemed to blame Drake; his conduct was normal.

On entering the narrows of the Channel, Medina Sidonia anchored his fleet in the open roadstead at Calais to await the crucial contact with Parma. The English anchored outside, a short distance away. The two fleets were at a deadlock. The Spaniards had used up nearly all their shot and could do little unless Parma could supply them. The English had a little shot left. In answer to Howard's piteous entreaties—"for the love of God and our country, let us have with speed some great shot sent us"—a trickle of shot and powder came from home.

The deadlock was broken by the proposal to send in fire ships to smoke the Spaniards out. Fire ships were uncertain weapons; there was always the risk that the wind could change and drive them back to their creators. But this time the tactic worked. The fire ships not only were stuffed with flammable material but they also carried double-shotted guns. As they burned, red-hot shot sprayed through the smoke in all directions. The blazing ships could not be approached for grappling and towing away, though the Spaniards tried every way they knew. Six fire ships broke through the Armada's protective screen. As these infernos swept toward their anchorage, the Spaniards had no choice but to cut the ships' cables and stand out to sea, where the English were waiting for them.

Off Gravelines, the English at last discovered that the Spaniards lacked ammunition. They closed range and inflicted terrible punishment. The Spaniards vainly tried to grapple and board their tormentors. Few ships escaped damage. Most supply ships

Recruiting with club and sword, an 18th-century press-gang plucks two new Royal Navy seamen from a London street. The gang's captain sizes up a short third. In ports, gangs were made up of sailors; inland, landlubbers did the pressing, with the promise they would not themselves be pressed. Gangs once got a shilling for each recruit. But quality fell off, and bounties were given only for collaring deserters.

Impressment, an ancient practice during time of war, survived the Magna Carta and other guarantees of freedom. By the early 19th century, when England needed some 75,000 seamen, well more than half of a typical crew had been impressed. The gangs seized men of other nations, including the United States. Her outrage over impressment triggered the War of 1812.

153

as yet acquired much experience with these weapons in a major battle.

The English, having windward advantage and nimbler ships, chose to fight beyond the range of Spanish heavy shot. But at that range the English fleet's own shot, if it hit the target at all, usually failed to penetrate. So both sides expended huge amounts of powder and shot without inflicting much damage.

The captains of Lord Howard's irregular navy were more interested in prize money than in following orders. They eagerly broke formation to chase stragglers in quest of riches. Drake himself left his position at the head of his squadron, at night without warning anyone, to pick up the damaged galleon *Rosario*. She was a big prize, for she carried the pay chest for much of the Spanish fleet. Nobody seemed to blame Drake; his conduct was normal.

On entering the narrows of the Channel, Medina Sidonia anchored his fleet in the open roadstead at Calais to await the crucial contact with Parma. The English anchored outside, a short distance away. The two fleets were at a deadlock. The Spaniards had used up nearly all their shot and could do little unless Parma could supply them. The English had a little shot left. In answer to Howard's piteous entreaties—"for the love of God and our country, let us have with speed some great shot sent us"—a trickle of shot and powder came from home.

The deadlock was broken by the proposal to send in fire ships to smoke the Spaniards out. Fire ships were uncertain weapons; there was always the risk that the wind could change and drive them back to their creators. But this time the tactic worked. The fire ships not only were stuffed with flammable material but they also carried double-shotted guns. As they burned, red-hot shot sprayed through the smoke in all directions. The blazing ships could not be approached for grappling and towing away, though the Spaniards tried every way they knew. Six fire ships broke through the Armada's protective screen. As these infernos swept toward their anchorage, the Spaniards had no choice but to cut the ships' cables and stand out to sea, where the English were waiting for them.

Off Gravelines, the English at last discovered that the Spaniards lacked ammunition. They closed range and inflicted terrible punishment. The Spaniards vainly tried to grapple and board their tormentors. Few ships escaped damage. Most supply ships

Officers of the future live
and learn in the midshipmen's
berth of a Royal Navy warship.
As men in training, they
worked with the crew. But, as
officers-to-be, they enjoyed
some benefits—such as these
relatively roomy quarters and

the likelihood of edible food.
Officers bought their own
victuals, and the wealthier the
officers, the better the food.
Separate and most unequal
menus were maintained by
the captain for his table, by the
officers for their wardroom,
and by midshipmen, who
lived in this room on a

lower deck. Seamen often got
bad food purchased with
royal funds by crooked pursers.
To avoid the sight of wormy
biscuits, men frequently ate
their meals in the dark. Some
chewed rigging grease to cover
the rotten taste of their grub.

154   were lost or burned. Finally, the invasion of England abandoned, the Spanish ships re-formed, by a magnificent feat of discipline and seamanship, and stood to the north in retreat. The English did not long pursue, for shrieking gales turned the retreat into a rout and strewed the coasts of Scotland and Ireland with Spanish wrecks.

Richard Hakluyt, the great English chronicler, did not call the event a victory. He wrote, "Why should I presume to call it our vanquishing; when as the greatest part of them escaped us, and were onely by Gods outstretched arme overwhelmed in the Seas, dashed in pieces against the Rockes, and made fearefull spectacles and examples of his judgements unto all Christendome?"

Medina Sidonia had been given an impossible task and had been defeated and humiliated. Long berated for the defeat, he is now seen in a more generous light. His judgment had sometimes been faulty, but not his leadership. He had kept the survivors of his fleet together. Fifty-four ships—two-thirds of his fighting strength—returned to Spain in company and under command.

The "great gun" of the Armada battle was to remain the essential weapon of sea fighting, with no radical change in its design or in the techniques of aiming and firing it, from Drake's day to Nelson's and even beyond.

To use the great guns effectively, navies needed fleets of new ships that could safely mount them, and they had to develop new tactics. The revolutionized navies also had to train a new breed of sea officer—fighting seamen, not simply gentlemen of the sword who happened to find themselves at sea.

The armed merchantmen and the privateers had to be excluded from the line of battle. Also excluded were small warships, too weak in firepower and too flimsy to fight on equal terms with "ships of the line"—warships that fought in a line and had to be standardized so that all performed equally.

In the 17th century, a set of conventions emerged about ships of the line. These conventions, common with variations to all the major navies, prevailed throughout the 18th century—the classic age of naval war, the battle fleet, and the sailing warship.

The standard battleship was the "seventy-four," which mounted that number of guns ranged on two decks, one tier above the other. Hundreds of these ships were built in the 18th century. Most navies had also a few "first-rates"—ships such as the *Victory*—carrying a hundred guns or more on three decks. No ship with fewer than 60 carriage guns was considered fit to stand in the line. Frigates usually mounted about 36 guns. Sloops and gun brigs carried still fewer guns, of smaller caliber.

The 18th-century ship of the line was an impressive monument to human industry, ingenuity, and belligerence. It had its own grim beauty, the intricate tracery of spars and rigging relieving the massive lines of the fortress hull. The ship was bigger than most country manors and far more complex. It took two years to build.

Woodsmen had to provide more than 3,000 loads of oak—each load, 50 cubic feet, the yield of a big tree—plus the elm for keel and bottom planks and pine trunks for the masts and yards. The ship needed 100 tons of wrought iron (not including the iron in the guns), 40 tons of copper, and many thousands of

Hammocks rock in the space seamen called home. Some captains let men share them—while in port—with "wives." Hammocks swung in the U.S. Navy until the 1920's.

Out of a merchant sailor's sea chest comes the stuff of his life—luxuries to a navy tar: accordion, whalebone ditty box, ship model in a bottle, knife and fork (for beef so hard that "it would take a good polish"), easily pocketed, short-stemmed pipes and twist of tobacco, bottles of medicine (usually alcohol-based nostrums), and letters. These were rare for most men of the sea. Those sailors who could write had little to write about. And, for many, home had long since vanished in their wake.

This Salem sea-chest owner stropped a straight razor and dipped from a soap dish to shave. As a weapon he wielded a slungshot, a lead ball wrapped in string. He had a fid (a hardwood pin) for splicing. He wore white linen pants and a tarpaulin hat, mended his clothes with a sewing kit and a sailor's palm, played checkers, read from his Bible, and studied navigation with the aid of a quadrant and The Practical Navigator by Nathaniel Bowditch.

Bowditch was also a sailor out of Salem. Self-taught, he passed time aboard ship by looking for errors in the standard English book of tables. He found 8,000 and published, at age 28, his own guide. Some seamen use it today.

156

ships, nor even bigger ships. The naval success enjoyed by Great Britain in the late 18th century was due not only to the experience and competence of many naval officers but also to the productivity of British dockyards and foundries.

Naval battles were won partly by tactical skill. A commander usually sought to keep to windward of the enemy, to have the initiative and choice of range. When he attacked, he tried to keep the enemy abeam, so that each ship could bring its whole broadside to bear. At all cost he tried to avoid presenting a vulnerable stern to enemy fire. All this required nimble seamanship and prompt attention to flag signals repeated down the line.

The tactical choices open to an admiral commanding a fleet were limited by the rigidity of conventional battle formations, by the rudimentary nature of signal systems, and by imperfect fleet discipline. Captains often failed to grasp what the admiral wanted them to do, especially if he wanted them to do something not precisely covered by Permanent Fighting Instructions.

These formal orders called for ships to maintain a strict "line of battle." Officers who deviated from the instructions risked their careers but often won battles. Nelson was one admiral who trusted his officers' judgment. "Something must be left to chance," he wrote just before his victory at Trafalgar in 1805. "But . . . no captain can do very wrong if he places his ship alongside that of an enemy."

When two fleets engaged, battle became a melee of fights between single ships and small groups. Inevitably, in the smoke and confusion, the admiral lost some control over his ships. It was then that

feet of hempen rope and cable. It housed 600 to 800 men, in some discomfort, and could carry enough food and water to keep them alive, somewhat unhealthily, for about six months.

Every few minutes during a battle, each of the ship's broadsides could throw half a ton of metal with lethal force against targets a quarter of a mile away. Adequately manned, it was reliable, efficient, and deadly.

The ship of the line in all major navies changed little through the 18th century. Worn-out ships were replaced by new ships that followed tradition and were of almost identical design. Technological considerations were rarely decisive in naval warfare.

Battles hinged on the condition of ships, their time out of dockyard, the state of their copper (if any), and hence their speed and handling qualities. Courage and determination helped win battles, as did professional skill in seamanship and gunnery, all of which determined a ship's fighting capacity. But with smoothbore cannon firing solid shot, accuracy was hardly possible. Effective fire had to be point-blank. What mattered was rate of fire, and that depended on drill. Admiral Nelson exercised his gun crews relentlessly. In a brief battle a well-drilled ship could get off a broadside a minute.

Above all, the outcome of a battle depended on superiority in numbers: more ships, not better

A New Nation's Fight for Its Rights On the Seas

Despite a Maryland delegate's misgivings—he called it "the maddest idea in the world"—the Continental Congress in 1775 launched what would become the U.S. Navy. Congress issued regulations (no swearing aboard ship, a daily rum ration of half a pint), purchased four ships, and commissioned the first naval lieutenant, John Paul Jones.

Most of the American ships that went to sea in the Revolutionary War were privateers. Fishermen and whalers manned them, inspired by patriotism and potential prizes. The privateers harassed British commerce to "the very chops of the Channel."

After the Revolution, Congress no longer saw a need for an official navy, since so many privateers were still around. But another kind of prize-seeker, the Barbary pirates, grew ever more aggressive. They prowled off Algiers, Tripoli, Tunis, and Morocco, demanding tribute for safe passage, seizing ships and seamen as hostages. In 1785 the pirates captured two American ships and held some 20 Americans for ransom. Privateers spawned by the French Revolution also preyed on the new nation's shipping. Strong action seemed imperative.

In 1794 Congress at last authorized the building of six frigates to protect American maritime commerce. Approval for more ships came in 1798, as the frigates *Constellation, United States,* and *Constitution* went to sea. Congress created the Department of the Navy and the Marine Corps later that year.

While the new Navy fought pirates, warring England and France hit each other with blockades that had the effect of jeopardizing American trade with both countries. Part of the British blockade reached the American coast and tested the new nation's resolve.

On June 22, 1807, the U.S. Frigate *Chesapeake,* sailing some ten miles off Norfolk, Virginia, was hailed by the British frigate *Leopard.* The American captain, believing the *Leopard* intended a routine rendezvous, hove to and took aboard a British officer. But the Briton then demanded the right to search the *Chesapeake* for British deserters. The American captain refused. The British officer returned to the *Leopard,* which fired on the U.S. frigate, killing three men. The *Chesapeake,* unprepared for a fight, struck her colors. She was searched, and the British took four crewmen.

The two countries managed to keep the incident from flaring into war. But impressment of American sailors and seizure of cargoes soon began anew. On June 18, 1812, America declared war with the rallying cry, "Free Trade and Sailors' Rights."

Baptized in the fire of the undeclared naval war with France and the Tripolitan War of 1801-05, the *Constitution* (page 160) and the *United States* fought victorious battles against the mighty Royal Navy. "What is wrong with British seapower?" asked *The Times* of London. The answer lay in what was right with the Americans: American frigates were bigger than British, had more firepower, and usually they were manned by better gunners.

Royal frigates now rarely cruised alone. But one British frigate did challenge an American "ship to ship." She was, fatefully, again the *Chesapeake,* caught unprepared for battle. In the duel, the British raked her with deadly fire and waited for her to strike her colors. She did not. The British had to board her to take her, for her dying captain, James Lawrence, had given orders that would never be forgotten: "Don't give up the ship!"

"I have not yet begun to fight!" shouts John Paul Jones in his memorable response to a demand for surrender in a Revolutionary War battle. He lost the Bonhomme Richard but boarded Serapis, his vanquished foe. Jones was commissioned, unlike most American sea warriors, who sailed as privateers. They fought again when America and England warred in 1812; the privateer brig Grand Turk (opposite) took 31 prizes. News of peace, ratified in February 1815, did not reach ships for months, and war at sea thundered on.

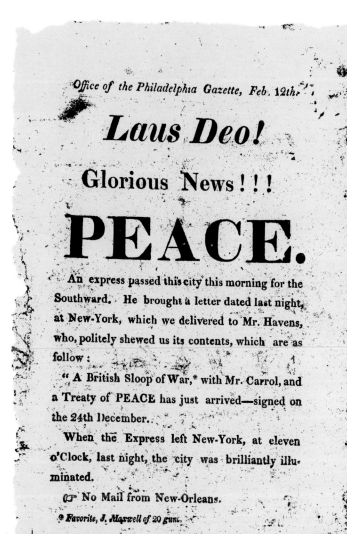

Office of the Philadelphia Gazette, Feb. 12th.

Laus Deo!

Glorious News!!!

PEACE.

An express passed this city this morning for the Southward. He brought a letter dated last night, at New-York, which we delivered to Mr. Havens, who, politely shewed us its contents, which are as follow:

" A British Sloop of War,* with Mr. Carrol, and a Treaty of PEACE has just arrived—signed on the 24th December.

When the Express left New-York, at eleven o'Clock, last night, the city was brilliantly illuminated.

☞ No Mail from New-Orleans.

* Favorite, J. Maxwell of 20 guns.

"Old Ironsides"—officially, U. S. Frigate Constitution—lives in remembered glory, manned by a U. S. Navy crew. Launched in 1797, she is the world's oldest commissioned ship still afloat. Out from her Boston berth, she fires a salute from a replica of one of her 24-pounders; sailors in 1812 uniforms line her bowsprit. Legend says she got her nickname from a gunner who saw shot bounce off her oaken side.

In 1812, just 16 minutes into close combat off Halifax, Nova Scotia, her guns toppled the mizzenmast of the British frigate Guerrière (below), then felled the mainmast and foremast. Unvanquished in 26 actions, she faced a final defeat by age. But a poem, "Old Ironsides" by Oliver Wendell Holmes, saved her, and pennies from schoolchildren later helped to restore her.

victories were won, by ships pounding one another at short range until one or the other struck its colors, ran, burned, or sank.

Ships of the line rarely sank in action unless a shot touched off a magazine. Their sides near the waterline were of tough, seasoned oak, two feet thick or more, and could stop solid shot except at very close range. A series of well-directed broadsides might cripple a ship, might reduce her decks to a blood-soaked shambles, but even that would not usually sink her.

The victor in a gunnery duel did not necessarily want to sink an enemy if he could intimidate him into surrender, or batter him into helplessness, then board and take possession. A damaged warship could be repaired and used by her captors. Many fine ships in Nelson's fleets had French names. And the *Berwick* and *Swiftsure,* captured from the Royal Navy, fought in the French fleet at Trafalgar.

Convention required that a surrender be made man to man. Most ambitious officers dreamed of receiving a defeated commander on the quarterdeck and accepting his sword, with the customary mutual civilities about honor and courage. These civilities emphasized the gulf that separated naval officers from merchants, privateersmen, and pirates. But both officers and men expected prize money to follow victory. Prize was a polite term for booty. In some naval officers, even in Nelson's day, the instincts of the pirate were not far below the surface.

The glamour and old tradition of boarding appealed to ambitious young officers; and boarding often seemed the only way to break the deadlock of a gunnery duel or the only way to attack a nearby

enemy at night. The tradition is not quite dead. In 1940 the German prison ship *Altmark* was taken off the coast of Norway in a boarding attack at night by men from H.M.S. *Cossack,* some of whom were said to have wielded cutlasses.

In the 18th century, many men on the lower deck thought of a boarding party as an outing, a relief from the tedium of lower-deck life. A walk round the gun decks of the *Victory* gives some idea of what that life was like.

The decks were smelly, low, gloomy caverns. A tall man could not stand or walk upright. The only fresh air and daylight came through the gunports, and in rough weather they were closed. However

carefully the carpenters fitted the port lids, they usually leaked, and in rough weather the sea seeped or spurted through the cracks.

Life on the gun deck was dominated by the guns, sullen black monsters ranged in rows along the ship's side and, when no action was expected, securely lashed down. A gun broken loose and hurtling between decks in rough weather could smash the men like insects.

The eight or ten feet between each pair of guns constituted a mess, in which 14 men lived in two shifts alternating between the starboard and port watches. Here at a collapsible table they ate their food, fetched in mess kettles from a brick-enclosed

ALSO
The schr.
CATCH ME IF YOU CAN,
A new vessel, has made but one trip, from Boston to this port, burthen 65 tons, sails remarkably well, and is well found in every respect—calculated for the West India or Bay Trade.
march 18   d8t

Skimming seas and centuries, the Baltimore clipper sails on. The War of 1812 enlisted these rakish ships, named for the city that built them and the time they clipped. Such ships ran the British blockade (below) and in peace advertised their speed. The Pride of Baltimore *(right), launched in 1977, shows skills that never died.*

galley on the lower gun deck. Between meals, the table was lashed overhead. Here the men slept in hammocks slung from hooks—canvas cocoons, 18 inches apart, swaying in unison with the ship. When not in use, the hammocks were tightly rolled and stowed in racks against the ship's sides, serving, when cannons roared, as protection against flying splinters, the shrapnel of the times. A man's best friend, the sailors used to say, was his hammock.

At their guns, every noon, they knocked back the daily rum ration—"up spirits," in the punning words of the traditional pipe. They played cards, gossiped, yarned, sang, and sometimes quarreled—"fell to loggerheads" in the old phrase. (A logger-

head, an iron bar used for sealing deck seams, was apt to be snatched up in the heat of an argument.)

In harbor, it was at their guns that they entertained such women as could be enticed on board, and sometimes a "son of a gun" was the result. Most commanding officers thought it was safer to let whores be brought on board than to allow the men ashore, where they might desert.

Desertion was a commanding officer's nightmare. Life on a warship was hard. Some men entered voluntarily, perhaps in the hope of becoming a petty officer, a warrant officer, even a commissioned officer. Some volunteered for the sake of the recruitment bounty. In war, however, *(Continued on page 168)*

Blood and Plunder: A Pirate's Mean Business

In the words of one pirate, the way to start a career was to seize "a small Vessel . . . make a black Flag, and declare War against all the World." The new pirate would then recruit from the crew of his first prize, and they would join him in search of bigger prey. In the heyday of piracy—from about the 1630's to the 1720's—a persevering freebooter could acquire a fleet.

Under the polite and patriotic label of privateering, piracy was an honorable calling in Elizabethan England and colonial America. Sir Walter Raleigh, who himself pirated for queen, country, and profit, noted that piracy was a matter of degree. "Did you ever know of any that were pirates for millions?" he asked. "They only that work for small things are pirates." And an American colonist noted that the few pirates hanged in Charleston were executed "because they were poor. . . . These rich ones appear'd publickly and were not molested."

One crew became so friendly with a colonial governor that he invited them to join him in a religious procession. The pirates, including two trumpeters and an oboe player, marched along to the tune of "Hey Boys Up Go We!" Then, as the pirate captain later wrote, "after Service our Musicians, who were by that time more than half drunk, march'd at the head of the Company."

Pirate crewmen were members of a kind of workers' collective. Men who joined up said they were "going on the account"—meaning they would become shareholders in the loot. The crew elected a captain, whose term ran as long as the voters permitted. One ship elected 13 captains in less than a year. Because many of the men had fled the tyranny of legal captains, they would not tolerate despots. Only in chase or in battle did a pirate captain have absolute

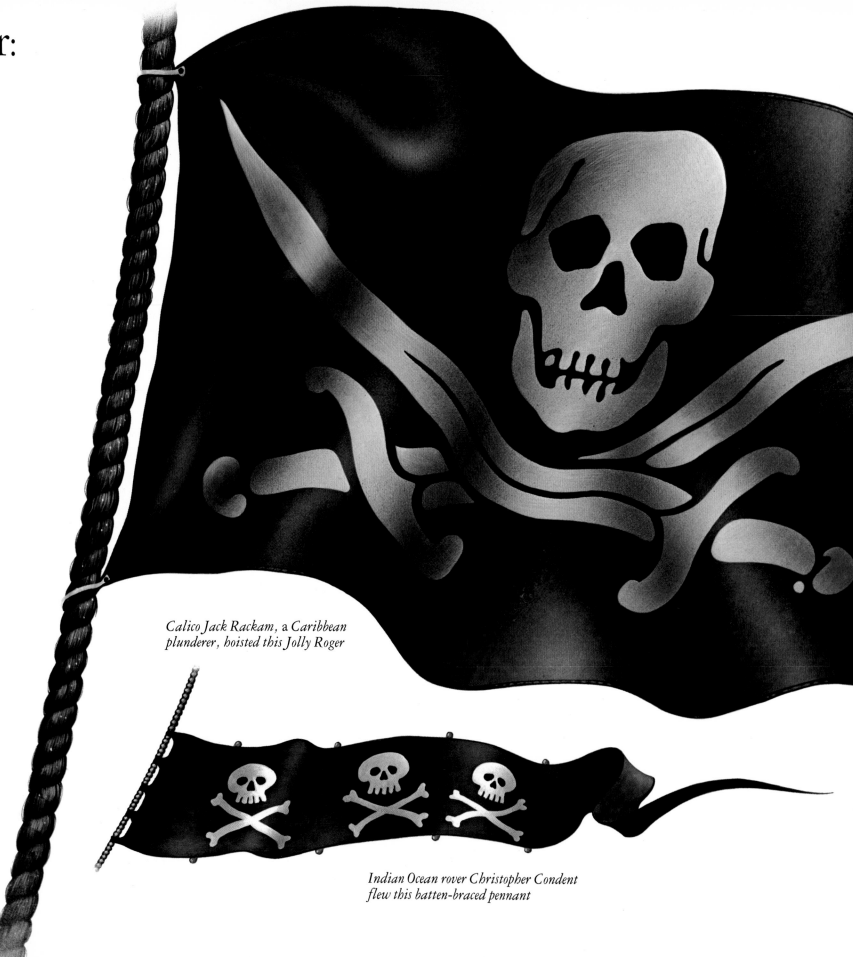

Calico Jack Rackam, a Caribbean plunderer, hoisted this Jolly Roger

Indian Ocean rover Christopher Condent flew this batten-braced pennant

Blackbeard's flag flaunted popular pirate symbols: hourglass, bones, and blood

The flag of the "Great Pirate" Bartholomew Roberts, who plundered some 400 vessels

ABH AMH

Another Roberts flag advertised his personal vendetta: "A Barbadian's Head, A Martinican's Head"

power—"drubbing, cutting, or even shooting anyone who does deny him command."

Pirates sailed under a constitution, "ship's articles," which decided the distribution of shares and the administration of justice. Most of the crew received equal shares, but the captain and such specialists as the surgeon, boatswain, and gunner got bonuses. Other typical articles prohibited fighting or gambling aboard ship. Anyone attempting to desert was usually marooned on some forsaken shore "with one Bottle of Powder, one Bottle of Water, one small Arm, and Shot." A man who robbed a shipmate might be put to death, or, under more merciful articles, have his nose and ears slit and then be marooned.

Pirates were covered by a primitive kind of insurance that provided payment for loss of limb, eye, or finger. But rarely did a captain go out of his way for a fight. It was bad for business, since shot and shell damaged the prize ship and its merchandise. Many successful pirate captains advertised their mercy because it was good for business. Believing only cargoes—not lives—would be lost, ships surrendered more readily. But a prize's captain might be killed, particularly if his crew denounced him for cruelty. And members of his crew often became instant converts to piracy.

Few were forced to join the pirate crew, though men with special skills—such as surgeons and carpenters—might be impressed. Draftees got the same share as volunteers but could not vote.

One pirate captain recruiting crewmen told them they worked for scoundrels who "villify us . . . when there is only this difference: they rob the poor under the cover of the law, forsooth, and we plunder the rich under the protection of our own courage."

Skull-and-cutlass flag and gleaming pieces of eight conjure up the age of piracy, when outlaws of the sea made crime pay. Blackbeard, one of the nastiest, stuck smoldering matches under his hat "to look more frightful." He betrayed his own crew, had about 14 wives in several ports, and pirated under the protection of the governor of North Carolina. Snared in 1718 by a British naval sloop, he quaffed a mug of his favorite brew—gunpowder and rum—and fought until his 25th wound felled him.

166 Some pirate crews banded together to set up organizations and engage in trade. Buccaneers in the Caribbean founded the "Brethren of the Coast" on the island of Tortuga and sold their Spanish loot to Dutch and French buyers. On the island of Madagascar, other pirates proclaimed the "republic" of Libertatia, which enjoyed a particularly friendly trade relationship with New England. The colonies imported loot and exported to Libertatia the two essentials of pirate life: ammunition and liquor.

Once a free-for-all erupted after the arrival of an ale and brandy ship. Some 500 carousers were killed in a prelude to the violent death of Libertatia. Madagascar natives then rose up against the invaders and wiped out the fledgling nation.

Pirate kingdoms flourished on the island. King James Plantain ruled from a castle around 1721. He took several native wives, gave them English names, and adorned them with silks and diamonds. Plantain warred against the native kings. One of them, known as King Dick, had a beautiful granddaughter, reputedly fathered by an English slaver captain. When King Dick turned down King James's request for the girl's hand in marriage, the pirate declared war. He won war, wife, and the island itself, which he ruled until he was overthrown and had to flee with his bride.

Women—"so dangerous an instrument of division and discord"—were not welcome on pirate ships as passengers or captives. (Pirates treated black women and men as people outside the code, slaves who could be molested or killed.) White women who were captured usually were well treated and speedily released. As a typical ship's article warned, "If at any time you meet with a prudent Woman, that Man that offers to

meddle with her, without her Consent, shall suffer present Death."

Two women who did find themselves aboard a pirate ship became pirates themselves. Mary Read, masquerading as a sailor for her own obscure reasons, was taken prisoner with the rest of the crew when her ship was seized. The captor was a sea rover of the West Indies known as Calico Jack Rackam.

Mary, still in her disguise, signed up with the pirate crew.

Now it so happened that Calico Jack himself had smuggled a disguised sailor aboard—his mistress, Anne Bonney. And she, thinking Mary a handsome young man, made advances and thus learned the truth about Mary. The women became friends and kept their secrets. Mary, meanwhile,

fell in love with a "young fellow of engaging behavior." (He *was* a man.) Before Mary could tell him of her love and her secret, the young man got into an argument with another crewman. The two men made a date to fight it out ashore. But Mary, fearing her man would be slain, picked a fight with his opponent, went ashore for a duel "at Sword and Pistol," and killed him. She "suffered the Discovery" of her true gender by the surprised young man, and "straight away they plighted their Troth," which she "looked upon to be as good as a Marriage."

Their honeymoon was interrupted by an armed sloop, which pounced on the pirate ship. In the fierce battle, Calico Jack and many of his crew fled below decks, leaving the fighting to Anne and Mary. Incensed, Mary fired into the cowards, killing one of them before she and Anne were captured.

The crew was put on trial and sentenced to be hanged. But Mary and Anne "pleaded their bellies," avoiding the noose because they were pregnant. On the day that Calico Jack was hanged, he was allowed to visit his mistress. Anne sent Jack off with heartfelt parting words: "that she was sorry to see him there, but if he had fought like a Man, he need not have been hang'd like a Dog."

Piracy swiftly waned after its apex, and by the early 1800's robbery on the high seas was no longer a major international problem. Unlike many of the pirates of the golden age, those of the 19th century were, with few exceptions, the scum of the sea.

One of the rare celebrities in that mean bunch was Jean Laffite, who ruled "hellish banditti" from a lair in the Louisiana bayous. In the War of 1812 the British asked him to fight on their side. He refused, choosing instead to fight at the side of Andrew Jackson in the Battle of New Orleans.

In 1817 Laffite founded a pirate town at Galveston. European adventurers, including two French generals, made it an outlaw social capital. Laffite seized more than 100 Spanish ships and hanged—for "piracy"—a captain who fired on an American ship. Facing forced eviction in 1821, he burned down the town and sailed off to an unknown fate in the sunset years of the age of piracy.

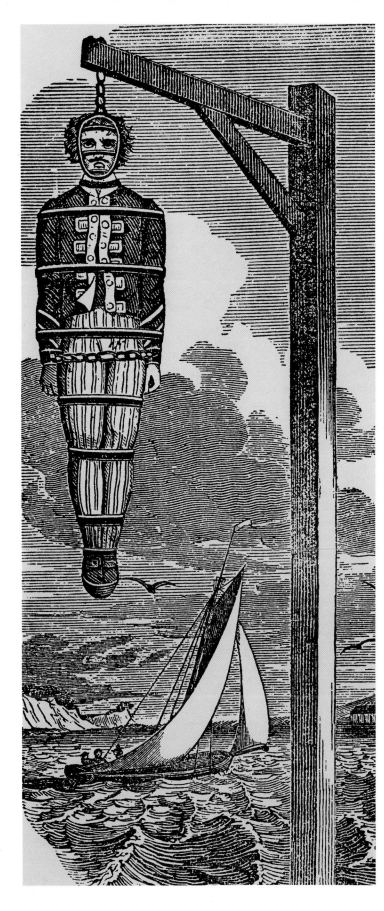

Businessman and businesswoman in the commerce called piracy, Captain Kidd and Madame Ching lived vastly different careers. Kidd, who sailed out of New York to hunt pirates, became one of them. He settled a dispute by killing an employee and, mostly for that, was put out of business at London's Execution Dock in 1701. Madame Ching took over her fallen husband's large fleet in 1802. She and her men—all two-bladed fighters—scourged the Chinese coast. She insisted on calling loot "transshipped goods."

Relatives of Hamburg sailors seized by Barbary pirates raised ransom with appealing art. These 17th-century statuettes stood at collection boxes in German churches. Religious orders also bought freedom for captives, then paraded them in chains to get more money. Such ransoming lasted into the 19th century.

there were never enough volunteers to man the fleets, and coercion was needed. In England the "press" kept tenders in the Channel to take men from inbound merchant ships. Sometimes gangs from undermanned warships roamed the streets and waterfront taverns, picking up anyone they could find—seaman, plowman, beggar, or thief. Usually the victims had no chance for redress.

All ships, particularly during the French wars at the end of the century, sometimes had to go to sea with a dangerously high proportion of incompetent, potentially mutinous conscripts. And so discipline grew harsher and punishment more savage. No wonder Samuel Johnson called a ship "a jail with the chance of being drowned."

It was a hard life: "Wooden ships and iron men" in the phrase of the time. Seamen made macabre jokes about dying in action, but few would joke about the horrors of the surgeon's table—the knife, the saw, the bucket of cauterizing molten tar.

It was an unhealthy life: Wet clothes and bedding encouraged rheumatism. Malaria and yellow fever attacked men in tropical harbors. For malaria, there was quinine; for yellow fever, nothing.

More deadly still was typhus, the dreaded "gaol fever," which often devastated fleets after a year or two of war, when the reserve of merchant seamen was exhausted and the press-gangs began to bring in verminous recruits from city slums. During an epidemic of typhus in the British Channel Fleet in 1780, the fleet could hardly be got to sea. Alarmed, the Admiralty set up receiving ships, where new entries could be examined, issued new clothes, and quarantined.

Barbary pirates fire a human bullet—the French consul— at the French fleet off Algiers in 1683. The warships had bombarded the city and killed 8,000 people. The pirates gave warning that if the bombardment did not stop they would begin using French captives as cannon fodder. The firing continued, and the Moslems loaded the consul, an aged priest, into the gun. Next, one by one, came 20 more prisoners. In 1688, after a similar French bombardment, the pirates fired a fusillade of 48 Frenchmen. Barbary atrocities went on until Algiers fell to the French in 1830.

By a characteristic irony of history, the belated measures taken at the end of the 18th century to control disease came at a time when the ships of the line were becoming less useful. The long story of the pre-eminence of the sailing battleship began with the Armada in 1588. It ended in 1805 with another great battle, this time between a British fleet on one side and a combined French and Spanish fleet on the other, off the Spanish cape that gave the battle its name—Trafalgar. This overwhelming victory for the English was the last fleet action of the classic 18th-century kind.

Throughout much of the 19th century there were no warships, other than British, in significant concentrations anywhere. No other power operated naval bases outside of its home waters to any significant degree. British ships of the line, like everyone else's, rotted gently at their moorings. From the Caribbean to the Pacific, the seas of the world were at peace.

Fighting other navies was not the only task that warships could perform. In The Naval Prayer read on Sunday mornings on the quarterdecks of H. M. ships, the petitioners ask that they may be not only "a safeguard for our most gracious sovereign lord . . ." but also "a security for such as pass on the seas upon their lawful occasions." Generally accepted convention allowed warships, of whatever flag, to stop and examine suspicious-looking craft at sea. In the 18th century the task of providing security had been entrusted mostly to small warships—frigates, sloops, gun brigs. They chased pirates, intercepted

U. S. Frigate Philadelphia *burns in Tripoli harbor, as the men who set her afire flee in their ketch. Seized by pirates, the frigate would have sailed under their flag. But Navy Lt. Stephen Decatur and 60 volunteers boarded her, routed her captors, put her to the torch, and escaped.*

Lord Nelson called their raid "the most bold and daring act of the age." Six months later, Decatur fought a pirate and killed him in hand-to-hand fighting (right) aboard a Tripolitan gunboat, one of three the Americans captured.

slavers, surveyed coasts, and "showed the flag" to friend and foe.

In the peaceful times of the early 19th century, there was little privateering, though it was not outlawed by general treaty until 1856. Slaving, though evil, was not a threat to maritime peace. Piracy was nearing extinction, and enough small warships patrolled the sea-lanes to prevent its revival.

Trouble spots remained. The Barbary States still engaged in semiofficial piracy after 1815. Most European governments had long decided that it was cheaper to pay modest subsidies and bribes than to mount repeated punitive expeditions.

The United States indignantly refused to accept this argument, and sent expeditions against Tripoli in 1801-05 and Algiers in 1815. The Americans had never attempted to build a line fleet, but in the early years of the 19th century they had built a number of large and powerful frigates. One of them, the famous *Constitution* ("Old Ironsides"), is still afloat, in Boston Harbor. Ships of this type were well suited to operations against the corsairs. But they achieved only temporary success, as did the heavy British bombardments of Algiers in 1816 and 1824. Algerine piracy was not finally snuffed out until the French conquest in 1830.

With these lingering exceptions, then, the oceans were at peace. The shepherds had driven the wolves to lurk in remote corners, chiefly in the China seas and the Malay archipelago. Almost everywhere, peaceful shipping could move with confidence, without guns and the extra hands that guns required. The 19th century, to a degree exceptional in human history, was a century of maritime calm.

Hard Diplomacy At the Gates Of Feudal Japan

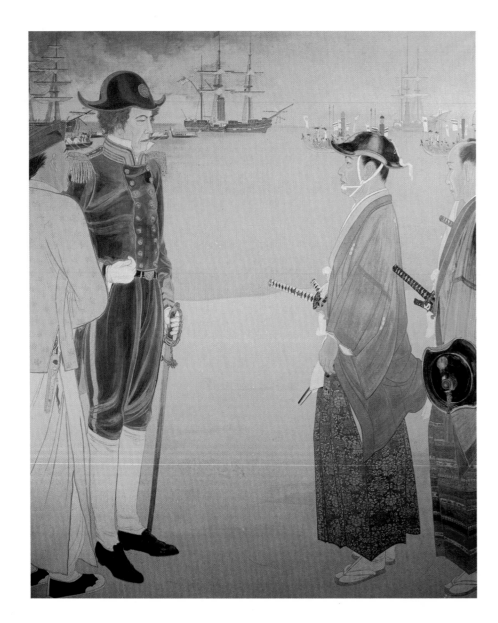

Four American men-of-war entered the channel to Tokyo Bay in July 1853, churning placid waters that had never known the clamor and smoke of a steamship. The ships coasted cautiously, leadsmen constantly sounding, for there were no reliable charts to these forbidden waters. Several Japanese junks spotted the warships—two ships steaming, two under sail, all bristling with guns—and darted to shore to spread the news: foreign invasion. The city of Yedo (as Tokyo was then called) panicked. A Japanese writer later told of "mothers flying with children in their arms, and men with mothers on their backs."

The American ships anchored off the village of Uraga about 30 miles south of Tokyo. Small coast-guard boats soon began flitting about, and Japanese officials attempted to board the American ships. Armed crewmen stopped them. Angrily, the Japanese tried to order the foreigners out of the sacred waters. The officials did not speak English, but they had ways to get their message across. A manual gave them phonetic expressions: "You must go way with first speedy wind. . . . It is a great prohibition of Japan to negotiate with strangers." One of them waved a scroll which, in French, ordered the ships to leave. Finally, from aboard one of the American ships came the voices of men speaking Japanese and Dutch, the only Western language that was then known in Japan.

The interpreters had been sent out on deck of the side-wheeler *Susquehanna* by Commodore Matthew Calbraith Perry, "Commander in Chief United States Naval Forces Stationed in the East India, China and Japan Seas." He remained in his cabin.

Perry had a basic mission: to peacefully open feudal Japan and negotiate a trade

長サ七十五間

船巾二十間

車六間半

帆柱三本

水ヨリ上ノ出

丈五尺

石火矢十挺

大筒裁十五挺

Steaming into the Japanese imagination, Perry's squadron inspired frightening art. Japanese sang of "The Black Ship . . . alien thing of evil mien." Perry (opposite) is portrayed with Oriental features. A translator at his side, he meets the commissioner who heads Japanese negotiators.

agreement for the United States. He was also to obtain guarantees of humane treatment of shipwrecked American sailors and the establishment of supply stations for American ships.

His career rose with sail and crested with steam. He fought as a youth of 18 in the War of 1812, and in 1837 he had taken command of a ship he called the "first American steamer of war," an oak-hulled, three-masted side-wheeler.

Diplomacy was not new to Matthew Perry. He had helped in the founding of Liberia for freed American slaves and had worked with other enlightened nations in the suppression of the African slave trade.

His father, four brothers, and three brothers-in-law had been naval officers. His brother Oliver, hero of the Battle of Lake Erie in the War of 1812, had given posterity a battle cry: "We have met the enemy and they are ours!" Matthew would triumph without bloodshed.

The official chronicle of his mission tells how he had decided to deal with the Japanese. He would meet them "on their own ground, and exhibit toward them a little of their own exclusive policy." Now, as the Japanese again approached the *Susquehanna*, his interpreters put his plan into action.

"We have the vice governor of Uraga aboard," a Japanese official called up.

"Why did you not bring the governor?" one of the interpreters asked.

"He is forbidden to board ships," the Japanese responded. "Will the Lord of the Forbidden Interior designate an officer of rank low enough to talk?"

The Lord behind the door designated his flag lieutenant who, when asked about the ships, haughtily replied, "We are armed ships, and our custom is never to answer such questions." The Japanese were told to remove their guard boats. After six days of negotiations, Perry decided that it was time to go ashore. The landing site chosen was the beach at Kurihama village.

Fifteen launches and cutters left the ships in formation. The boats carried some 300 officers, sailors, marines—and two brass bands. Perry followed in his barge. A master showman, he glittered in full-dress uniform and sword. He stepped ashore as one of the bands struck up "Hail, Columbia!"

The beach was lined with fluttering pennants and screens that bore the emblem of the shogun of Japan, who ruled in the name of the emperor. Thousands of Japanese soldiers guarded a reception house hastily erected near the shore. Perry strode along this avenue of pomp and power while his bands kept playing. Flanking him were two tall, muscular black sailors, both armed. Before them walked two ship's boys carrying gold-hinged rosewood boxes. They contained Perry's credentials and a letter to the emperor from President Millard Fillmore, proposing to his "Great and Good Friend" that the two countries "live in friendship and have commercial intercourse."

Perry said he would return in spring for the answer. He sailed away to what the Japanese called the "Dark Interior." To the far north was "the country of the night people"; the polar south was "impossible to know." Isolation had given the Japanese people this image of the world.

Europeans first heard of "Zipangu"—Japan—from Marco Polo in the early 14th century. But there was no sustained contact with Europeans until Portuguese traders and missionaries settled in Japan in the 16th century. The first Englishman to live there, Will Adams, was carried to Japan by a

横濱海
岸蒸氣
鐵道
車圖

One of Perry's gifts to Japan—a quarter-size locomotive, tender, passenger car, and 370 feet of track—grew in an artist's eye. The toy train and other gifts showed Japan the benefits of trade. Within 20 years, real trains were chugging along 18 miles of track linking Tokyo and Yokohama.

175

storm-ravaged ship in 1600. Unlike Perry, Adams did not sail away. He became a confidant of the shogun and lived in Japan until his death in 1620. He set up trade with England, built two oceangoing ships for the shogun, and taught him gunnery and world geography.

Adams, who married a Japanese woman (though he had a wife in England), was dubbed "The Pilot," a name later given to a Tokyo street. Soon after Adams's death, the British trade offices were shut down, and within a decade or so the Japanese expelled all Europeans except the Dutch. Already strong in what would become the Netherlands East Indies, the Dutch were allowed to cling to a Japanese trade depot on a tiny island off Nagasaki.

That was still the only Western toehold when Perry returned to Japan in February 1854. He went ahead of schedule because of rumors that Russia was planning a similar trading incursion. This time Perry's flotilla numbered nine ships, and this time he brought presents: weapons and tools, several clocks, a telescope, two telegraph instruments, 100 gallons of whiskey, cherry cordials, Irish potatoes, a miniature train, a daguerreotype camera, and a Noah Webster dictionary.

After another ceremonial landing—with the added touch of booming salutes for the emperor and his negotiator—Perry quickly got down to talks. He won a treaty that opened two ports to American ships and, ending Japan's isolation, authorized limited trade between the two countries. Their representatives celebrated by introducing each other to native entertainments: "unnumbered glasses" of champagne and a minstrel in blackface; 300-pound sumo wrestlers and geisha girls.

Sea Hunters and Harvesters

"There she blows!" At the cry of the lookout from the masthead, crews scramble to launch the whaleboats. They cast off the gripes and let run the falls. Thumping into the water, the boats—each with five men at the oars and a mate in the stern, steering—race toward their quarry, a sperm whale dawdling in the distance, unaware. Keeping careful silence so the prey will not be "gallied," or alarmed, the first boat draws near.

Within a few fathoms, bow close to the whale's flank, the mate at the steering oar calls softly, "stand up." The harpooner in the bow rises, puts down his oar, and snatches up the first harpoon. Bracing himself with a leg jammed against the "clumsy cleat" notched into the foremost thwart, he darts his iron. The aim is true. The needle-sharp harpoon, attached to a coiled line, penetrates blubber and muscle, and the barbs hold fast. "Stern all!" The

boat backs out of the way of the flailing flukes as the whale rushes off at panic speed, 10 or 12 knots, towing boat and crew on a wild "Nantucket sleighride." It could be an exhilarating experience if it ended well for the whalemen. Often it did not.

The fish and mammals of the sea are wild and unfettered. When man exploits them he does so not as farmer or herdsman but as a hunter pursues his prey—in its own habitat and on its own terms.

Some of the world's most bountiful fishing and whaling grounds lie in areas least hospitable to man—the tempestuous North Sea; the ice-clotted waters off Iceland, Greenland, and Spitsbergen; the Bering Sea; the Grand Banks of Newfoundland. Here the water— murky gray or green or blue, depending on the light—is rich with plankton and algae, providing sustenance for an array of sea creatures that draw flotillas of shipborne hunters and harvesters.

Hunters become the hunted as a sperm whale, surfacing under their boat, turns the tables on its tormentors.

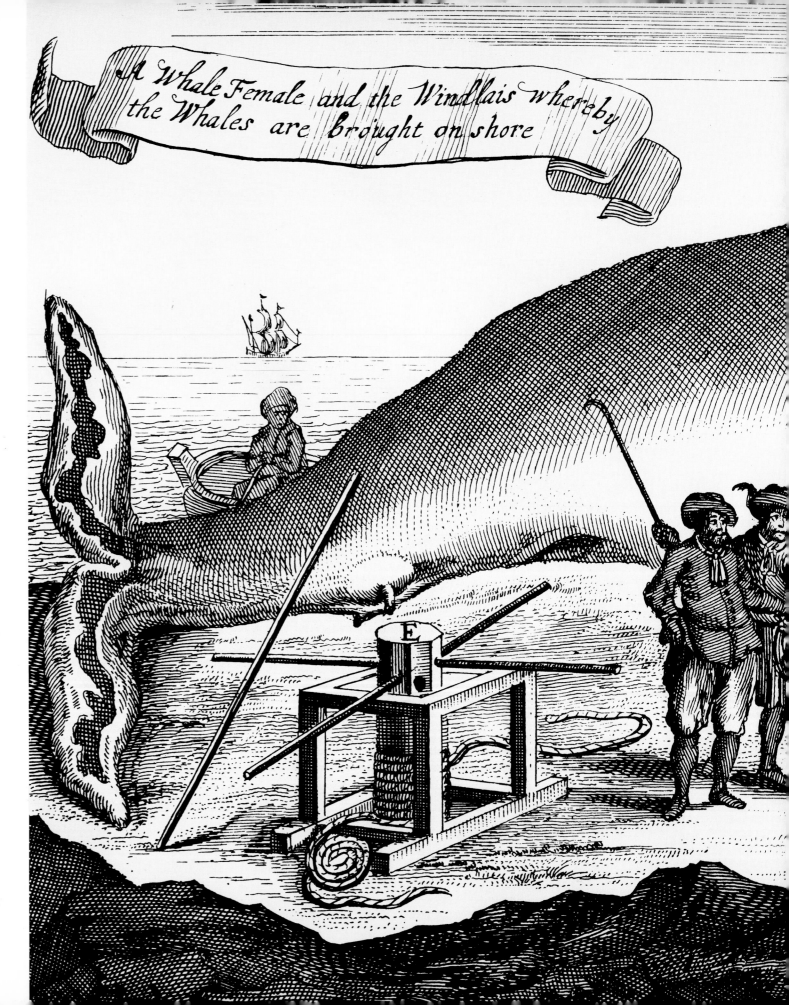

A Whale Female and the Windlais whereby the Whales are brought on shore

The most celebrated hunters of the sea have been those who pursued its biggest and most formidable quarry: the whale. As Herman Melville, who wrote the whaling classic, *Moby Dick,* phrased it, no man "can feel stranger and stronger emotions than that man does, who for the first time finds himself pulling into the charmed, churned circle of the hunted sperm whale."

Whale hunting in small boats is an ancient skill, the subject of Paleolithic drawings scratched on rock faces in shallow caves in Norway more than 10,000 years ago. The quarry shown includes dolphins, porpoises, and killer whales—small, toothed species.

The earliest written accounts describe ninth-century whale hunts in the Bay of Biscay, which touches the shores of France and Spain. Here the Basques, using harpoon and line, sought the Atlantic right whale, a slow-swimming species that feeds on plankton near the surface. These and other plankton-eating whales have hundreds of comblike plates of baleen—"whalebone"—growing from the palate. The baleen acts as a strainer to extract minute morsels of food from seawater.

People hunted similar species in other parts of the world. The Japanese used enormous nets with casks as floats to entangle the humpback whale before moving in to spear it. The Eskimos, among the most skillful of marine hunters, chased arctic bowhead whales in skin-covered umiaks. They attached their harpoon lines to sealskin floats to tire the animal and to enable them to follow its movements.

Capt. George Waymouth, reconnoitering New England shores in 1605, reported seeing Indians off

179

Prize in hand, 17th-century Dutch whalers on the desolate Spitsbergen coast begin flensing operations. Windlasses and gaffs have drawn the quarry—a right whale—ashore. The flenser slices blubber into foot-thick slabs called "horse pieces," which will be rendered in the tryworks. Right whales are slow swimmers. They could be caught by small boats and they floated when killed, which avoided loss. Yankee whalemen found a better way to peel the blubber: stripping it from the carcass in a spiral.

the Maine coast hunting whales: "They go in company of their King with a multitude of their boats, and strike him with a bone made in fashion of a harping iron fastened to a rope . . . then all their boats come about him, and as he riseth above water, with their arrowes they shoot him to death."

As maritime horizons widened in the 16th century, enterprising whalemen began to make longer voyages in bigger ships, into the arctic seas of Iceland, Greenland, and Spitsbergen. Throughout the summer months these plankton-rich waters teemed with right whales.

With the shift to the arctic region, the industry changed. Early coastal whalers had hunted chiefly for the meat. Now the by-products, oil rendered from the blubber and whalebone cut from the mouth, became increasingly valuable.

The English were first to exploit these seasonal feeding grounds, but the Dutch soon outnumbered them and were more successful. Both learned their business from the Basques, and initially they employed Basques as harpooners. So valued were their skills that British captains were ordered to treat them "kindly and friendly, being strangers, and leaving their own country to do us service."

Smeerenberg Bay in Spitsbergen became the most productive arctic station in the 1600's. It was a forbidding place, barren and ringed with glaciers. Ships anchored in the bay in spring, and lookouts posted on the cliffs watched for whales. Ships' boats pursued the quarry and towed carcasses back to the ships for flensing, or peeling off the blubber, and chopping out the whalebone. Blubber strips were towed ashore, cut up, and rendered in huge copper

Driven far to sea by a storm, he found himself amid a crowd of great black shapes. Not the familiar right whales with their V-shaped spout, these had squarish heads, and their spout arched forward in a single jet. They were sperm whales. Hussey killed one and towed it to shore.

Nantucketers had seen sperm whales before, but not many, and they had assumed they were rare wanderers, perhaps mutants. In fact, the sperm whale was one of the commonest of the big whales but, because of its deep-sea habits, it rarely came close to land. A fish-eater, the sperm whale has formidable teeth in its lower jaw. A favored prey is squid, which it pursues in the cold depths thousands of feet down. It can dive deeper and stay down longer than any other whale. To resist the cold and the pressure at such depths, it is enveloped in thick insulating blubber, making it a valuable oil-producing whale: some 2,000 gallons from a 60-foot bull. Besides ordinary blubber oil, the sperm whale yielded finer and more valuable "case oil" from the reservoir in its head—the precious spermaceti from which were made the clearest and longest-burning candles. The sperm whale quickly became the principal quarry of the New England whalemen.

They hunted this valuable beast in mid ocean, sailing out in 60- and 70-ton sloops, and towing whaleboats astern. The Nantucketers became the pioneers of true pelagic whaling. They devised a technique for rendering blubber at sea. Cauldrons and fireboxes were enclosed in a fireproof structure of brick which stood in the "duck pen," a shallow tank of water that kept the decks from catching fire. Of course, oil slimed the deck, smoke from the

kettles. In late August or early September ships laden with oil and whalebone sailed home to the Netherlands. At the height of whaling operations, in the mid-1600's, some 300 Dutch ships summered in the bay. Smeerenberg resembled a bustling Dutch town with shops, warehouses, and "good inns" where, according to a chronicler, crews enjoyed a touch of home—hot rolls for breakfast.

The pace could not continue indefinitely. Whales mature slowly and have a slow rate of reproduction—usually no more than one calf every second or third year in most large species. By the late 18th century they were becoming too scarce in the exploited areas to be hunted in profitable numbers from the shore stations. But as European whaling slid into depression, a whole new whaling industry was growing up in New England.

For 120 years the center of New England whaling, and initially its cradle, was Nantucket Island,

off Cape Cod. Its Quaker population, frugal and tough, had settled there to escape religious persecution. Largely a sandbank, Nantucket offered little in the way of a livelihood. But their island, the settlers soon discovered, lay within reach of a main migration stream of right whales. Watching the whales go by one day, one elder is said to have remarked, pointing to the sea: "There is a green pasture where our children's grand-children will go for bread." Before long, watchtowers were strung along the seaward shores, and the cry "Whale off!" would send crews scampering to a dozen boats. Dead whales were towed ashore to be rendered, scores of them every spring and fall.

After several decades, migrating whales began to avoid the coast. The islanders had to go farther out to sea to find them. In 1712 Christopher Hussey, out for whales, made the first of a series of discoveries that transformed the New England industry.

A tangle of spars, rigging, and oil casks crowds New Bedford wharf in the 1870's. At its peak 20 years earlier, the port handled 155,000 barrels of oil a year. Its whaling fleet of more than 300 ships (put end to end they would have stretched 10 miles) employed some 12,000 seamen. Here, bluff-bowed whalers with oversize davits flank a dark-hulled cargo ship.

Whale-oil lamps lighted streets and homes during the 19th century. Oil softened rope fibers and lubricated machines. Baleen, known as whalebone, stiffened hoopskirts, corsets, and parasols—and made buggy whips. Spermaceti, the white waxy substance from a sperm whale's head, made superior, non-wilt candles. And ambergris, formed around indigestible tidbits (such as squid beaks) in a sperm whale's intestines, found its way into perfumes and spices—and brought up to $400 a pound.

183

For Light Sperm Oil & Candles   For Food   The Whalebone   Manufacture Oil Works   Commerce Spermaceti, Ambergris

tryworks smutted sails and blackened spars and rigging, and the whole ship stank; but the gain in economic efficiency was enormous.

On-board processing became even more necessary to exploit the Pacific whale fisheries revealed by Cook's expeditions. Nantucket whalers had been hard hit by the loss of ships during the Revolutionary War and subsequent exclusion from Britain's market for oil. British whaling revived, but the firms found it hard to man their ships. Whaling was dirty and dangerous, the voyages long, and, except on lucky voyages, it paid poorly. On these counts even slaving was preferable. In a time of expanded shipping in England, experienced hands could choose their berths, and they avoided the "floating stinkpots." To find expert harpooners and boatsteerers was almost impossible—except in Nantucket. The first whaler to round Cape Horn into the Pacific, the British ship *Amelia* in 1789, carried

mates and harpooners from Nantucket. Britain's industry, though it made good profits for about 50 years, never outgrew its dependence on foreign skill.

The British market for whale oil declined as cheaper coal gas came into use to light streets and factories. New England whalemen enjoyed an expanding, chiefly rural home market, so that by 1820 they had reasserted their old predominance. By the middle of the 19th century three-quarters of the world's whaling fleet flew the American flag.

Nantucket's days as America's foremost whaling port were numbered. Its small harbor could berth only a limited number of ships. Worse, a sandbar spread across the entrance so that heavily laden ships could not enter. The resourceful islanders devised pontoon rigs called "camels" to overcome the barrier. These were large wooden boxes ballasted to ride low in the water. The camels were lashed to the sides of a ship and their ballast jettisoned, so that they

buoyed the vessel across the bar. But the device had its limits, and by the mid-1800's Nantucket had been eclipsed by mainland New Bedford.

In the 1850's New Bedford counted only 20,000 inhabitants, but it was home port to nearly 400 whalers—four-fifths of the American whaling fleet. New Bedford ships each year brought back five or six million dollars' worth of whale oil and baleen. Oil served as local currency: Parsons and schoolmasters often took their pay in casks instead of cash.

But times were changing. New England, like England itself half a century earlier, was becoming industrialized. New Bedford grew into a mill town, as well as a port, in the second half of the century. The great expanses of the Midwest also opened up for enterprising farmers. Young New Englanders had no need to go to sea in whalers, and most of them preferred not to. Ships sailed with skeleton crews and rounded out their complement as they went—with

Hove down for hull repairs, New Bedford whalers undergo a ritual: careening, caulking, and "coppering." Men work the capstan, winding a line tied to the mast of Sunbeam (below), hauling her on her side for work on keel and bottom.

James Arnold, *keel freshly undercoated with "bright varnish"*—a tarlike substance derived from turpentine—awaits new metal sheathing.

Such repairs were mandatory every voyage or two. Besides ordinary wear and tear, ships fought teredos, or shipworms. Burrowing into exposed wood undetected, these voracious warm-water mollusks could riddle the stoutest oak, leaving it spongy in a matter of weeks. Partly to stave off teredos, wooden ships were clad with thin sheets of "yellow metal," a copper-zinc alloy. But sheathing could be damaged, and another ship might vanish without trace, its timbers sabotaged by shipworms.

Portuguese from the Azores, "Bravas" from the Cape Verde Islands, "Kanakas" from the many islands of the Pacific. At the same time the demand for whale oil, spermaceti, and whalebone shrank as kerosene, paraffin, and flexible steel replaced them. By the 1870's the industry was slowly dying. The last square-rigged whaler to sail from New Bedford, the *Wanderer,* was wrecked in 1924, only 13 miles outward bound from home.

One New Bedford sailing whaler survives more or less intact, the bark *Charles W. Morgan,* 351 tons, 105 feet overall. Launched in 1841, she saw 80 years of service and is said to have earned more than a million dollars for her owners. The *Morgan* now lies preserved at Mystic Seaport, Connecticut.

No ship of sail can escape beauty altogether, and the *Morgan* is the principal attraction of the waterfront museum; but as sailing vessels go, a whaler is an ugly lump of a ship. In this respect, the *Morgan* is probably representative of her kind.

Whaling vessels did not need speed or high weatherly qualities, and certainly not an elegant appearance; in their line of work even ordinary cleanliness was hard to achieve. What they did need was solid construction and big hold capacity. In striking contrast to the tubby, undercanvassed, and slow mother ship, the boats that hung in her davits were slim, graceful, and deadly.

The New England whaleboat was a highly specialized craft, superbly designed for its purpose. It measured about 28 feet long and 6 wide. A whaleboat was strongly but lightly constructed of cedar planks only half an inch thick. It was double ended so that it could back quickly away from a flurrying

Morgan Recalls the Heyday Of Whaling

186 "May kind Neptune protect us with pleasant gales and may we be successful in catching Sperm Whales." The hope expressed by the second mate in the log of the *Charles W. Morgan* as she set out on her maiden cruise in September 1841 was destined to be fulfilled. No other whaler would travel as many miles or bring home as many barrels of oil as the *Morgan* did in a seafaring career that spanned 80 years.

The *Morgan* undertook 37 voyages between 1841 and her retirement as an active whaler in 1921. The first voyage alone, a 40-month cruise of the Pacific whaling grounds by way of Cape Horn, brought in a cargo of oil and bone worth $56,000—enough to repay the $52,000 it cost to build the ship. The *Morgan's* most profitable voyage—the sixth, undertaken during the Civil War—yielded a cargo valued at $165,000. Altogether, the ship netted her various owners 54,483 barrels of oil and 152,934 pounds of whalebone.

Built in New Bedford by Jethro and Zachariah Hillman, the ship bears the name of one of her first owners, Charles Waln Morgan, a Quaker merchant from Philadelphia who came to New England and married into a wealthy whaling family.

Originally, the *Morgan* wore ship rig, with square sails on all three masts. Later, to facilitate handling, she was re-rigged as a bark, with fore-and-aft sails on the mizzenmast. Thus she served for 54 years.

The ship normally carried about 33 crewmen, including officers, seamen, and the "idlers"—cook, carpenter, cooper, and the ship's boy—who remained aboard to handle the ship while the boats chased whales.

Twenty-one skippers commanded the *Morgan* through the years. One, James A. Earle, took her on nine cruises, but most served only one or two turns. Five captains took their wives to sea. One, Tom Landers, installed the gimbal-mounted bunk in the captain's quarters so his wife would not feel the roll of the ship. Charles Church's wife served as an assistant navigator.

Among the crewmen, George Parkin Christian, great-grandson of the *Bounty's* Fletcher Christian, held the longest record of service—12 voyages between 1893 and 1913, during which time he rose from boat-steerer to first mate.

San Francisco became the *Morgan's* home port from 1887 to 1906. After numerous Pacific cruises, the ship returned to New Bedford for her last seven whaling voyages.

Through the years, the *Morgan's* luck held. She survived typhoons, hurricanes, near-mutinies, and groundings. Lightning blasted her three times and, on one occasion, a disgruntled crewman tried to set her ablaze. The fire was doused and the crewman was clapped in irons.

Another time, while becalmed near Sydenham Island in the South Pacific, the ship was surrounded by canoes filled with "whooping, roaring ugly devils." The crew, using harpoons and cutting spades, repelled several attempts to board. Then a new danger: A reef suddenly loomed under the hull. But at the last instant the current veered, carrying the ship clear of the island and beyond reach of the cannibals.

Moviemakers discovered the *Morgan* after her retirement as a whaler. In the early 1920's she starred in two movies, *Down to the Sea in Ships* and *Java Head*.

Mystic Seaport acquired the venerable whaler in 1941. Moored there, she heads a fleet of wooden ships that each year attracts more than half a million visitors.

Finale for a bowhead whale: More than a ton of baleen— a tough, hornlike substance also known as whalebone—swings aboard an arctic whaler off Alaska, the final curtain in a drama of man versus leviathan. Hundreds of these flexible strips | *fringe a baleen whale's upper jaw, enabling it to strain krill and other food from the sea. Victorians paid a pretty penny for baleen—up to five or six dollars a pound. Then, in the early 20th century, came spring steel—and baleen prices plummeted to 50 cents.* | *Another victim, this one a sperm whale, lies belly up beside the* California *(opposite). Crewmen line the cutting stage, a retractable scaffold, to carve away its tooth-studded lower jaw. Then, using razor-sharp spades, they will decapitate the whale, flense its carcass of* | *blubber, and haul the head, or "case," aboard (far right) to ladle out valuable spermaceti oil. The teeth, embedded in cartilage, will be stripped out— raw material to fill odd hours at sea scrimshawing.*

whale. A whaleboat could be sailed, and sailed fast, when the wind served; otherwise it was pulled by five oars and steered, when in action against a whale, by a sixth over the stern. With a good crew springing it along, a boat could travel about five knots under oar in calm water—fast enough to outstrip a right or sperm whale swimming on the surface at about the speed of a walking man.

The boat's equipment was as specialized and deadly as the boat itself. The harpoons rested in a crotch on the starboard side forward. The first to be used was bent to the whale line coiled down with care in its tub amidships. The coiling was crucial. The line must run out free; a kink or turn when fast to a whale could drag the boat under or drown a man or take off his arm. From the tub the line led aft, around a snubbing post called the loggerhead, forward to the chock, or fairlead, in the bows, and then to the harpoon. All this gear was kept ready for instant use when the whaler cruised the grounds with lookouts at the mastheads.

Once harpooned, the whale might run on or near the surface, towing the boat after it. The "sleigh-ride" could cover many miles; a right whale once towed a ship, the *Royal Bounty,* at two knots for an hour and a half. But sooner or later the whale would tire and the boat could be hauled up on the line for the final attack. Or the whale might sound—dive deep. When that happened, it had to be allowed line, or the boat could be pulled under.

Other boats might have to be called on to help, to bend on additional lines. A skillful mate could play a "fast" whale as a fisherman plays a salmon, using the loggerhead to check the animal's rush. Sooner

or later, out of breath, it would have to surface again.

Harpooner and mate, meanwhile, had changed places, the harpooner taking the steering oar, the mate the lance—a long, broad-bladed spear. By custom, the mate's seniority entitled him to make the final thrust, with the boat's bow almost touching the exhausted animal's flank—"wood on black-skin." If the mate succeeded in finding the "life," the vital heart or lungs, the whale would die quickly. Even so, its final flurry could be harrowing and dangerous. Describing such a scene, a 19th-century seaman recalled that the whale "beat the waters with his flukes, and darted hither and thither at immense speed, in his death struggle. From the distance to which we had removed for safety from an accidental stroke, we could not see his actions; and it was fearful to list to the swift blows of his flukes, and know that but a little way from us, in the thick darkness, a leviathan was parting from life."

That was how whale hunting went, according to the book. In practice it might take many darted irons and many lance thrusts to kill a single whale. And many of them escaped.

If whales had the same instinct for vindictive counterattack as a wounded elephant or buffalo, hunting whales would have been prohibitively dangerous. But whales are peaceable on the whole. On feeling the iron their first reaction usually is to escape rather than retaliate. Even so, 60 tons of blubber, bone, and muscle in a hurry to escape can wreak havoc. The whale might rear in the air and, falling back, swamp the boat. Or it might lash out with its tail, smashing a boat to kindling with a single flick of those mighty flukes.

Scrimshaw: A Lonely Whaleman's Shipboard Art

"By the time we had gotten a month's experience of the cruising ground," wrote seaman-author Charles Nord-hoff in 1856, "I no longer wondered at the wandering, lack-luster look . . . of your regular old whaleman. His mind has been gradually killed out by lack of use."

Boredom may have been a chronic occupational hazard among whaling crews, but it also contributed a type of folk art called scrimshaw—ornamented whale teeth (G) or useful or decorative objects made from whale teeth and baleen or walrus tusks. A scrimshander—as the practitioner was called—worked with a jackknife and an awl made of a nail or a sail needle. Talented hands turned out the latticework carousel—a swift for winding yarn into a ball (A), knitting needles, and intricate clock case (C). Fancy corset stays (B), wheeled piecrust crimpers (D), cane head (E), and ditty box (F) also were inspired by the boredom—and loneliness—of life aboard a whaler.

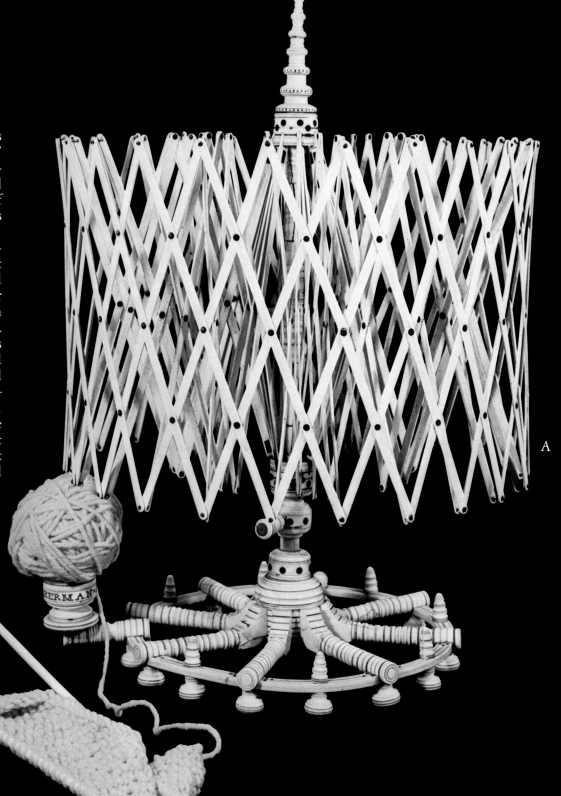

A

B

C

G

E

D

F

Whaling Wives:
Loneliness Ashore
Or Danger Afloat

If whaling was hard on the men who pursued their quarry to the farthest reaches of the globe, it was no less so for those who stayed behind, waiting for loved ones who might be gone three or four years at a time—or perhaps forever. Whaling was hard on *anyone* involved with it, which perhaps accounts for the stoic expressions on these wives of New Bedford whaling masters, whose names are lost to history.

"We have been married 10 years," wrote Helen Brown, wife of Capt. Samuel Brown, "and for two thirds of that time the oceans and the continents have separated us." Lydia Gardner, for 37 years the wife of Capt. George Gardner of Nantucket, noted that during that time he had spent less than 5 years at home. The wife of yet another captain figured that she had seen her husband less than a year in an 11-year marriage.

But by the mid-1800's certain changes began to take place, at least for spouses of ships' captains. No longer were they relegated to years of loneliness and solitary vigils from the "widow's walks" on the rooftops of their seaside homes. As one shipowner noted in 1849, Capt. Prince Ewer "will probably go again in the *Emily Morgan* and Mrs. Ewer will accompany him. This custom is becoming quite common and no disadvantages have been noticed, though there are some, but the advantages overpower them. There is more decency when a woman is on board."

Mrs. Ewer was not the first wife to accompany her husband on a whaling voyage. Credit for that goes to Mary Hayden Russell of Nantucket who, in 1817, sailed aboard the *Hydra* on a three-year Pacific cruise. Accompanying the Russells was their 12-year-old son, William, who was signed on as cabin boy. On a subsequent voyage, Cap-

tain and Mrs. Russell took their 7-year-old son, Charles, and William, now a strapping 17-year-old, occupied a harpooner's billet.

The decision to follow their husbands to sea was not an easy one for whaling wives to make. The thought of forsaking the comforts and conveniences of home for the rigors and dangers of life aboard a cramped and reeking whaleship was more than most women raised in Victorian gentility could endure. So they stayed ashore and whiled away the months with family and friends, or ran shops and stores in seaport towns largely bereft of men. For a time Nantucket's Centre Street was known as Petticoat Row because so many of its businesses were managed by wives of absentee sea hunters.

But for other women the decision to go a-roving was easy. As Mrs. Brown put it: "Samuel is all the world to me and why should we live with half the globe between us?" By the last half of the 19th century more than a hundred other wives who had never been as far away as Boston or New York found themselves at exotic ports such as Talcahuano, Chile; Hakodate, Japan; Ponape in the Caroline Islands; and Great Loo Choo, as whalemen called Okinawa. Martha's Vineyard alone numbered more than 40 seagoing wives.

For some of the women a single voyage was sufficient, especially if accompanied by incessant bouts of seasickness. But others were undaunted by any amount of danger

and discomfort. Adelaide Mayhew Cottle was one of them. She spent 20 years of her life aboard her husband's ships and sailed farther north than any other white woman of her time. In 1913 she and her husband, then aboard the *Belvedere,* rescued members of an Arctic expedition that had been forced to abandon their ships in a gale. The winter that was coming on proved a severe one, and for the next 18 months the *Belvedere* stayed locked in ice north of the Arctic Circle.

A few seagoing wives bickered with officers and crew, earning their ship a dubious reputation as a "hen frigate." One woman complained that her husband's first mate was the "nearest to a *savage* of anyone I ever met." And the young mate of another ship characterized his skipper's wife as "the meanest, most hoggish and the greediest female that ever existed. . . . The whistle of a gale of wind through the rigging is much more musical than the sound of her voice."

But most captains' wives were content to be with their husbands, sharing in his life, rearing their children, attending sick and injured crewmen, and baking treats for special occasions. "I should never have known what a great man he was if I had not accompanied him," wrote Mary Chipman Lawrence of her husband, Samuel.

Some women distinguished themselves as competent mariners. Caroline Mayhew, a doctor's daughter, not only nursed the *Powhatan*'s crew when smallpox swept the ship, but also navigated and commanded the vessel when her husband fell ill. Charity Norton won the gratitude of her ship's company by courageously shielding them from the wrath of her fiery-tempered husband. On one occasion she halted the flogging of a dozen men being punished for trying to jump ship in South America.

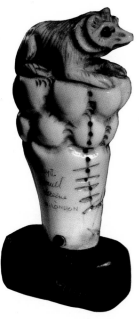

Logbook stamps carved of whale ivory kept idle hands busy and told the story at a glance: Here, within a five-day span, the William Baker *captured two dolphins and a right whale yielding 60 barrels of oil. Five other whales—signified by upturned flukes—were chased but escaped unharmed. Had they been wounded, upturned whale heads would have stated the fact. Such stampings embellished the margins of many a whaleship's log—and enabled the owners to gauge quickly the success of a voyage.*

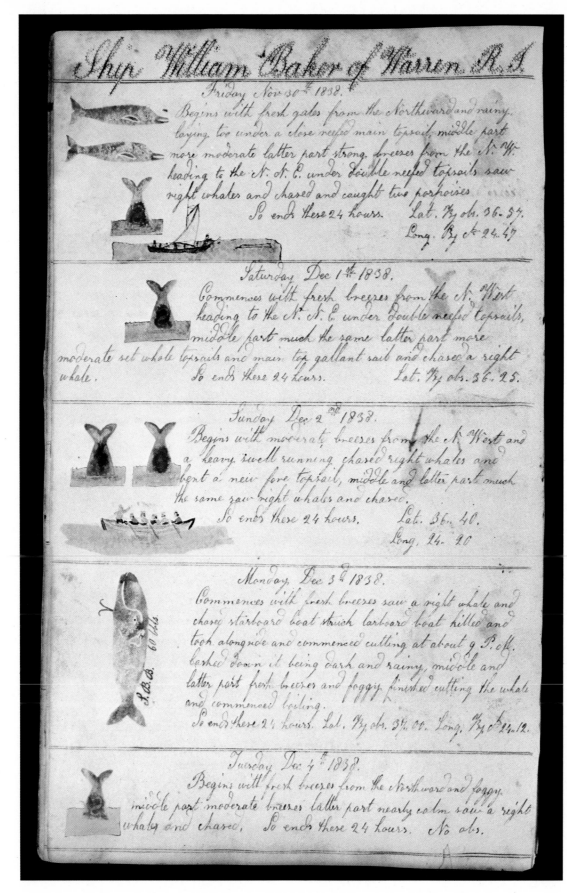

Sperm whales sometimes attacked head-on, crushing boats and men in their jaws. They even attacked ships. Three are known to have been sunk by whales. The most famous, the *Essex* of Nantucket, sank in minutes after being rammed by an enraged sperm whale in 1819. Her people drifted in boats for weeks, and those who survived did so by resorting to cannibalism. All three of these attacks appeared to be deliberate, and in at least one case the whale was subsequently killed—and found to have old harpoons rusting in its hide.

One huge sperm whale, Mocha Dick, was a veteran of scores of encounters which took a toll of 30 men and dozens of whaleboats. Mocha Dick was the real-life counterpart of Herman Melville's fictional great white whale, Moby Dick.

Killing the whale was only the beginning. Then came the backbreaking tow to get the huge inert carcass back to the ship; the labor of securing it alongside, tail forward; and the gory, greasy butchering: cutting in, rigging the blubber hooks, manning the capstan, stripping off the thick strips of blubber, chopping them into lumps called "horse pieces," and slicing the lumps into "bible leaves" to be tossed into the kettles and rendered into oil. Describing the scene in the blubber room below decks, where the fat was minced before being fed into the try-pots, the wife of one whaling captain wrote: "The Mate came to me and wanted me to go with him and take a look down in the reception room, as he termed it. I went, and I could not refrain from laughter, such a comical sight! There the Men were at work up to their waists in blubber. The warm weather had tried out the oil a good deal and made it soft. I don't

see how they could stand in among it, but they were laughing and having a good deal of fun."

But danger was the aspect of 19th-century whaling that most impressed stay-at-homes. It became the theme of popular prints of the period. It is revealed in whalemen's epitaphs on the walls of the Seaman's Bethel in New Bedford: "carried overboard by the line, and drowned," "killed by a sperm whale," "towed out of sight by a whale." The whalemen themselves accepted the dangers as part of their job: "a dead whale or a stove boat." A successful whaleman, especially a harpooner, took pride in fighting a potentially dangerous animal with handheld weapons. It made him a hero in his hometown.

However exciting the chase, one aspect of whaling could not be avoided: tedium. Voyages lasted three or four years, and for most of the time there was not a whale in sight. It was boredom that peopled the South Sea islands with beachcombing deserters, including Herman Melville.

Many of the surviving relics of old-style whaling reflect these simple facts. Widow's walks—those little lookout galleries that straddle the roof ridges of houses in old whaling towns—are mute monuments to long separations. Scrimshaw was the solace of enforced idleness and a refuge from tedium. A fad for collecting it in recent years has called into being a whole new trade in factory-made fakes. Genuine scrimshaw is moving because it can invoke nostalgia. Those artless scratchings on bone, those swifts and piecrust crimpers, are the poignant expressions of a sad and profound homesickness.

All this, of course, is long gone. Modern whale hunters, seeking the raw material of soap and

MASTERS OF VESSELS!

And all others interested, are hereby publicly cautioned against shipping the following officers of the "LANCASTER," of New Bedford, as it was through their ignorance, inefficiency and utter incompetency that the "Lancaster" was "SKUNKED!"

WILLIAM HENRY ROYCE,
SECOND OFFICER,

Was 3d mate and boatsteerer of the Bark "Black Eagle" for the season of '55, during which time he distinguished himself as an excellent DO-NOTHING, whilst as 2d officer of the "Lancaster" he won for himself the reputation of an extensive KNOW-NOTHING! Too ignorant to catch a bow-head, and afraid as death of a right whale. Would make a good deck walloper.

CHAS. BUSHNELL,
THIRD OFFICER,

Is equally incompetent and worthless. Was boatsteerer in the "Washington" when lost--no oil! Then 4th mate of the "Wm. Badger--no oil! Again 4th mate of the "Huntsville," brought no oil to the ship! And finally 3d dickey of the "Lancaster"--SKUNKED! Was fast six hours to a ripsack which drove him out of the head of the boat and from which he finally cut. Would make a good blubber room hand.

Of the mate we will say nothing, preferring to consign him to the tender mercies of Captain Carver.

Before shipping any of the above worthies, Masters of Vessels are requested to ascertain their true characters.

(Signed by the entire Crew.)

Ships on Ice:
The Terrible Winter
Of 1871

By September 8 it was clear that disaster loomed. For days, westerly gales had roared across the Arctic Ocean, sending giant slabs of ice drifting and grinding toward the 32 whaling ships huddled off Alaska's northwest coast. Two ships, the *Comet* and the *Roman,* already had been caught, crushed, and sent to the bottom by converging floes. Other ships, too, had sustained serious damage, and that same day the *Awashonks* and the *Elizabeth Swift* had been driven aground by ice.

Now, with the barometer falling and reports that "offshore is one vast expanse of ice," the masters of all the ships convened aboard the *Gay Head* to decide on a course of action. Should they abandon the fleet, escaping southward in open whaleboats before the ice cut them off completely? Or should they stay on, hoping that the wind would veer and open a channel wide enough for the fleet to navigate? Ride out the winter where they were? No chance. Supplies would not last, and pack ice would demolish the ships. Besides, there were several women and children to consider—the families of captains.

The summer cruise to the Arctic whaling grounds began inauspiciously that year of 1871. One ship, damaged by ice, had to be abandoned, and her gear and men assigned to other ships. The pack ice was slow to retreat, and it was not until August that the fleet could work its way to Point Belcher along a 20-mile-wide strip of open water.

But bowhead whales were plentiful and there was space in the holds. Eskimo warnings of an early freeze-up went unheeded. Then the wind shifted and the channel began to narrow. Still the ships lingered. By early September the floating ice had bottled the fleet into a shallow anchorage along the shore. The whalers were trapped.

On September 10 three whaleboats were sent out to reconnoiter an escape route along the shallow coastal waters. They returned two days later with heartening news: Seven whalers were 80 miles down the coast, below the southern edge of the ice shelf. They would stand by.

On the morning of September 14 the fleet was abandoned. Whaleboats loaded to the gunwales with men, women, children, and supplies set out on a two-day haul through ice-clogged channels to the waiting rescue ships. They made it without loss of a single life. But the fleet perished.

A Newfoundland fishery of the 18th century processes cod. The parka-clad fisherman in the foreground holds a baited hook similar to those being used by the men fishing from suspended barrels. Unloaded from a boat, the fish are dressed, washed, salted, and spread to dry on a platform. A press extracts "ye oyl from ye Cods Livers."

margarine, run no excessive risks and incur no serious hardships. Factory ships are reasonably comfortable. Whalers do not now make unbearably long voyages. Their crews do not go in for scrimshawing. Yet something, perhaps, has been lost. If there was ever any romance at all in whaling, factory ships, steam catchers, and harpoon guns have killed it—as they have also killed most of the world's whales.

The Grand Banks of Newfoundland, an underwater plateau measuring some 400 miles by 350 miles, ranks among the world's richest and most extensive fishing grounds; certainly it is among the most exacting and the stormiest. In its wide expanse of shallow water any wind can kick up a steep, lumpy sea in a very short time. But the biggest hazard to navigation on the Banks is fog. The Labrador Current keeps the water cold. For much of the year, warm moist air from the nearby Gulf Stream drifts across the cold gray surface of the sea on the Banks, condensing in thick, dripping, clinging fog that can last for days. It is a place for seamen to avoid, if they have a choice. But fishermen must go where the fish are, and for 500 years, perhaps longer, they have gone to the Banks.

The earliest recorded report of prodigious quantities of cod here was made in 1497 by John Cabot, sailing from Bristol under license from Henry VII. He reported that the natives caught fish with nets and weighted basket traps and that they called codfish *baccallao*—the Basque word for the same fish. Bristol fishermen, too, probably had frequented the Banks years before Cabot's voyages and, after the fashion of their calling, had kept their mouths shut.

By the early 16th century, despite the long voyage and rough conditions, fishermen from many nations—Basques and Bretons, Englishmen and Normans, Spaniards and Portuguese—were sailing out to the Banks every spring in large and increasing numbers. By 1626 Devonshire alone was deploying 150-ship fleets on the Banks, and the French were even more numerous.

When not actually fishing, the crews camped on the beaches of southern Newfoundland and dried and salted their catch on "flakes"—scaffolds of rough timber cut on the site. In the autumn they loaded their catch and returned to Europe.

European fishermen brought their methods with them. Cod, bottom feeders, were caught on handlines over the side or, increasingly from the 18th century, on longlines suspended just above the ocean floor. Made of thin, but extremely strong, tarred fiber, longlines ranged from two thousand feet to nearly a mile long. Along the length of these "ground lines" were spliced 20- to 30-inch "snoods" or "gangions," each bent to a steel hook baited, typically, with whelk. There might be 500 to 800 hooks per longline. Floats attached at intervals kept the longline from sinking to the bottom; flag buoys marked each end of the line so that it could be located and hauled in.

Flaked out on a bed of boughs, codfish dry beneath a pallid Newfoundland sun. Cod flesh, unlike that of most other fish, is rich and gelatinous without being fatty. Its high protein content makes cod "the beef of the sea." Properly salted and

dried, the flesh keeps almost indefinitely. Spruce boughs covering the "flake," a platform made of poles, allow air to circulate freely during the bleaching process. In fog or rain, or as night approaches, the cod are covered or piled skin outward in small heaps. After curing, they are placed on skids

(below) and baled in bulk or packed into small casks.

To avoid bruising the flesh, which promotes decay, the fish must be handled gently— even when stowed in the hold of a fishing vessel (opposite).

As colonists settled New England, Nova Scotia, and Newfoundland, they too took to fishing. Nearby residents often competed violently with fishermen from Europe, who regarded Newfoundland as their private domain. New Englanders arrived later in the area, having first exploited their own excellent fisheries nearer home. But by the 1800's these American groups predominated in the Banks fishery, using their own fishing methods and distinctive types of fishing vessels.

The earliest New Englanders had been poorly equipped for offshore fishing and at first relied on shallops, dugouts, and birchbark canoes. Later they built mostly square-rigged ketches and sloops, handy both for fishing and for coastal trading. These boats, deckless and ballasted with stones, carried one or two masts without stays to brace them. They provided no protection from the elements. Three-man crews took them out along the coast for three or four days at a time, sometimes a week. Rations for a week-long fishing excursion might consist of a few pounds of flour, fat pork, sea biscuit, half a gallon of water—and a jug of rum.

As the need arose to fish farther at sea, larger craft were devised. One type, the pinkie, of 20 to 60 tons, carried two fore-and-aft sails, but no headsails or jibs. It had decks, a tiny cabin aft, and a forecastle with two bunks, one of which was reserved for the cook. A plank running along the waist served as a bulwark in heavy weather. The forecastle fireplace, made of brick or mud-daubed wood, served both for cooking and for smoking part of the catch.

Everyone on a pinkie fished, including the skipper. Each had his place at the low rail and handled

one or two lines weighted with a heavy lead sinker. Each man shared according to the number of fish he caught, the captain keeping a daily tally by the number of fish tongues or tails turned in.

New England fishermen began voyaging to the Grand Banks near the end of the 17th century. A trip there lasted ten or twelve weeks and, if successful, resulted in a ship so heavily laden that its decks nearly ran awash. Under such circumstances, it is

surprising that any vessel returned. Many did not. As the town record of Gloucester laconically reports: "On the 14th day of October . . . a number of fishermen were on their way to Gloucester, some of them within 30 or 40 leagues of our Cape. . . . There arose on said day a very extraordinary storm, which lasted all that day and a great part of the night following. A few days after, four of our vessels arrived, some of them much broken, like wrecks; and four more are not yet heard of. . . ."

Hand-lining left its mark on a man—if he survived. In many a fishing port a handline fisherman could easily be distinguished in a crowd—by his hunched and rounded shoulders.

It was the development of a different vessel that would ultimately turn the tide of Banks fishing in favor of the colonists. In 1713, when Capt. Andrew Robinson's new ship slid down the ways at Gloucester, an admiring spectator supposedly exclaimed, "See how she scoons!" The expression, which describes the graceful flight of a stone skipped across water, seemed appropriate. The trim lines of the hull were complemented by two tall masts rigged with fore-and-aft sails. Even though schooner rig was not an American invention (Dutch fore-and-afters plied the North Sea in the 1600's), it would reach perfection as an American rig—and the name stuck.

Schooner rig had several advantages over square rig. Sails behind the masts enabled schooners to run close to the wind and to tack quickly in narrow waters—or to pick up dories in an emergency. And they could be handled by smaller crews.

The L. A. Dunton, *one of the last Grand Banks fishing schooners, lies at her moorings in the Mystic Seaport harbor. She was launched in 1921. The 124-foot Gloucesterman—known as an "Indian Header" because of her rounded bow—* shipped a 22-man crew and nested 10 dories. She was converted to diesel power, her hull shortened, masts cropped, and bowsprit removed.

The vessel served her last commercial owners as a coal and general cargo carrier, plying between Nova Scotia and Newfoundland. Restored to her original condition, the Dunton *recalls days of glory.*

Visitors marvel at the ship's compactness—and wonder how crewmen found room to stow their gear in a forecastle (opposite) shared with the foremast and the cook's stove.

In modern times Banks fishing schooners ranged from 100 to 150 feet long and from 80 to 175 tons. Well-ballasted and deep-keeled aft, they stood up to a tremendous press of canvas. The main boom on some schooners reached a length of 75 feet.

Most Banks schooners stepped two masts and carried a mainsail, foresail, forestaysail, and a jib, known collectively as "the lowers." In summer topmasts were added and additional sails set. In heavy weather a small, triangular canvas, called the riding sail, or storm trysail, was hoisted on the mainmast. This sail was also set when the ship lay at anchor or when it shifted from berth to berth on the fishing grounds. A vessel under riding sail, foresail, and forestaysail was said to be "under Bank sail."

Trim as a Banks schooner might look, life aboard it was decidedly cramped. Up to sixteen bunks were sandwiched together in the forecastle, where most of the crewmen lived, and another four to six in the captain's cabin aft. The galley stove, kept lit day and night to cook meals and to dry out soggy clothing, kept the forecastle warm.

At sea the skipper took charge of all navigating and shiphandling. The men were primarily fishermen, but all took orders from the captain and had to help sail the ship, steer, keep a lookout, and handle the sails. During the run to the grounds, the men busied themselves with the dories, the fishing lines, and other gear. When on the Banks a fishing schooner usually stayed there—fair weather or foul. During a blow, the usual practice was to heave to under foresail and forestaysail, or even bare poles. A schooner bucked and kicked like fury against the buffeting waves, but if its anchor held, it could ride out all

The Grand Banks yields its treasure—a cache of mackerel that brings smiles to these fishermen as they dip a sample from their seine. Aboard ship, the fish are beheaded, gutted, and split. A dory makes a handy washtub for the fish (far left) before they are salted and stowed below.

Heeled to the breeze under easy sail, the Bluenose scoons for her home port in Canada. The starboard watch, clad in oilskins and drenched with spray, searches for a landfall.

but the most ferocious storms in relative safety, scarcely taking water over the side.

In winter, ice could become a problem. Freezing spray could quickly coat a vessel, making it top-heavy and vulnerable to capsizing.

Fisherman's pay on the Banks was often a matter of luck. On some vessels all hands drew equal shares after a certain portion—usually a fourth or a fifth of the catch—had been set aside to pay for the ship and supplies. Other skippers paid "by the count," keeping record of the number of fish landed by each dory. A lucky dory was known as the "high liner" or "high dory." With luck, a fisherman of the 1920's might draw $70 a week. Without it, he could fish all season—and bring home $45.

Before the advent of powered trawlers, long-lining from dories became standard practice for Banks fishing. Dories are sturdy, flat-bottomed boats with removable thwarts that can be nested one inside another on the deck of a parent vessel—up to 20 or so on a big schooner. Each was usually handled by one or two men.

When the ship reached the fishing ground, it hove to or anchored, depending on the weather, and at first light lowered its dories. Dorymen sailed or rowed away from the ship, each in a different direction. Most of them were soon out of sight, for convention decreed that fish would not be found near the ship. Arriving at his chosen spot, each man paid out his longline, a task requiring deftness and speed. Each hook was baited before it was dropped over the side. The line, carefully coiled in a wooden tub, ran out smoothly; a carelessly coiled line could tangle, or jab needle-sharp hooks into a man's flesh.

Pride of Nova Scotia, the Bluenose, *fastest of the Grand Banks fishing schooners, trails Gloucester's* Gertrude L. Thebaud *in this 1930 race. In later years the Canadian vessel triumphed, successfully defending the international title she held for 17 years.*

The doryman ran a real risk of losing his way in the fog; he had only a small boat's compass to help him return to his ship if it drifted or blew off station. He might be run down by a steamer in the fog or smashed against his own ship's side in a heavy seaway. He might be swamped—or overturned by a passing whale. On one occasion more than two hundred dorymen were lost in a single gale. But dorymen were a hardy lot and sometimes survived in the face of overwhelming odds. Such was the case with Howard Blackburn, a halibuter who, with his dorymate Tom Welch, strayed from the schooner *Grace L. Fears* during a bitter January blow in 1883. Howling winds kicked up the sea and dumped a blizzard of snow. Between squalls the two men caught glimpses of their ship in the distance, and tried desperately to row to her. No use. Wind and tide prevented them from making headway. That

Britain's Livonia *reaches for a* 207
*marker buoy during the 1871
America's Cup race off Sandy
Hook. Hard on her heels comes*
Sappho, *the American defender
that went on to win the event.
Yachting's most venerable
trophy, the America's Cup cost
$500 in 1851, the year the
schooner* America *won it sailing
against the Royal Yacht
Squadron. Millions have since
been spent vying for the cup.*

Close-hauled on wings of wind, Freedom *(foreground) and the challenger,* Australia, *vie for a lead during the 1980 America's Cup contest off Newport, Rhode Island. Here both sloops tack into the breeze, relying on giant-size genoa jibs to drive them along an upwind leg of the 24-mile course. The*

Australian yacht forged ahead to win this race by seconds, but ultimately lost the match— leaving unbroken a string of 24 American victories since the first contest was held.

208   night they lost sight of the ship. There was only one hope: row for Newfoundland, about a hundred miles away. But between rowing and bailing, Blackburn's mittens went over the side and his hands began to freeze. Realizing his fingers would soon be useless, Blackburn wrapped them around the oars—and let them freeze in rowing position.

On the second night Tom Welch died—frozen in the bow where he had sought shelter from the wind. Blackburn propped the corpse on the stern seat and rowed on, bailing, rowing, clubbing ice from the gunwales with his frozen hands. Blackburn's feet froze, and still he rowed. For four days he rowed and bailed and rowed, until he made land. Blackburn lost his fingers and toes—but he lived.

Another man, a Portuguese doryman, became hopelessly lost and drifted for five days in pea-soup fog and shrieking wind. He rowed and bailed constantly, with only a few cupfuls of beans and whatever moisture he could wring from his fog-drenched cap. Finally, on the morning of the sixth day, long after the crewmen on his ship had given him up for dead, the doryman crested a wave and saw the mast of a ship in the distance. It was his own ship, and when he stumbled aboard to pick up more bait and get on with his work, his legs gave way beneath him. He was compelled to rest a few hours before resuming his duties.

Tales of bravery and self-sacrifice were legion on the Banks. In one case, two men hit by a huge wave were thrown clear of their dory and left floundering in the sea. One of them grabbed hold of a thwart floating past and held on. His companion, who couldn't swim, called for help. "Here, take the thwart," shouted the first man, tossing it to his dory-mate. The drowning man grabbed the dory seat and kept himself afloat long enough to be rescued. But his companion, a man named Jennings, had vanished. Jennings couldn't swim either.

Such hazards the doryman always accepted. The possibility that he most resented was weather too foul for fishing.

On a good day the doryman shot his line three or four times. When he was ready to haul in his long-line in the evening, the fisherman located his marker buoy and hauled it aboard, along with the anchor holding his line in place. Standing at the bow, the doryman hauled his line out of the water, dexterously flipping his catch into the boat and disengaging the hook all in the same motion. As the line came aboard, the unused bait was knocked off the hook and the line was coiled carefully back into its tub. Unmarketable species such as sculpins and dogfish were knocked back into the sea by slatting them against the dory's gunwale.

If he were lucky, the doryman returned to the mother ship with his dory loaded down, knee-deep in wet, rubbery cod. The heavy fish would then be gaffed onto the deck and the dories hoisted in, stripped, and nested. After a hasty meal, the real work began—gutting, splitting, salting, and stowing the fish, with hands already cracked and raw from baiting hooks and hauling lines in the icy wind. The work might take half the night, and at dawn, if the weather held, the dories would go out again. Not until the holds were full, or the season too far advanced for fishing, did the vessel weigh for Lisbon or Lunenberg, Gloucester, Saint John's, Saint Malo, or whatever port she had sailed from.

The most celebrated fishing schooners came from Lunenberg, Nova Scotia, and Gloucester, Massachusetts, for more than 100 years competing centers of fishing and shipbuilding. The craft were admired as much for their beauty and speed as for economic advantage; the first fish back to market fetched the best price. Local pride and racing instinct impelled skippers and crews to drive these lovely ships to their utmost, with every stitch set, spars whipping and bending, lee rails awash. They were the precursors of ocean-racing yachts.

Perhaps the most famous of the fishing schooners, the Nova Scotian *Bluenose,* was so admired that her image graces the Canadian dime. She sailed her last race in 1938, defending and narrowly retaining her title against Gloucester's *Gertrude L. Thebaud.* These two schooners were among the last of their type. By 1938 both had retired from fishing and, with cut-down rig, became humdrum freighters. Both were eventually wrecked, *Bluenose* off Haiti in 1946, *Thebaud* two years later off Venezuela.

Today the Banks belong to giant factory trawlers—300-foot-long leviathans that catch fish with electronically guided efficiency, and process and freeze them right on board. Within the ranks of these supertrawlers a keen-eyed observer may still detect an occasional relic of Portugal's "great white fleet" of dory schooners. A few of these vessels, shorn of masts and fitted with diesel engines, still ply waters too shoal and rocky for the large trawlers. But powered launches, not dories, are let down from their decks. The schooner hulls are all that remain of the great age of dory fishing.

Flying on Clouds of Canvas

"We never saw a vessel so perfect in all her parts as this new celestial packet," raved a column in the *New York Herald* in 1844. The vessel was the *Houqua*—so named for a rich Canton merchant who had befriended Yankee traders—and she was the realized dream of Nathaniel Palmer, former blockade-runner, sealer, explorer, packet master, and now a crack skipper on the China run. She was about 600 tons, sharp as a cutter, rakish in rig as a pirate ship, neatly arranged as a lady's boudoir—so the *Herald* said. Palmer, who had designed her, carved the model, and got promises from a builder, believed in her merits and set out to prove them.

But the celestial *Houqua* was launched into celestial company. By the time Palmer sailed her back from her maiden run to Macao, eclipse was imminent. On the way was *Rainbow,* 750 tons, of even finer entry. A sharp front knifed the water, tending to bury the bowsprit in heavy seas, and people said she would plow right under. She clipped days from the record for a round trip to China. Glorious and ephemeral as her name suggests, she lived four years, then vanished. But by then there was *Sea Witch.* And so it went.

Year by year more new clippers took to the seas, each a little bigger, sharper, more heavily sparred than the last. In the middle years of the 19th century, the biggest, fastest, most beautiful sailing ships the world had yet seen were racing halfway round the globe. Racing each other. Steamers, burdened with having to fuel ravenous boilers, still chugged in the wake of the flying windships.

Speed was their hallmark and speed their demon. To the men who had to handle their towering pyramids of canvas, clippers often were beautiful hell ships.

Skysails gleaning the lightest airs, Ariel *and* Taeping *race cargoes of tea to the London market.*

West goes East—to China. *Flags of Denmark, Austria, the United States, Sweden, Great Britain, and Holland flutter over* hongs, *or trading stations, in Canton. In 1784 the* Empress of China *pioneered America's entry into the rich mercantile field long dominated by the British and Dutch East India Companies.*

By edict, the Chinese confined foreigners to the waterfront area, alive with ferryboats, sampans, junks, and barges. Sailing traffic, routed to use favoring winds and currents between major ports, plied well-defined arteries on the international highway (below).

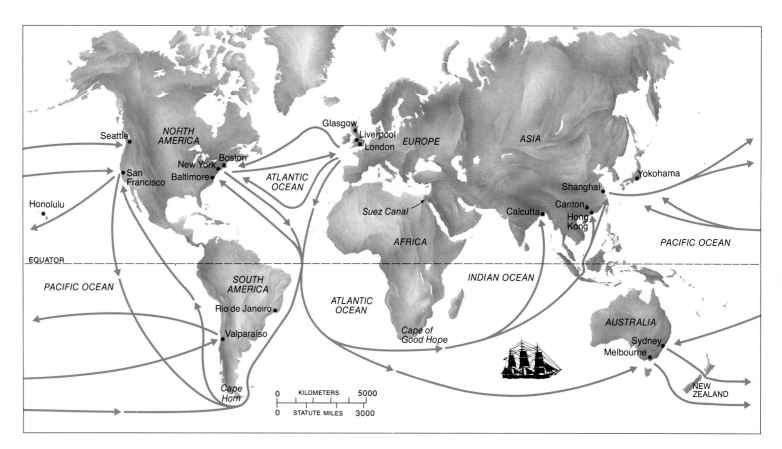

A clipper type of ship was not invented; it evolved. Speed has been a feature of American shipbuilding tradition since colonial times. In the early 19th century, Baltimore shipyards had turned out some notably fast, sharp-hulled sailing vessels, some of which carried ship rig—square rig on all three masts. One of those, the *Ann McKim,* launched in 1833, is sometimes loosely called the first true clipper, though she retained some features of the schooner. The hull form of *Ann McKim* and her predecessors was one strain in the clipper ancestry. The French privateers of the Napoleonic Wars also had sharp clipper lines.

The classical clippers of the middle 19th century all had certain features: a fine entry, with the hull increasing to its greatest width at or behind the midlength point, a pronounced rake to the stem, and an overhanging counter. For such streamlined vessels, they were heavily sparred and carried a big area of canvas in proportion to length. To many enthusiasts of sailing ships, clippers were perfection.

Perfection, however, means different things to different people. Ships have to earn their keep. Desirable qualities of a cargo vessel have always been large capacity, low operating costs, and speed—but the mix varies. For clippers, clearly, speed was paramount. A new pattern of trade was largely responsible for this new emphasis in design.

After 1815 the Western world emerged from decades of sea warfare into a century of almost unbroken maritime peace. Merchant ships in most parts of the world no longer needed to carry heavy guns or crawl along in convoy. The seaborne trades, fed by industrialization in Europe and growth and prosperity in America, increased by leaps and bounds. Trades long pursued as protected monopolies were thrown open to competition.

The most sought-after trade was the carrying of goods, especially tea, from China to England and North America. Though not the largest in total volume of cargo, the China trade yielded a high return per voyage. Merchants paid for the tea with metals, manufactured goods, opium from British colonies in India, and gold and silver coins called "treasure." Competition called for speed.

Not long after the East India Company lost its exclusive franchise for shipping tea to England in 1834, a fashion spread for drinking new tea, rather than aged. The first shipments of the new season's picking to reach New York or London commanded a premium price and the best freight rates. Ships with a reputation for speed—including the *Ann McKim*—began to be diverted to the China run about 1840.

The Opium War, begun by England to gain easier trading access to China, was then in full swing. Opium from poppies grown in India was one of the products involved. When the war ended, the Treaty

Treasures From the China Trade

Captain John Green needed ballast. The *Empress of China* lay in Macao harbor in 1784, ready to take on tea and bales of silk for New York. More weight was needed—and so a cargo of porcelain came aboard.

It was made of clay, yet you could see your hand through it. Marco Polo called it *porcellana* after a lustrous seashell. New Yorkers took one look at Captain Green's "ballast," snapped up every piece, and placed orders for more. They could choose a stock pattern or send their own design to a shop in Canton. George Washington owned china-ware decorated with the Order of the Cincinnati, honoring French and American friendship during the Revolution.

As colonists, Americans had not been allowed to trade directly with China. But as free men, American skippers could turn their bows where they pleased. The *Empress of China* launched a cross-cultural exchange. To the Orient the tall ships brought such American wares as furs and ginseng, prized as a medicinal herb. From islands on the way they gathered sea slugs to delight many a Chinese gourmet. Skippers' pockets bulged with shopping lists: "Two Canton Crape shawls of the enclosed colors," if you please, or "one Tureen 14 by 10 inches, China." It was the men who battled with storms, pirates, and bribe-prone Chinese officials with a hand out for the customary *cumshaw*. But it was the womenfolk who set them sailing for silks, ivory, china, furniture, and a host of fashionable luxuries.

And what luxuries they were! Modern eyes still drift with wonder over a silver punch bowl (A) whose dragon handles seem about to bear it aloft. Fans by the hundreds of thousands fluttered away the summer heat, some at a cost of less than a penny, others fetching $20 or more. Mother-of-pearl ribs grace this hand-painted arc (B) adorned with a fitting subject: ships riding at anchor near Canton, among them the *Empress of China* herself.

The real-life empress may be portrayed at the far right in this group of clay figurines (C) with heads that nod. Each stands about 26 inches tall. A 23-inch white jade pagoda dangles its gilded bells (D), and a view of Macao waits inside a sewing table lid (E).

Ironically, the clipper ships helped end this golden era. Goods from their copious holds eventually flooded the market.

A

B

C

D

E

216 of Nanking also eased trading in China for other nations, including the United States. Enterprising firms in New York began building ships expressly designed to make fast passages to China. Among them were *Houqua, Rainbow,* and *Sea Witch.*

The glorious ten-year career of *Sea Witch* spanned the heyday of American clippers. Launched in 1846, she was wrecked near Havana in 1856. She broke more records than any other ship her size has ever done. In 1847 she returned to New York from Canton *against the monsoon* in 81 days. Outbound via the Cape of Good Hope she had averaged 206 miles a day for more than 40 days. And no sailing ship has ever beaten her 1849 passage from Canton to New York, which astonished the shipping world. Sails taut, her dragon figurehead gleaming, she arrived two weeks before any China ship was expected. Her master was Robert "Bully" Waterman, a hard-bitten former packet captain who had gone to sea at twelve and commanded ships in his twenties.

The notice of the astounding passage by *Sea Witch* filled less than three lines on an inside page of the *Herald* for March 25, under arrivals at the Port of New York: "Ship *Sea Witch,* Waterman, Canton, 74 days 14 hours, passed Anjier Jan 15, Cape of Good Hope Feb 15, with teas, to Howland & Aspinwall."

There was a reason for the meager publicity: California gold had claimed the front pages along with the hopes and dreams of thousands of people.

California gold gave a powerful impetus to the clipper boom in America. News of the discovery filtered through to the eastern seaboard late in 1848. The rush was on. Before 1849 ended, 775 vessels of every description had left eastern ports for Califor-

nia. Not all got there. Some hobbled into Rio de Janeiro or Valparaiso; some piled up on poorly charted coasts; some simply disappeared.

The losses, split sails, and dismastings came as much from carrying too much sail for the sake of speed as from the frequent violence of the weather; but even with care and skill, ships could be lost. Neither the strong, cold winds off the Argentine pampas nor the gales of Cape Horn spared weaklings or the unlucky.

At the peak of the gold rush, 20 or 30 ships might pass the Golden Gate in a day. As each ship rounded to, off North Beach, people poured over her sides into the boats as if the ship were about to explode, hurrying ashore to keep in the forefront of the race for gold. Sometimes the ship's company deserted too, leaving master and mates wondering how they could discharge cargo and sail the ship back to New York, on to China, or wherever she was bound.

The population of San Francisco grew from about 1,000 to 20,000 within the year. They all had to be fed, clothed, and equipped. With an egg or a four-month-old newspaper selling for a dollar, a pack of cards for five, a barrel of flour for fifty, it paid as well to carry goods as passengers. The rush for shipping space was as hectic as the rush for gold.

Speed was the key to profit. The *Sea Witch* was the first vessel to make the passage around Cape Horn to California in under 100 days. Few passages on that run took less than 120. But shipowners advertised impossible 80-day passages, and gullible souls believed them. The performance of known ships and the potential of new ones was avidly discussed in the press and along the waterfront. For shipowners,

Goliath of the clipper ships, McKay's Great Republic *was built in 1853, in anticipation of round-the-world voyages to Australia. She held 6,000 tons of cargo, twice as much as her sisters. The dream went up in smoke. The* Great Republic *lay in New York, loaded for her first Atlantic crossing, with Lauchlan McKay, Donald's brother, in charge. A fire swept the waterfront buildings and windblown sparks set the sails afire. She burned to the waterline. Though salvaged and rebuilt, she never matched her original magnificence (opposite).*

Vessels lacking refrigeration could keep some meat fresh on long passages by taking along live animals: a cow, sheep, pigs, or chickens. Livestock were penned on a roofed part of a deck until the day appointed for the crew's seaborne feast.

more than bets and vanity were at stake; every day clipped off the run to San Francisco might add thousands of dollars to the profit. In that frenzied time, it was said that a new ship could earn her construction cost in a single voyage.

More and more ships were needed, powerful ships that could make rapid passages and yet face Cape Horn weather with confidence. They could not safely be scamped or cheapened, and cost was no object. Steamers of the time were not racers; most of the brigs and schooners were too small and slow. Clippers were the cry. Nearly all the fastest and most celebrated American clippers were built between 1850 and 1854, and many of them sailed for California: *Surprise, Game Cock, Witchcraft, Challenge, Flying Cloud, Sovereign of the Seas, Great Republic, Rapid,* and *Neptune's Car. Champion of the Seas, James Baines,* and *Lightning* were built in America for British owners, and there were others almost as famous.

No two of the ships were exactly alike, but they all had the clipper's characteristic overhanging stern and raked stem. They were much bigger than clippers of the 1840's, most of them ranging from about 1,100 to 2,500 tons.

They sailed under great clouds of canvas: courses, topsails (sometimes divided into upper and lower), topgallants, royals, skysails—with the corresponding studding sails for fair weather. Skysails were the highest sails normally carried, but occasionally a captain might indulge his vanity by having his sailmaker make a small sail to set on the short top end of the mast above the skysail. This extra sail might be called a moonraker, cloud-scraper, star-scraper, or even an angel's footstool. These fancy kites probably

added to speed only in very light airs, but they were part of the clipper mystique.

In the 1850's one of the important centers of clipper building was Boston, where Nova Scotian designer Donald McKay had established his yard. Henry Wadsworth Longfellow frequently visited the McKay yards, finding inspiration for his poem, "The Building of the Ship":

> *Built for freight, and yet for speed,*
> *A beautiful and gallant craft;*
> *Broad in the beam, that the stress of the blast,*
> *Pressing down upon sail and mast,*
> *Might not the sharp bows overwhelm.*

McKay's beautiful and gallant craft set records on sailing routes around the globe. The *Flying Cloud* made two record passages between New York and San Francisco in just under 90 days. *Sovereign of the Seas* in 1853 sailed from Honolulu to New York in

One-way to El Dorado! Aged vessels left to rot crowd a boneyard by the Golden Gate. Many of the ships—crammed with picks, pans, bedrolls, tents, and hordes of fevered forty-niners—had survived the 15,000-mile marathon voyage

from the east via Cape Horn to San Francisco. On arrival, some crews jumped ship and sprinted for the goldfields. The hulls of derelict ships furnished some of the wood to raise a boomtown by the bay. Beached hulks saw use as warehouses, saloons, banks, churches. The Niantic became the ground floor of the Niantic

Hotel; and the brig Euphemia, the new city's first jailhouse. Shipbuilding thrived, as new, faster vessels replaced the old. A ship's card of 1864 (below), an advertising handout used to attract passengers and cargo, still thumps a gold-rush drum.

A rapid passage was not necessarily evidence of improved design, even by the narrow criterion of speed alone. Other things being equal, greater length adds to speed. But several more factors contributed: the trim of the ship, the nature of her cargo, the condition of her bottom. There was also the time of year, the luck of the weather, and—even more important—the route. The right choice of route for the time of year might make the difference between a spanking passage with fair winds, and weeks wasted beating against head winds or slatting about in flat calms.

There was no avoiding calms altogether, particularly in the doldrums near the Equator. The wise navigator planned his passage in order to cross the belt at its narrowest and seek the most favorable winds and currents, even if the route was more circuitous. The data that helped him do this was collected and distributed by a U. S. Navy officer, Lt. Matthew Fontaine Maury. Grateful captains nicknamed him the Pathfinder of the Seas.

Maury was appointed in 1842 to the Depot of Charts and Instruments in Washington, D. C. There he began to analyze, condense, and distribute the experience recorded in the thousands of ships' logs collected in the depot. By 1854 Maury had analyzed more than a million observations on the direction and force of sea winds and currents, nearly 400,000 of them on the Gulf Stream. This mass of information was published in 1855 in Maury's *The Physical Geography of the Sea.*

It was this systematic knowledge of the oceans, as much as the genius of designers, that enabled clipper captains to make the (Continued on page 226)

A NEW AND MAGNIFICENT CLIPPER FOR SAN FRANCISCO.
MERCHANTS' EXPRESS LINE OF CLIPPER SHIPS!
Loading none but First-Class Vessels and Regularly Dispatching the greatest number.
THE SPLENDID NEW OUT-AND-OUT CLIPPER SHIP

CALIFORNIA

HENRY BARBER, Commander, AT PIER 13 EAST RIVER.

This elegant Clipper Ship was built expressly for this trade by Samuel Hall, Esq., of East Boston, the builder of the celebrated Clippers "SURPRISE," "GAMECOCK," "JOHN GILPIN," and others. **She will fully equal them in speed!** Unusually prompt dispatch and a very quick trip may be relied upon. Engagements should be completed at once.

Agents in San Francisco,
Messrs. DE WITT KITTLE & CO.

RANDOLPH M. COOLEY, 88 Wall Street, Tontine Building.

NESBIT & CO., PRINTERS.

82 days. The *James Baines,* one of the few clippers designed primarily to carry passengers, in 1854 set a record from Boston to Liverpool: 12 days and 6 hours, and on to Melbourne in 63 days, a passage only once equaled, by the British clipper *Thermopylae.* McKay's *Lightning* returned from Melbourne to Liverpool in 63 days, also a record.

McKay was the most famous clipper designer, but not necessarily the best. William Webb, the designer of *Challenge,* turned out more clippers. John Griffiths, who designed *Rainbow,* was perhaps more inventive than McKay. Samuel Pook, working with Samuel Hall in Boston, created some of the fastest hull models. McKay kept abreast of developments, picked up ideas and methods wherever he could, and improved on them. He remarked late in life that he had never designed a ship that came up to his ideal. But in performance his ships spoke for themselves.

Cutty Sark, "A Ship Both Stout And Strong"

From the day she slid off the ways, she rode the seas under a cloud, doomed by the times. It was 1869, the year the ribbon was cut on the Suez Canal, threatening the clippers with obsolescence. Useless to ships that needed wind and sea room, the shortcut virtually handed the China trade over to steamships. With the canal, a steamer could run from London to China in only six or seven weeks; and a lighter fuel load left more cargo room.

For some, the great tea races had already lost much of their appeal. After 1866, when *Ariel* and *Taeping* had raced home to the Thames in a dead heat and split the prize money, the premium was discontinued.

But the competitive drive of John Willis and one or two other British shipowners was undiminished. In ordering his new clipper, Willis seemed less interested in the business of transporting tea than in owning a ship fast enough to beat the *Thermopylae*, the new champion of the clippers. Willis named his ship *Cutty Sark,* or short shirt, for the skimpy garb worn by the amorous young witch Nannie, who chased the hero of Robert Burns's poem, "Tam O'Shanter."

> *Her cutty sark, o' Paisley harn*
> *That while a lassie she had worn,*
> *In longitude tho' sorely scanty*
> *It was her best, and she was vauntie.*

It was a busty wooden Nannie who rode as figurehead under *Cutty Sark*'s bowsprit.

Willis's new ship earned a solid but not sensational record in the tea trade. Only once, in 1872, did *Cutty Sark* and *Thermopylae* leave Shanghai together to race to the Thames. The *Cutty Sark* lost her rudder in a gale in the Indian Ocean. She was 400 miles ahead of the *Thermopylae* at the time, but with an improvised rudder she limped home

to the Channel a week astern. It was considered a moral victory and made her a national heroine if not a winner—small consolation for her owner.

Capable seamen, not racers, commanded *Cutty Sark* through the 1870's. She needed a genius to get the best out of her. She found him in Richard Woodget.

By 1883 the clipper had left the China trade and—14 years old, with her rig cut down—had settled into the Australian wool trade. The wool clip in those days was shipped and sold at auction in London from January to March. Wool from remote hill stations took a long time to reach Sydney. A fast ship that would wait in Sydney to load the late clip and rush it to England in time for the auctions could earn a high freight rate. Clippers, using the westerlies of the southern oceans, could sail out via the Cape of Good Hope in 70 days or so, and home in 80 via Cape Horn. This became *Cutty Sark*'s routine. Under Woodget, she seemed to revel in it. Her rounded counter proved ideal for running before the mountainous seas of the roaring forties, each sea lifting her stern and passing harmlessly under her.

Cutty Sark won the wool race year after year. She made 12 round trips between 1883 and 1895. She broke record after record. In 1885, in a straight race, she beat her old nemesis *Thermopylae* at last.

In 1889, as *Cutty Sark* headed for Sydney in light winds, she was overtaken by the new mail steamer *Britannia,* then said to be one of the world's fastest ships. Woodget and his crew watched her smokestack fade in the distance. When the wind freshened, *Cutty Sark* was ready. During the night she gained on the *Britannia,* finally passed her, and beat her to the dock. The Australians, always interested in faster mail service,

China's green gold, tea, is packed for export. Strong wooden chests, lined with lead foil and then with paper, shield the cargo from moisture and strong odors. Buyers often watched workers pour a chosen batch from the baskets into boxes, so inferior leaves would not be substituted.

Aging the crop up to two years had been standard. A new fad favored fresh tea. The first of four pickings from the shrubs, show-chun—early spring— was most valued. The first load to reach New York or London commanded a premium price. Chinese stevedores stowed the chests tier on tier, carefully leveling the ballast so a given

number of tiers exactly fit the space up to deck level. Half chests and smaller catty boxes filled odd spaces so tightly the cargo could not shift. A ship out of trim lost speed. And speed meant cash and glory as clipper captains cracked on sail for frenzied passages to market.

7

6

5

4

3

1

2

18

17

16

11

15

10

9

14

8

13

12

23

26

22

25

21

20

24

19

29

28

27

32

31

30

36

35

34

33

37

38

39

Jibboom

Bowsprit

Dolphin Striker

Cutwater

Counter

Rudder

Sternpost

Keel

Ship Rigs:
A Medley of Masts
And Sails

In the 1840's clippers took wing on soaring masts, all square-rigged, an arrangement called ship rig (left). A visual delight, they were the epitome of speed and grace under sail. Each rope, or line, served a purpose: Halyards were for hoisting and lowering sail; braces controlled the angle of the yard; sheets held the foot of the sail taut. Sailors adjusted sail to make the best use of the wind to drive the ship on its course. A man experienced on one ship-rigged vessel soon "knew the ropes" on another. Square-riggers tried to avoid sailing dead before the wind because the after sails would blanket those on the foremast, causing them to flap and chafe. Greatest speed usually was attained with a quarterly wind.

Of the vessels at right, the sloop (a racing type) and schooner have fore-and-aft rig; the others combine square rig and fore-and-aft.

1. Spanker
2. Crossjack
3. Mizzen Topsail
4. Mizzen Topgallant
5. Mizzen Royal
6. Mizzen Skysail
7. Mizzen Moonsail
8. Mizzen Staysail
9. Mizzen Topmast Staysail
10. Mizzen Topgallant Staysail
11. Mizzen Royal Staysail
12. Main Spencer
13. Mainsail
14. Main Topsail
15. Main Topgallant
16. Main Royal
17. Main Skysail
18. Main Moonsail
19. Main Staysail
20. Main Topmast Staysail
21. Main Topgallant Staysail
22. Main Royal Staysail
23. Main Sky Staysail
24. Main Topmast Studding Sail
25. Main Topgallant Studding Sail
26. Main Royal Studding Sail
27. Foresail
28. Fore Topsail
29. Fore Topgallant
30. Fore Royal
31. Fore Skysail
32. Fore Moonsail
33. Lower Studding Sail
34. Fore Topmast Studding Sail
35. Fore Topgallant Studding Sail
36. Fore Royal Studding Sail
37. Fore Topmast Staysail
38. Jib
39. Flying Jib

Sloop

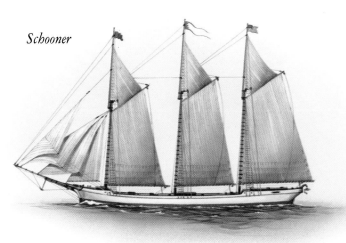

Schooner

Topsail Schooner

Hermaphrodite Brig

Brig

Bark

Stripped to a third of her sails, the Pamir (opposite) beats against a gale. Fully clothed, the four-masted bark sported 34 sails, more than an acre of canvas. Although she rode out this squall, a mid-Atlantic storm claimed Pamir in 1957, with the loss of 80 lives. Choice of sails was critical, but no two ships handled alike. A captain's judgment depended on the wind, sea conditions, the strength of the vessel, cargo, experience of the crew, and his own character. Generally, winds of around 25 knots required furling the royals, the upper staysails, and gaff topsail (first diagram, below). As the weather grew heavier, the ship would shed layer after layer, down to the minimum needed (bottom diagram) to maintain stability and steerageway.

230 long, simmering mutiny. The *Challenge's* mainmast towered 200 feet above the waterline, and her lower sails, including studding sails, stretched 160 feet from leech to leech. Such a ship, with such a master, should have broken every record: Indeed, the owners had promised Waterman a $10,000 bonus for a 90-day passage.

Waterman was a superb seaman who could "smell a wind." He had broken earlier records on the China run in the *Natchez,* a ship that was not even a clipper but an old New Orleans packet. In his years on Howland & Aspinwall's *Sea Witch,* he had cemented his reputation as a driver of clipper ships and men.

In the *Challenge,* Waterman sailed with a crew of 56, half of whom had never been to sea before. Some knew no English; many had never stood a trick at the wheel. Earlier sailings had stripped the port of New York of seamen, and Waterman's sorry crew was the best the crimps could do. Many had no clothes but those on their backs. At least one man had no shoes. Wooden ships were unheated, and they were headed for the antarctic winter. Waterman remarked, "I'll make sailors of 'em, or else mincemeat."

The mates seemed competent, but the first mate, James "Black" Douglass, was a bully; the second, Alexander Coghill, a shifty nondescript. The two quarreled from the first day out. Four weeks out, a group of men leaped on Douglass with drawn knives. Waterman came to the rescue. He dispersed the attackers with an iron belaying pin. Those who could be identified were flogged, though the suspected ringleader was hidden by his shipmates before he finally had to come out for punishment. After this incident the officers went armed.

No more overt mutiny occurred. Instead, most of the crew tried to keep to their bunks, pleading sickness. Some were genuinely sick, some more or less incapacitated by beatings they had received. Others, including Coghill at times, malingered. On some days, only 3 or 4 out of 27 men turned out for their watch. Waterman and Douglass had to work the ship between them, and did not condone shirking. Nine men died during that appalling passage, four of illness or exposure, two as the result of ill-treatment. Three were killed by falls from the rigging, having been kicked by one or another of the mates (so the others alleged) while working aloft.

The passage took only 108 days. On arrival in San Francisco the crew fled ashore, except for the sick and the eight mutineers handed over to the shoreside authorities to await trial. Exaggerated stories of the horrors of the passage circulated in the waterfront bars and got into the local newspapers. Waterman and Douglass managed to escape lynching by a mob of angry seamen.

Both eventually stood trial, Waterman at his own request. Douglass was convicted on a charge of murder, Waterman on one of assault. Neither was sentenced; the threat of mutiny was held to justify almost any severity, and Waterman's passengers, who must have been frightened for their own lives while on passage, testified in his behalf. "Black" Douglass never shipped out again as mate; he was too well known. Waterman bought a cattle ranch in California, sent for his wife to come out and join him, and retired from the sea.

As for the *Challenge,* under a new captain and crew she made some fast runs (Continued on page 239)

"Most Mad Seas" And "Intollerable Winds" Of Cape Horn

Decks awash and a wall of water towering astern, crewmen on the Grace Harwar *(above) struggle to square a yard while doubling Cape Horn in 1929. In heavy seas, such work was difficult and dangerous; with the vessel rolling her rails under, seamen working the side of the ship risked being swept overboard.*

From the heady gold-rush days of 1849 until the opening of the Panama Canal in 1914, hundreds of clippers and other sturdy sailing ships hazarded the treacherous route around Cape Horn.

Perhaps no other passage has inspired such dread among sailors, or sowed so much alarm and despondency among marine insurance underwriters, as the trip around the southern tip of South America and the island headland dubbed "Cape Stiff."

In the last half of the 19th century, the Lutine Bell at Lloyds of London tolled regularly for ships reported overdue or missing while "doubling the Horn."

The vital sea-lane passed through a region of seemingly nonstop westerly squalls known as "Cape Horn snorters" and of 60-foot seas called "graybeards." Doubling the Horn meant antarctic freeze and stinging hail, dense fog and the gleaming threat of icebergs. It meant long hours aloft on a pitching yard, back to the wind, struggling with ice-stiffened canvas.

It was a region where an oilskin-clad man could be catapulted to sudden death in frigid waters too violent to launch a lifeboat. It was a voyage to the bottom of the world, the ultimate test of man and ship, where the baleful albatross enshrined the souls of dead seamen and Saint Elmo's fire danced, fizzed, and crackled about yard and masthead.

"Right down to the date of the Great War," wrote Basil Lubbock in *The Last of the Windjammers,* "this grim sentinel of the Southern Ocean watched the everlasting fight between sail and sea and wind; and it was by no means uncommon in the last days of sail for thirty or forty ships to be in sight at once off the pitch of the Horn."

Sir Francis Drake may have been the first mariner to sight the cape. After negotiating the Strait of Magellan in 1578, he was blown far south and complained of "most mad seas" and "most intollerable winds." But the first men to double the Horn were Dutch navigators Willem C. Schouten and Jakob Le Maire in 1616.

Until the middle of the 19th century, the few ships to brave its stormy waters were mostly South Sea whalers, copper ore traders, and some hide carriers.

But with the onset of the gold rush in 1849, the great square-riggers began to choke the storm-tossed seas of the cape, holds bulging with men and equipment bound for California.

When the gold rush subsided, the ships continued to make the arduous voyage round the Horn, whether to pick up grain from the Pacific Northwest, nitrates from Chile, frozen meat from New Zealand, or wool and grain from Australia.

Outward bound from the Atlantic seaboard or Europe, the square-riggers hauled coal, textiles, iron rails, machinery, guns, liquor, and manufactured goods.

"From the sixties to the nineties that gateway to the Pacific . . . was thronged with a great fleet of clippers and carriers," Lubbock wrote.

But what made the 1,400-foot cliff on Horn Island, the meeting place of two great oceans, so notorious? Why did seamen shun ships bound round the Horn? The answer lies in the area's unique combination of wind, wave, and shelving ocean floor.

Between 40° and 60°S latitude, the prevailing winds blow strongly from the west, often at gale force.

From the Pacific, this eastward flow of air runs squarely into the unyielding mass of the Andes, a sheer 1,200-mile-long mountain wall. Diverted south, the winds finally

OVERLEAF: *Clinging like a limpet to the handrail, a sailor edges aft as the bark* Parma *weathers a squall on a passage between New Zealand and Cape Horn in 1932. At times like this, it was often more dangerous for the crew to be working on deck than aloft.*

Seething brine churns around the men of the Parma *(left) as they wrestle with a portside winch. A safety net sags above, limited protection at best against cresting "graybeards" of the Horn. With stormy weather finally behind them, five members of the* Grace Harwar's *crew (above) strain at capstan bars to hoist the main topsail.*

Seamen on the Parma *(left)* hustle up the vessel's mizzen shrouds to furl the crossjack. Sailors normally climb shrouds to windward, where the force of a gale will press a man into the rigging rather than pry him away from it. Heels to the footrope and wind at their backs, Parma's crew balance over the yard *(right)* to make fast the mainsail in heavy weather.

funnel through Drake Passage, a 500-mile breach between Cape Horn and the South Shetland Islands of Antarctica.

The same westerly winds also produce a strong ocean current flowing eastward at the rate of 10 to 20 miles a day or more. This powerful flow, like the wind, boils between Cape Horn and Antarctica.

The problems for sailors presented by the water turbulence and strong wind are compounded by the shelving ocean floor between Cape Horn and the South Shetlands, which throws up the huge graybeards.

Most fearsome for the sailing ships was the westward passage, square in the face of the current and the prevailing winds. But even driving east, ships bucked mountainous seas and ran before murderous gales.

The ships' engines were canvas, which was graded according to strength. Grade 0, the heaviest material, weighed about two pounds per square yard—roughly twice the weight of the lightest, grade 4.

Basil Lubbock, who went to Canada during the Klondike gold rush of 1896 and returned as an ordinary seaman on a vessel that rounded the Horn, described the preparations for the encounter:

"The stoutest canvas was bent, all standing and running rigging overhauled, and replaced with new rope or wire wherever it was at all worn, spars and boats were double lashed, hatches rebattened down, skylights weather boarded, new purchases rove for rudder tackles, [and] life-lines stretched along the maindeck. . . ."

Despite these precautions, tragedy often stalked the square-riggers as they drove along the roaring forties of latitude and finally made the passage around the cape, from 50°S latitude in one great ocean to 50°S in the other.

Captain Alan Villiers, a veteran of many voyages around the Horn, wrote in *Men, Ships, and the Sea* about the death of a friend during a 15,000-mile trip aboard the Finnish ship *Grace Harwar.*

It was May 25, 1929, and the *Grace Harwar* was 38 days out of Australia, laden with grain and bound for England.

Ronald Walker, who had shipped out of Wallaroo, Australia, with Villiers, was hit by an upper topgallant yard whose halyards had snapped and sent it crashing.

"We rushed up the shrouds and found him between the yards, and we thought he was unconscious," Villiers wrote.

"There was no sign of a wound, save for some blood oozing from his mouth. I tried to bring him to with water. But he did not come to. We rigged a gantline, got it under his armpits, and lowered him gently.

"Captain Svensson took one look. 'He is dead,' he said.

"Nowhere is death more painful than at sea. Ashore there are diversions; one forgets. But at sea on a windjammer there is only the little band of men. And when one goes, no one comes to take his place.

"We buried him from the poop next day. The Finnish ensign flew at half-mast, and the crew were white-faced. At sea you know the 'innards' of a man—no subterfuge, no pretense. You see all. We knew poor Walker and we liked him well.

"The captain read prayers; we sang hymns. Someone made a short talk. The ship was hove to, the moan of wind in her rigging now stilled by her deadened way, the surly wash of the sea about her decks softened. We carried him to the rail, tilted the hatch, and there was a dull plop. Then we put the ship before the wind once more and we drove her."

More masts, more sail, more space for goods, and almost as fast as clippers, boasted the steel-hulled windjammers, the ultimate sailing ships. The square-rigger Preussen (left), built in Hamburg, measured 440 feet in length, 54 abeam. She carried up to 60,000 square feet of canvas on five masts and could handle nearly 8,000 tons of cargo. She was launched in 1902, the same year a Massachusetts yard built the Thomas W. Lawson (below), a schooner with a mast for every day of the week. The only seven-master ever built also had eight engines to aid with steering, pumping, handling cargo—so she needed only 16 men. But her size limited the ports she could fit into. Caught in a storm, she broke up on the Scilly Isles in 1907.

in the China trade but never lived down her reputation as a troubled ship. She suffered two more mutinies. She had her rig cut down three times. Her life was a long one, as clippers went. She foundered off the coast of France in 1876.

Other fast clippers had personnel problems, even the proud and lovely *Flying Cloud.* She was commanded by Josiah Creesy, a noted driver like Waterman, though somewhat less likely to strike out with a belaying pin.

On her maiden voyage a few days out from New York, she ran into a gale and lost her main and mizzen topgallant masts. The men worked frantically to send up new spars, only to find later that the main topmast itself was sprung. Despite the damage, Creesy cracked on sail, and the *Flying Cloud* flew on toward Cape Horn. Her crew, like the *Challenge*'s, included many landsmen who seemed less mutinous than scared. As the sprung mast strained and creaked above him, one greenhorn took an auger and drilled two holes in the ship's side, presumably hoping that the leak would force her into Rio for survey and refit. But no—the leak was found and plugged, the culprit identified and manacled. He had been foolish enough to drill holes under his own bunk. The *Flying Cloud* pressed on—sprung mast, saboteur, and all—round Cape Horn and on to San Francisco. She made it in 89 days and 21½ hours, the first of her many speed records.

The British began building clippers later than the Americans, but sailed them longer. New rules of measurement made it possible to build ships longer and narrower, with extravagantly raked bows, without greatly increasing their register tonnage, on

which British harbor taxes were based. After 1848, yards in Aberdeen built ships that could properly be called clippers, meant for the China trade: *Reindeer, Chrysolite, Stornoway,* and others.

In 1850, with the arrival of the clipper *Oriental* at the London docks, Americans first entered the English tea trade. For the next ten years they sent an average of a dozen tea ships a year. Their participation lasted until the Civil War effectively ended the American clipper era. The arrival of *Oriental* had aroused competitive alarm in England, where British designers studied her lines. By quickening the pace of trade, the *Oriental* and her successors stimulated a burst of shipbuilding in Britain. Ships built at Glasgow in the 1850's were as graceful and fine-lined as the sleekest American clippers, but much smaller. They rarely exceeded 1,000 tons.

In light airs, the best of the British clippers were probably the fastest sailing ships ever built. The *Thermopylae* was said to fan along at seven knots in a breeze too slight to extinguish a lighted candle on her poop. In strong winds the Americans were faster. No British-built ship ever equaled the great bursts of speed achieved by the *Flying Cloud* or the *Sovereign of the Seas.* The fastest day's run ever reported for a sailing ship was 465 nautical miles, by the *Champion of the Seas*—a British ship built in America—running before the westerlies on passage from Liverpool to Melbourne in 1854. The *Cutty Sark's* best day's run was 370 miles.

But a fast passage—not bursts of speed—mattered more. Over a long passage, fair winds, gales, and calms tended to cancel each other out. The 1854 passage to Melbourne by *Champion of the Seas,* apart from the one miraculous day's run, was unremarkable. It is difficult to compare the passages of American and British ships, because they rarely competed over the same course at the same time.

All the American clippers were made of wood. British builders, short of timber, tried iron on their new clippers. The experiment was at least partially successful; one of the ships was notably fast. Iron hulls proved stronger and more durable than wooden, but they tended to "sweat the cargo" and cost more to keep clean. Hulls fouled underwater, and foul ships were slow. Unlike wood, iron hulls could not be protected with copper sheathing. Dry-docking for cleaning cost both time and money.

The solution for a decade or so was a composite ship: an iron frame covered with wooden planking. The composite hull could be coppered. The iron frame was strong, flexible, and less bulky than wood, leaving more inside *(Continued on page 245)*

Figurehead: A Ship's Spirit At the Bow

It was more than just a wood carving, more even than a work of art. A ship's figurehead was almost an incarnation of the vessel's personality; it was guiding spirit, symbol, the very soul of the ship it led over the hazardous sea. Carvers of these icons were honored artisans, and every major port needed their patient hands.

Their art traces into deep antiquity. On Egyptian pottery and rock carvings 5,000 years old, crudely drawn barges float timelessly. Palm fronds decorated the bows of many barges; horned animal heads adorned others. Ornaments, perhaps—but it is more likely that they were talismans to appease the powerful sea gods.

The Vikings mounted fierce dragons on the stemposts of their ships to help tame storm and seaborne foe. But near landfall the Vikings would take them down lest they terrify the local spirits ashore.

The Apostle Paul put to sea from Malta on a ship with a figurehead of Castor and Pollux, the "twins" revered by Roman mariners. Eighteen centuries later, a more earthly pair of twins took shape under a ship carver's chisel (right). And down through those centuries the waves have lapped at a proud procession of figureheads—the gilded lions snarling on the blunt bows of Elizabethan naval vessels, or the folk heroes on ships of a young America.

Unlike the Vikings, crews of the 1800's displayed their figureheads in port. But at sea they sometimes stowed the figure—or its most delicate parts—in crates to protect it from the ravages of ocean voyaging, ravages that kept carvers busy repairing and repainting figureheads that dared the sea.

And often, when the sea broke a ship into pieces, its buoyant figurehead might be the only survivor.

"The girl had a kind face," commented Captain William Smith of the figurehead adorning the square-rigger Falls of Clyde; "wooden-faced," was his opinion of the image that replaced it after a collision in 1913. A kind face again graces the restored ship's bow (right). Gilding lends subtle sparkle to a figure all in white.

Twins entwine in a splash of color befitting their tender years (below). Time has long since erased all memory of their names, their ship, and even the carver who gave them immortality.

A

B

Masterworks of the wood-carver's art nestled
under many a proud ship's bow. In the classical
robes of ancient Greece, the namesake of the
Scottish bark Mary Hay (B) leaned into the waves.
American carvers also put classical style in
such figures as the draperied maiden adorning
the clipper Glory of the Seas (E). But patriotism
burgeoned as the new nation's maritime fortunes
rose; Indians, folk heroes, and the national
emblem took their place on her ships of war and
commerce. Pocahontas (A) carried a cameo of
Capt. John Smith to sea in the early 1800's; no one
now knows the ship the Indian princess graced.
But there is no doubt that the fur-capped figure
of a frontiersman (D) was carved for the 1853
clipper David Crockett—nor that the great gilded
American eagle (C) took up its perch on the
new bow of the U. S. Frigate Lancaster in 1881.

C

D

E

Whispers in the Mist: What Happened On the *Mary Celeste*?

Mariners still yarn of her in wardroom and fo'c'sle. She was a smart little half brig named the *Mary Celeste,* and a right good master and crew took her out of New York on that November morn in 1872. Seventeen hundred barrels of alcohol filled her hold. Capt. Benjamin Briggs had his wife, Sarah, and their two-year-old daughter aboard with him. The *Mary Celeste* was bound for Genoa, a port she never raised.

Four weeks later, about 2,700 miles down her easterly course line, she yaws aimlessly *westward* as the brigantine *Dei Gratia* hauls up and heaves to. Capt. David Morehouse—or maybe it was the mate Oliver Deveau—cups hand to cheek and "speaks" the lolling vessel. Someone puts a spyglass on her. A boat is lowered away. The rowers ship their oars, bump alongside, and step into history as they board a ship sailing the ocean without a crew. A derelict. And to this day, a mystery.

No sign of violence. Sail has been shortened. There is a little storm damage, some three feet of water in the hold. Several hatch covers are off—one of them lying on deck. Plenty of fresh water in the casks and provisions in the storeroom. The log book on the mate's table shows its last entry at noon, November 24. There is also a temporary log slate entry at 8 a.m. on the 25th; the *Mary Celeste* then lay a few miles off the island of Santa Maria in the Azores. With not a soul aboard, she has sailed ten days and nearly 600 miles for her rendezvous with the *Dei Gratia* and immortality.

A few dark spots spatter the deck; a souvenir sword is found under the skipper's berth. The spots are spilled wine, says a chemist, and the stains on the sword blade are only rust. But the queen's proctor who

is in charge of the inquiry at Gibraltar insists that both are blood.

Folks here and there begin to whisper about pirates. Or a crazed crewman. Even about a conspiracy by Captain Morehouse to claim salvage rights to the ship.

Time passes. Legends grow until they encrust the facts like barnacles on a piling:

Man-eating sharks got the *Mary Celeste's* skipper and mate while they were swimming in the sea; a huge wave then bore away the others as they watched.

No, a monster octopus seized the ship and devoured all hands, one by one.

No, it was a floating island that rose under her keel and lifted her high and dry;

when all aboard stepped ashore to investigate, the accursed island sank.

Was it nothing more than alcohol fumes that sent ten souls scuttling for the lifeboat in fear of a great explosion—and then a sudden squall that snapped their towline and set them drifting into oblivion? So speak the facts, brought out in a formal inquiry. But who will listen? For the sea is no docile milkmaid but a stormy mistress to all who court her. Aye, mystery suits her best.

Do the facts tell only of a stubborn Dutch captain who cursed Cape Horn and the God who made it stormy? Let such a man vanish while rounding the Horn and in mystery his doomed ship sails on forever as the *Flying Dutchman,* evil omen to all who sight her ghosting through a fog bank or scudding hull down in a distant squall line. To keening widows the poet offers scant solace, for "They who see the Flying Dutchman never, *never* reach the shore."

Suppose the facts do show heavy traffic in the seas and skies between Bermuda and the Antilles, and an accident rate no worse than we would expect of such traffic in those latitudes? Let five U. S. Navy planes vanish together over those waters; let ships and yachts and aircraft disappear without anyone receiving an SOS, without even the flotsam that almost always marks a wreck—and sailors begin to mutter of a vaguely defined Bermuda Triangle. In this place there be flying saucers . . . a civilization on the seafloor . . . a door to another dimension.

Ancient mariners feared monsters beyond Gibraltar, the Pillars of Hercules. Not too many centuries ago seamen feared they might blunder off the edge of the world.

Old terrors pale, yet the new ones chill our marrow. For do we not sail the same dark seas as they?

space for cargo. Nearly all of the best clippers built in the 1860's—*Ariel, Taeping, Thermopylae, Cutty Sark*—were composite built. All of them were well under 1,000 tons. They were fast, sensitive, and graceful, yet tough and durable.

By the 1860's the annual tea race from China to the Thames had taken on all the aspects of a major spectator sport, including a handsome premium paid to the winner. The 1866 race was the closest and most exciting. A dozen clippers took part. *Ariel* and *Taeping* left Foochow on the same day. They frequently passed within sight of one another over the 15,000-mile course. The two ships came up the Thames on the same tide, watched by throngs of fiercely partisan enthusiasts. *Ariel* and *Taeping* shared the premium. Clipper racing was better than horse racing from the owners' point of view because, win or lose, the tea paid for it.

Later the focus of seafaring sport shifted to Australia, where the annual wool race got the attention once reserved for the Chinese tea chase. In the 1880's and 1890's *Cutty Sark* won it year after year. Her most famous captain, Richard Woodget, became a legend in his day. He shared with Waterman and Creesy the seaman's genius for finding a wind. Like Waterman, Woodget was a driver, but he did not much resemble Waterman in other ways. He was gentle and quiet-spoken, with a twinkle of humor that shows in photographs. He would amuse himself by roller-skating in the 'tween decks when the ship was empty. When that diversion palled, he pedaled around the deck on a bicycle.

Woodget was known for his way of handling apprentices. One boy, a story goes, kept reporting sick

Amid a raging brawl of wave against rock, North Pier Lighthouse stands firm off England's shore. The surf here can break as high as 100 feet. Lighthouses, lonely sentinels, have helped keep mariners on course—and off the rocks— since ancient times. Generations of keepers tended oil lamps or kept candles burning in days before radar and automated lights. When their efforts were not enough, bold rescue teams launched oar-driven surfboats or shot a line to survivors. Heroic exploits won fame for many—among them this crew from Hull, Massachusetts.

246

with an illness that seemed to be imaginary. Summoned to the saloon, he found Woodget and the ship's Chinese cook (known as "the doctor") stretching out a length of cod line. On one end of the line was a small lead sinker and on the other a stiff spiral brush used for scouring bottles. Woodget said, "The doctor and I have been discussing your symptoms and we think we know what to do. You swallow this sinker. When it comes out the after end we pull the whole rig through—give your innards a thorough clean-out—do you a world of good." The boy fled, instantly cured.

The boy's name was C. E. Irving. When his time on *Cutty Sark* expired he joined the P. & O. (Peninsular and Oriental Steam Navigation Company) and eventually rose to command several of their larger ships. He was climbing the career ladder that would lead other clipper-hardened seamen into the new era of seafaring, a route followed by many of Woodget's apprentices. The saying was: "He left the sea and went into steam."

The pall of smoke from the steamships that had driven the clippers from China now drifted over Sydney. A network of new coaling stations enabled steamers to reach almost anywhere in the world. The *Cutty Sark*'s career in the wool trade amounted to little more than a defiant gesture. Australians applauded; but they sent their wool by steamer.

A calm anchorage in Puget Sound mirrors the masts of square-riggers and schooners against a misted backdrop of towering evergreens. To the cove at Port Blakely, Washington, pictured in 1900 (opposite), came sailing ships old and new, of every nationality, to load cargoes of lumber from forests of the Pacific Northwest.

After the railroads came, more lumber for domestic use was hauled by land than by sea. But sailing ships still made long passages across the Pacific or around Cape Horn to Europe well into the 1920's.

Shipmasters' cabins, austere at sea, became homelike in port when captains' wives traveled with them. Amid Victorian elegance—caged bird, flowers, family mementos—Captain and Mrs. E. Gates-James are pictured aboard the British four-masted bark Lynton at Port Blakely in 1905 (below).

Windships are diehards. Sailing vessels and sailing men fought a tenacious rearguard action against the encroachments of steam for fifty years after the clippers had gone the way of cogs and triremes. Stout, no-nonsense square-riggers were built in the 1860's, 1870's, and 1880's. Those built in New England were called down easters. Owners often advertised these ships as "clippers," but they were closer akin to the later, more refined Atlantic packets. The down easters were somewhat slower than clippers, but more durable and more capacious.

The sailing ships that survived longest in the competition against steam were built in Europe in very small numbers in the 1890's and early 1900's. Steel hulls and wire rigging made these deepwater vessels much stronger than any clipper. The biggest could stow 8,000 tons of bulk cargo such as grain, coal, nitrates, lumber, or canned goods. Such were the mighty *Preussen,* a five-masted ship built in Hamburg in 1902 for the Laeisz Line; and the *Kφbenhavn,* the last five-masted bark built in Scotland, in 1921 for the Danish East Asiatic Company.

These windjammers were obliged to compromise with the mechanical age. Their gear—wire halyards and braces, blocks as big as wrecking balls—was too heavy to be manhandled easily. Sometimes steam donkey engines helped with the heaviest jobs: weighing anchor and discharging cargo. Bracing the yards had always been a sailor's bugbear. It was especially hard and dangerous work to square the yards in heavy weather when the ship was rolling her rails under. Hand-operated brace winches, invented about 1890 by a Scottish shipmaster, J.C.B. Jarvis, enabled two men to do work that might have taken

the whole watch. The British scorned these winches, but the Germans appreciated and used them. A logical next step was to lead the brace to a donkey engine. But even on a ship that had one, the donkey engine was seldom fired up at sea. Using manpower was cheaper than buying wood or coal.

Windjammers were worked with pared-down crews. The *Preussen* had only 47 men. In economy, capacity, reliability, and speed, she and her like were the ultimate expression of deepwater sail.

With more comfort on steamers, fewer and fewer seamen wanted to ship out under sail. Gradually, the windjammers were confined to trades the steamers had left as unprofitable or inconvenient. They hauled grain to Europe from Australia, grain and lumber from the Pacific coast of North America, nitrates from Chile, coke from Hamburg, coal from New South Wales.

In 1910 there were still 300 big sailing ships operating under British registry alone. By 1923 there were only 23 of more than 1,000 tons. Numbers were similarly reduced in other parts of the world.

After World War I big sailing ships were becoming curiosities. Yet they still attracted adventurous young men eager for the experience of sailing on an aged windjammer. Wages mattered little; some youths even paid for the privilege. To cut costs, at least one owner ran the old ships uninsured and without union rules and benefits for the sailors. But without the cheap labor and corner-cutting, owners could not have stayed in business. A few ships struggled on almost until World War II. One by one they wore out or were wrecked and abandoned.

Today, between 30 and 40 sailing ships of small to moderate size—mostly square-rigged ships and barks—are regularly employed as specialized training ships. Some navies train their officers in sail: the Portuguese in the big bark *Sagres II,* the Argentine in the *Libertad,* the Chilean and the Spanish, respectively, in the twin topsail schooners *Esmeralda* and *Juan Sebastián de Elcano.* The British and U. S. navies have long abandoned sail training on this scale, partly on grounds of expense. But the U. S. Coast Guard still operates the trim bark *Eagle.* Most of the school ships train officers for careers in the merchant services.

Besides ships and barks that give vocational sea training, a growing number of small barkentines, brigantines, schooners, and ketches take young people to sea for shorter periods for experience and character development.

At two-year intervals beginning in 1956, fleets of these diverse types have assembled in tall ships regattas, and thousands of people have flocked to admire them. Beauty and romance apart, square-rigged vessels, with their intricate arrangement of sails, offer training in agility, self-reliance, quick thinking, and understanding of the sea that no powered ship can equal.

Sailing ships have not disappeared from the oceans, nor are they likely to. High fuel costs in the past few years have encouraged experiments with sail-assisted powered ships. Though it is too early yet to know the prospects of success, the idea is not likely to be abandoned. The wind is free.

"The Liner She's a Lady"

They were the largest moving objects ever built by human hands. In their golden age, each of the great ocean liners was a city afloat, a posh resort hotel, a society in microcosm, a symbol of an era. Their like had never been seen before— and until great starships take colonists by the thousands into the fathomless seas of space, we shall not see their like again.

A big liner was a self-contained town, population perhaps 3,000 or more. Somewhere in its labyrinth there would probably be a printshop grinding out a newspaper . . . a beauty parlor, or two or three . . . a library, a clinic, a kennel, a post office, a restaurant . . . swimming pools, nightclubs, game courts, boutiques.

On the outside, a liner was a ship; on the inside, she was a grand hotel to rival those ashore. "Why don't you make a ship look like a ship?" queried Arthur Davis when asked to design interiors for the

Aquitania in the early 1900's. He later recounted the answer: "The people who use these ships are not pirates, they do not dance horn-pipes; they are mostly seasick American ladies, and the one thing they want to forget when they are on the vessel is that they are on a ship at all. . . . If we could . . . get people to enjoy the sea, it would be a very good thing; but all we can do, as things are, is to give them gigantic floating hotels."

Each liner carried a scale-model society. It was a society layered into classes: The rich luxuriated in first class, surrounded by the most elegant of staterooms and sculpture; the rest kept to the lower classes of accommodation—sometimes below the water line.

Above all, a liner was a symbol—sleek and luxurious, yet complex and powerful, a marriage of art and technology. Now we jet about, cramped, hurried, often bored. Back then we *traveled*.

Empress of an era, the Mauretania *could knife the waves at better than 25 knots—and did in 1909 for a transatlantic record that stood for 20 years.*

"How this glorious steamer wollops and gallops and flounders along!" exulted a passenger on the Great Western, *shown below leaving Bristol, England, in 1838. "She goes it like mad." Indeed she did, for those days: better than 8 knots average, and New*

York in 15 days. Built to steam the Atlantic, she honored an odd ancestry. Jonathan Hulls of London had patented a tug in 1736; it steamed in a sketch (upper left) *but never in fact. Half a century later, John Fitch's steamer* (center) *dipped its dozen paddles; six stroked in unison as the rest swung forward for the next*

stroke. Jeers turned to cheers in 1807 when Robert Fulton's Clermont (upper right) *chugged from New York to Albany in 32 hours. Its rivals, the sloops, could promise no such speed. Paying passengers soon made "Fulton's Folly" a financial success —the first for ships of steam.*

254

The ocean liners, in large measure, owed their genesis to a single idea: predictability. That is hard to achieve in ships dependent on the wind. Passengers on a long voyage in a sailing ship can never be sure within days, or even weeks, when they are likely to arrive. Before the 1820's they often could not even be sure when they would leave.

Voyagers in those days had to seek passage in freight-carrying ships, often haggling over fares with the ship's master, who took travelers aboard as a sideline. Some masters looked after their passengers and set them a lavish table; some didn't. But freight always came first. A ship sailed when her hold was full, when official formalities and paperwork were complete, and when wind and tide served. Passengers signed on, claimed their cabins—and then might spend tedious, expensive weeks in dockside inns waiting for the ship to sail.

In the mid-18th century, the British Post Office began a regular mail service between Falmouth, England, and New York. The little brigs carried no freight, but they did accept a few passengers. "Coffin brigs," the sailors called these small, rather unstable vessels that took on the temperamental Atlantic on the first Thursday of every month. Those that were not lost at sea might spend nearly three months crossing it. In 1816 the January brig took 81 days, the February brig took 43—and they arrived in New York on the same day. But they offered transatlantic passengers an important advantage: regular departures.

That set a vital precedent for the commercial packet lines. Originally a packet was a mail boat; later the term meant any vessel that sailed a regular run at regular intervals. In 1818 the Black Ball Line gave "packet" a more precise meaning: a monthly service between New York and Liverpool with sailings not merely on a fixed day but at a fixed hour. At the appointed time for the eastbound departure, the mailbag would be brought over from the Tontine Coffee House in Manhattan, where it had hung for a month; as soon as it was on board and stowed, the ship would cast off. Some freight was carried, but passengers and mail were not kept hanging around while the holds filled. That risked some financial losses, but in the long run, punctuality brought prosperity as the Black Ball siphoned business away from its competitors.

As the Black Ball Line grew—from 4 to 13 sailing ships in its first 5 years—it inspired imitation. Edward Knight Collins, an American, founded his famous Dramatic Line in 1836. Soon it was a favorite among travelers for its good food and attentive service. Many of the ships in Collins's splendid fleet bore the names of well-known actors—hence the name Dramatic. Other owners later followed the Collins example of keeping to a single theme in christening their vessels.

Of all the great oceans, the North Atlantic is probably the most punishing, the hardest on ships; nowhere else are busy shipping lanes so beset by gales, fog, and floating ice. Modern-day ships are required to have load lines painted on their sides, showing the depths to which they may safely be loaded in various conditions. The lowest of these lines, the lightest loading, is marked WNA, which stands for Winter North Atlantic.

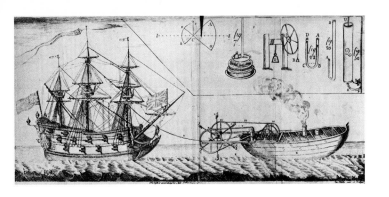

Sails set and paddles wet, the Savannah takes the sea in 1819. She was first to span the Atlantic under both steam and sail. She could carry little fuel and thus used steam only as an aid. Here her paddles slow to a stop as sailors unfurl the last of her canvas. The elbowed stack that guides sparks away from the sails soon will grow cold as the 99-foot vessel's crewmen snuff her fires, fold up her paddles, and stow them on deck until they are needed again. Even the paddle-wheel housings came apart for stowage while the ship was under sail.

The packets undertook to sail through this dangerous waste, on pre-announced dates, whatever the weather, winter or summer, without fail. For more than 60 years they fulfilled their promise—and won the admiration of the entire shipping world.

In those days about 90 seagoing American ships were wrecked each year. But, out of nearly 6,000 transatlantic packet crossings, only 22 ended in disaster. Collisions occurred, but the packets' strong hulls usually shrugged off serious harm. Packets, in short, were not greyhounds of the sea; they were the covered wagons of the Atlantic: reliable, indomitable, tough. The best were like well-run warships, with an esprit that was not won by knocking sailors down with handspikes.

Passengers who paid "thirty guineas, wines included," expected the master to be a gentlemanly host as well as a fine seaman. After a good trip they might present him with a silver tray or an elegant sextant. Grateful survivors of one stormy shipwreck gave their captain a family Bible, suitably inscribed.

Dozens of passenger journals describe a high standard of comfort and cuisine. Most masters provided the food and drink, for a goodly share of the passenger's fee. Every packet had its "farmyard," and greens were sometimes grown on board. But steerage passengers, berthed 'tween decks on narrow shelves, brought their own food and cooked it on grates set up on the upper deck—unless bad weather put the fires out. They got little for their money, so their fares were almost pure profit. But their noise and smoke could offend cabin passengers, and freight 'tween decks was more profitable. Not until the steamers appeared and began to lure away cabin

Bostonians cheer in the chill as trial turns to triumph in 1844. Only four years earlier, Nova Scotian Samuel Cunard (right) had founded the Cunard Line on four fine sister ships—among them the 228-foot side-wheel steamer Britannia.

Like clockwork the Cunarders chuffed in and out of Boston Harbor, swelling civic pride and businessmen's purses alike. The clock scarcely missed a beat when ice locked Britannia in the harbor—and Bostonians chopped a 7-mile channel to get her out. An artist caught this view of a ship and city victorious,

but for a time Boston suppressed the painting as a bad ad for a seaport. Charles Dickens was an even worse ad for the ship; his cabin, he grumped, was an "utterly impracticable . . . and profoundly preposterous box."

In 1843 a revolutionary ship floated from her berth in Bristol, England, and sat for a photograph (opposite). Today the Great Britain *rests again in the selfsame berth, welcoming visitors to a hull filled with history. Once she dwarfed all else afloat and* embodied in her design all that would later be called modern: a metal hull and rigging, a balanced rudder, a bow that cut the water instead of pushing through it, a steam power plant that drove not two paddle wheels but a single screw propeller.

She circled the globe 32 times in three decades as a passenger ship. Stripped of her worn engines, she then hauled cargo under sail. Finally, in 1937, she was beached in a backwater of the Falkland Islands—whence restorers in 1970 towed her back to glory.

passengers and fine freight did the sailing packets start packing immigrants into steerage.

The year 1837 was a bad one. Gale after gale battered shipping. One sailing packet after another came in long overdue. "Multitudes cry out for a steamer," wrote shipping magnate Junius Smith. In April 1838 they got two; both arrived at New York on the same day. One was the tough little *Sirius,* an Irish coastal steamer 19 days out from Cork. The other came thudding up the harbor a few hours behind. She was the *Great Western,* 15 days out from Bristol, a big powerhouse designed by that daring genius of early steam, Isambard Kingdom Brunel.

At a board meeting of the Great Western Railway, convened to discuss the line then building from London to Bristol, Brunel had suggested the idea of building a steamer to continue the line to New York. The directors had taken him up on his visionary idea. So there she was in New York, on St. George's Day 1838, in all her sooty majesty.

"If the public was stimulated by the arrival of the *Sirius,*" said one newspaper, "it became intoxicated with delight upon view of the superb *Great Western.*" A passenger described the scene: "Flags were flying, guns were firing, and cheering rose from the shore, the boats and all around loudly and gloriously as though it would never have done. It was an exciting moment, a moment of triumph."

More steamers soon followed. In 1839 the *British Queen* replaced the little *Sirius,* which duly returned to her coasting duties. A year later came the *President,* at 2,366 tons; some people said that a ship that large was too big to be safe. In 1840 the canny Nova Scotian Samuel Cunard began a regular steamer

S.S. GREAT BRITAIN

Great Britain
Showed What a Liner Should Be

In iron and imagination, the *Great Britain* defined the true luxury liner. The imagination was Isambard Kingdom Brunel's; the bold British engineer conceived a supership and a tublike dry dock in which to build her. The iron was in the shipwrights' hands, and with it they reared a tight and mighty hull. Wrought plates formed the skin; rows overlapped (A) in a technique called clinker-built. Seven bulkheads, two of them running lengthwise beside the engine room (B), buttressed the hull and divided its interior into compartments made watertight by stout doors. The mainmast (C) pierced the decks; other masts were stepped in pivots (D) and could be angled as needed. But sail was secondary, a fuel-saver when the wind was right. Coal and water moved this marvel. Coal bunkers (E) fed 24 furnaces (F) firing a huge boiler; water boiled to steam and hissed into four engine cylinders (G), each more than 7 feet in diameter. Huge pistons (H) turned an 18-foot

wheel (J), its rim hidden here by a chain belt (K) that powered the propeller shaft (L). Some 1,800 horsepower drove Brunel's unique propeller (M)—yet passengers noted little noise or vibration as they strolled the promenade deck (N) or feasted on "Chevaux de Frize Lamb" in the first-class dining saloon (O) and "Boiled Mutton, Caper Sauce" in second cabin (P). A piano lulled the cultured ear; yards of specially loomed Brussels carpet pleased both eye and foot. Daylight gladdened it all, spilling into upper decks through "light boxes" like horizontal windows (Q marks four of many).

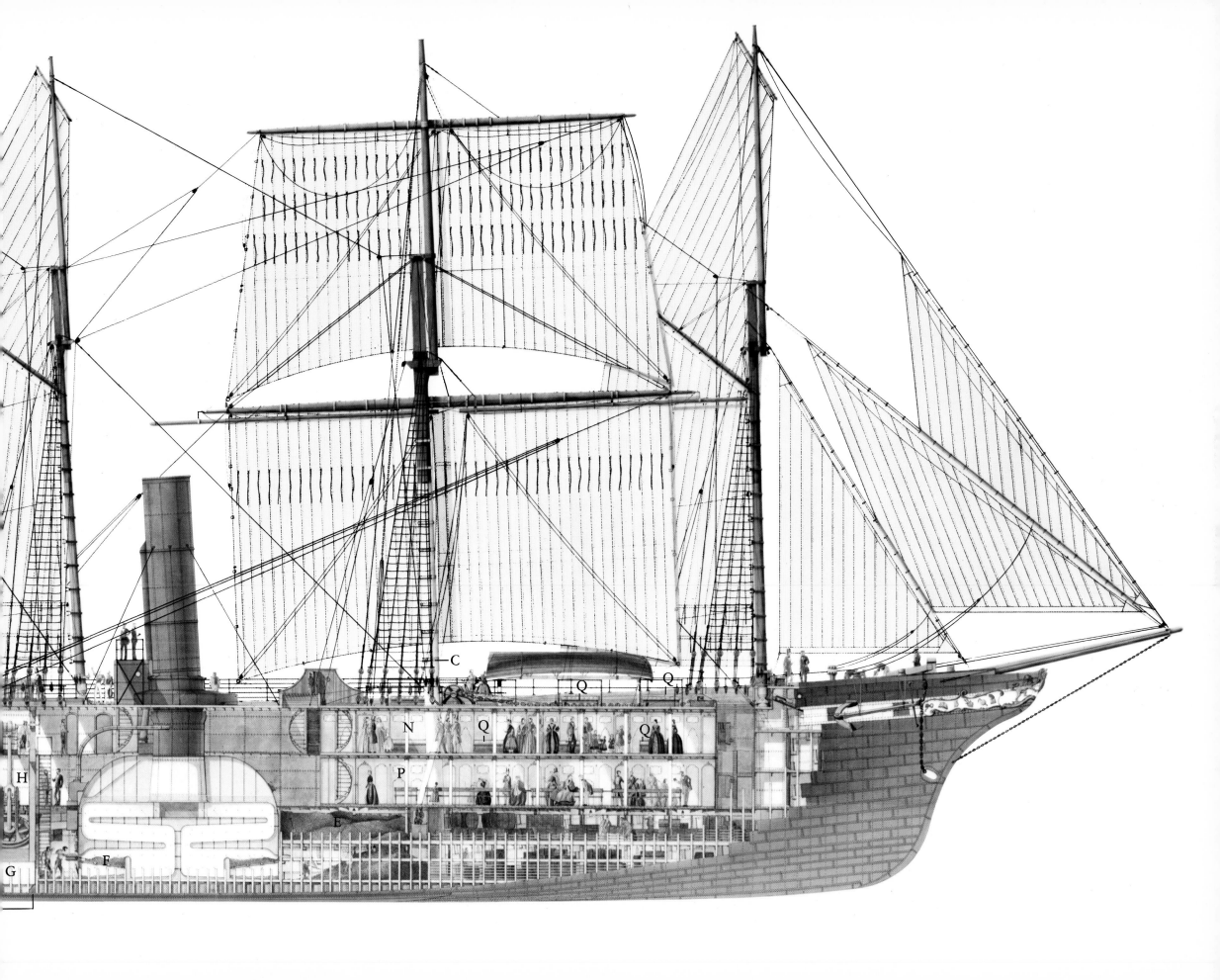

Anchor chains of his last and largest ship form an apt backdrop for I. K. Brunel, for a chain of events dimmed his *Great Eastern's* glory. With paddles and propeller the 692-foot giant could round Africa for the Orient nonstop. But the proposed Suez Canal, too tight for her, would get her rivals there faster. So the *Great Eastern* turned west, trudging the Atlantic until her size won her a berth in history: the laying (right) of the first transatlantic cable.

 262 service out of Liverpool, not to New York but to Halifax and Boston. So began the famous Cunard Line, which was to sail dependably, year in, year out, from that day to this.

All of these early steamers were wooden side-wheelers. In 1845 a new kind of ship appeared on the Atlantic: the *Great Britain,* second of Brunel's majestic experiments. At 3,270 tons she was by far the biggest ship afloat. She was the first iron-hulled transatlantic ship and the first to cross the Atlantic with a propeller, though she still carried sail on six truncated masts. Like many majestic experiments, she showed signs of becoming a massive white elephant. Indeed, it had been proposed—not wholly in jest—to name her *Mammoth.* She was over four years from the laying of her keel to her trials. She got stuck in the lock through which she was to reach open water; she left on her maiden voyage with only one-sixth of her cabins occupied; and a year later she ran aground in the Irish Sea.

That mishap, curiously, made her reputation. The pounding she endured on the rocks off Dundrum Bay demonstrated the soundness of her design and the durability of her iron hull. She was hauled off eventually, but the cost of repairs was too much for the company to bear. The *Great Britain* was sold and went to work for her new owners, first on the North Atlantic run, then for many years carrying immigrants to Australia. She lies now, partially restored and repainted, a shapely and much-visited relic, in the very dock in Bristol from which she originally sailed more than a century ago.

The *Great Britain* was a harbinger. But screw propellers did not oust paddles until about 20 years lat-

er, nor did steamers immediately drive the sailing packets out of business. The packets were familiar, they offered frequent service and choice of routes, and they were immune to boiler explosions. The steamers were not invulnerable to the hazards of the Atlantic; the much touted *President* had vanished in a storm in 1841. Steamers were also expensive, and in the 1840's there were not enough of them to maintain frequent transatlantic service or stick to the schedules that the packets had pioneered.

Against these drawbacks, and the nuisance of smoke, smells, and clattering machinery, early steamers at least offered the passenger the advantage of predictability, not only of departures but also of arrivals. In time this advantage would prove decisive, but not in the early days. It held good only where the distance between coaling stations was not too far. The North Atlantic run came within these limits, but only just. Side-wheelers consumed immense quantities of coal. Sometimes they ran out and had to finish voyages under sail.

Steam's advantage was doubly limited on the eastbound run; with the favoring winds, the bigger packets often made as good time, sometimes better. Seasoned travelers went west by steamer, east by sailing packet. Thus the packets often sailed westward with most of their cabins empty, though for a time they could offset the loss by filling up steerage with immigrants forced to the New World by unrest and famine in the Old.

Among the seasoned travelers was Charles Dickens; he traveled to the United States in 1842 in Cunard's *Britannia* and returned in the sailing packet *George Washington.* From his account of the journey,

"Some Made The Crossing By Rail."

In the halcyon days of ocean travel that was the standard joke, told and retold at the expense of nauseated shipmates reeling to the rail in one of the most venerable rites of the sea. Since man first threw a leg over a floating log and invented boating, landlubbers upon the waves have reserved their darkest epithets—and their keenest ingenuity—for the ancient affliction of mal de mer, better known as seasickness.

Landlubbers are not alone in their sufferings; the roster of the afflicted includes some salty old sea dogs as well. Lord Nelson, the British naval hero, could put a French fleet to flight, but he never won a battle against the malady that beset him at every weighing of the anchor.

Few have died of seasickness, although many believe that they will. Sweating, aching, retching violently, they hug the ship's rail or huddle miserably in a bunk, enduring symptoms wrought not by disease but by the confrontation of their own built-in balance mechanisms and the immutable laws of wave-motion physics.

Pluck a harp string and you hear energy made audible. Watch an ocean wave slide under the keel of your ship and you see energy made visible. A cork bobbing alongside stays behind, about where it was, for the wave is not a traveling mass of water but a traveling pulse of energy.

Most of that energy comes from wind. Waves radiate outward from a storm like rings of ripples on a pond. Swells can travel thousands of miles—a distance referred to as fetch. But as the waves roll by, rank upon rank, the cork simply bobs up and down in an elliptical, rope-skipping motion.

A boat does more than that. Aligned with the swells, it rolls from side to side; perpendicular to them, it pitches fore and

aft like a seesaw. And if it quarters into the oncoming waves, pitch and roll blend in a motion called yawing.

Boats are built to withstand wave motion, but humans are not. We sense our position by signals from our joints, our eyes (especially what they say about the horizon), and our inner ears, where fluid-filled tubes sense even slight movement. When all the signals agree, we can run, walk, stand, sit, or lie with our stomachs well under control. But motion can fool the inner ear and distract the eye from the horizon. Beset with signals now confused, the system responds with malaise.

And to that, people have responded with remedies wise and wacky. Gulp a pint of seawater; eat mustard pickles; sip water and vinegar; force down, if you can, some fat pork and garlic. "Don't go to the table,"

counseled a guidebook for liner passengers, "unless confident of your ability to stay there." A Cunard Line commodore voiced the ultimate cure: "Separate the passenger from the ship."

Until that could happen at voyage's end, the ship's queasy riders could only try one remedy or another, or simply tough it out. For many, the misery passed in a few days, when they "got their sea legs." And some never suffered it at all. "Alas!" complained one hardy swain. "All the young girls are sick—devilish sick. . . . I like to have my love returned, but not my dinner."

In the early 1900's, German liners triggered a craze for sports at sea. Violent exercise, according to the ships' doctors, cured the sickness that surely must be the wages of slothfulness anyway. Elaborate gymnasiums began to blossom on liners of every flag. And still the railbirds retched.

In 1947 a Baltimore woman seeking relief from hives began taking an experimental drug. It cured the hives—and also the carsickness she had felt on her way to the clinic. Thus was Dramamine born, the best known of a family of drugs that can quiet fluttering stomachs and make travel more enjoyable for millions. Perhaps it would not have for Mark Twain, who with tongue in cheek observed that "we all like to see people seasick when we are not, ourselves." But it might have made a better traveler of humorist Irwin S. Cobb, who recalled that in his misery "there passed in review before my eyes several of the more recent events of my past life—meals mostly."

Today the malady is called motion sickness, for it can happen in a lurching airliner, a jouncing automobile, a bobbing rowboat, or even a rocking chair in a living room, slowly teetering to and fro, to and fro.

Few cures for seasickness worked—but none flopped quite so grandly as did the Bessemer Saloon, brainchild of Henry Bessemer of steelmaking fame. His idea: Balance the saloon on pivots so it stays level as the vessel rolls around it. But his saloon rolled more than the ship. After two Channel crossings in 1873, the idea died.

he seems to have enjoyed the packet voyage much more. Not only was he seasick on the steamer; he also found the food indifferent, the service minimal, and his bed "a very thin mattress, spread like a surgical plaster on a most inaccessible shelf."

Samuel Cunard saw no reason to pamper his passengers. Nor was he interested in breaking speed records; safety and punctuality were his watchwords, and his captains were so instructed. For many years after Cunard's death in 1865, the public's image of the line he founded remained one of cold-boiled-mutton dependability.

Thus, throughout the 1840's, the sailing packets held their own against steamer competition and kept the public's respect. The sailing ships were approaching their peak of beauty, speed, and glamour. New clippers were coming off the ways; bigger and faster ships were joining the packet lines; the New York newspapers were loud in their contempt for "British smoke-boxes."

The enduring enthusiasm for sail was justified, for sail still had about half a century of useful life. But beneath the newspaper trumpetings was an undercurrent of anxiety, an attempt to reassure. In the special conditions of the North Atlantic passenger trade, sail was under threat. Events combined at the close of the decade to hasten its end.

In 1847 Cunard decided, at last, to extend his operations to New York. The homespun dependability of steam challenged the glamour of sail in its very capital. But steam could be glamorous too, as well as dependable. And the man to make it so was E. K. Collins, already seasoned in the passenger business and rich through the operations of his packet line.

Cunard's commercial success and his move to New York had touched off a burst of patriotic alarm in Washington, which Collins skillfully exploited. Congress wanted reliable transatlantic mail service in American ships. The Navy wanted them to be fast steamships that could be readily converted to use as military transports. And the public wanted steamers with the panache of the sailing packets; they wanted captains whose clear-eyed rectitude and bewhiskered dignity would be fitting models of American manliness; they wanted speed records, big statistics, awesome dimensions.

Collins, with his experience and a generous governmental subsidy, undertook to please them all. And for a few hectic years he succeeded. In his steamers, as in his packets, only the best would do: the best ships, the best officers, the best food, the best service. The line was a brief triumph and a pacesetter for the future. More than any other man, Collins created the tradition of the floating grand hotel.

Part of Collins's agreement with the government stipulated that he must submit the design of his ships for the Navy's review and approval. The appointed inspector was Commodore Matthew Perry (pages 172-75), later famous for forcing the opening of Japan, but now a conservative officer with a prejudice against screw propellers. He thought paddles more reliable—as many officers did, and many

Life at sea: Some passengers loved it, some loathed it. American painter Jasper Cropsey portrayed his family at ease in homelike comfort in a cheery stateroom of the eastbound Devonshire *in 1856 (opposite). Charles Dickens painted too—but in livid language that pictured his "thoroughly hopeless" cabin aboard the* Britannia *in 1842. A candid hand sketched the tiny cubicle (left) with its claustrophobic dimensions and its narrow shelflike bunks. "Nothing smaller for sleeping in was ever made," fumed Dickens, "except coffins."*

266 passengers; they felt more confident if they could actually see the wheels going around. So Collins's ships, like Cunard's, were side-wheelers. But they were much bigger than Cunard ships, bigger than anything afloat except the *Great Britain,* and much better appointed.

Breathless press descriptions greeted the *Atlantic,* the first of them. And no wonder. The *Atlantic* was steam heated throughout. She had bathrooms, an amenity which few private houses then enjoyed. She had bellpulls to summon servants. An ice room held 40 tons of ice and a prodigious quantity and variety of food. She offered a hairdresser's shop; reporters who saw it waxed lyrical over the adjustable padded patent-leather chair and the ranged bottles of perfumes. She provided a separate smoking room; no longer need gentlemen go "behind the barn" to smoke. The room, it is true, was a bare, rancid, claustrophobic den in a small house on the upper deck. But it was a potent social innovation, and for more than a century no liner would be without one.

The ship had its critics, of course. One genteel traveler railed at the size of the rooms that served as quarters for two. For "single men to be made double, Siamese for the voyage," he felt, was "utterly abominable. . . . Dressing is a mystery, when two men, strangers, are up in such quarters. . . . Some could only get along in putting on a coat by opening a door, and so thrusting an arm into the corridor; and by a jump from the bed shelf get into their pantaloons." He saw only one answer: *"Take a whole state-room to one's self.* No matter what the cost. Sacrifice a month or more of foreign travel, wear old clothes, eat but one meal a day, rather than have a

fellow-citizen so near you as to breathe half your air, and make you breathe all his."

The grand saloon, everyone could agree, was magnificent. On one of the walls was a huge painting of Liberty trampling a feudal prince. Even the spittoons were works of art; one passenger said they were fashioned like seashells and painted "sea green or sky blue."

The Collins ships had more than superficial virtues. They were fine ships for their day. All were a knot or two faster than their Cunard rivals, and their masters (who received more than double the salaries paid by Cunard) drove them hard. This attracted

publicity and ministered to national pride, but it led to trouble. The engines were too powerful. They wracked the wooden hulls, necessitating frantic and expensive repairs between voyages. A thirst for speed records may also have contributed to disaster. Two of the five Collins ships were lost at sea: the *Arctic,* in collision with another ship in fog in 1854; the *Pacific,* presumably in an ice field in 1856.

The line might have survived these disasters, but not its ruinous financial losses. Congress was at first sympathetic; in 1852 it more than doubled the Collins subsidy. But politicians grew weary of pouring money down an apparently bottomless if nicely-appointed well. In 1858 the subsidy was withdrawn. The line collapsed, and Collins abandoned ships to pursue other ventures. But he had left an indelible mark. Nothing on the transatlantic route was ever quite the same again.

Even careful Cunard learned the lesson, built bigger and faster ships, improved the mail service, and paid more attention to passengers' wishes. In 1856 the Cunard Line—which had never been thought of as especially innovative—put its first iron-hulled ship into service.

The *Persia* was Cunard's answer to Collins's *Pacific.* Her master, C.H.E. Judkins, did not quite fit the tradition of Cunard caution, and once expressed a preference for cracking on speed in a fog because that way you are "sooner out of it." On her maiden voyage his ship pounded head-on into the same ice field that probably sank the *Pacific,* but her stout iron hull got her through without major damage.

Six years later, more daring still, Cunard introduced its first screw-propelled steamer on the North

Inman Line, that specialized in transporting them.

William Inman operated a fleet of small, economical, screw-propelled iron ships. He was no luckier than Collins in avoiding marine disaster; two of his ships, the *City of Glasgow* and the *City of Philadelphia,* were lost in the mid-1850's. His line survived by offering services that no other steamship operator had thought of. He was quick to realize that there could be a lucrative market in carrying impoverished immigrants across the Atlantic at a cheap rate by steamer, and he was the first to capitalize specifically on that market. He was also the first to send his ships into Queenstown, thereby sparing Irish immigrants the misery and expense of the crossing to Liverpool. He fed his steerage passengers, although somewhat basically: oatmeal and milk for breakfast, beef for dinner, gruel and tea for supper. "Three thousand miles at a halfpenny a mile, and this nourishment thrown in for nothing," boasted his advertisements. He even provided soap and towels. No wonder immigrants deserted the packets and flocked into Inman's steamers.

Gradually the once-proud packet fleets aged. Fewer new ships were added, and as those in service grew older they could not be driven as hard. Crossings became slower. More and more the packets fell back on the ordinary freight they had once disdained. The last line packet, a Red Swallowtail Line ship, cleared from London in 1881. She was aptly named: *Ne Plus Ultra*—Nothing Further.

In 1859 the third and biggest of Brunel's great shipbuilding ventures appeared, a giant of a ship at almost 19,000 tons. Nearly 700 feet long, the *Great Eastern* was five times as big as the next biggest ship

Atlantic run: the *China.* Characteristically, Cunard matched her with a new paddle wheeler, the *Scotia,* which proved to be the faster ship, though vastly more prodigal with fuel and therefore less profitable. These ships went far to dispel the Cunard Line's reputation for fussy conservatism. And they kept its reputation for safety intact.

Collins's competitive drive had been aimed chiefly at Cunard; but Cunard survived it and steamed serenely on. The losers in the competition of the 1850's were the sailing packets; they lost nearly all their cabin passengers to the steamers. By the middle of the decade they were also losing steerage passengers to a new British steamship company, the

Hurrah—
Off at Last!"

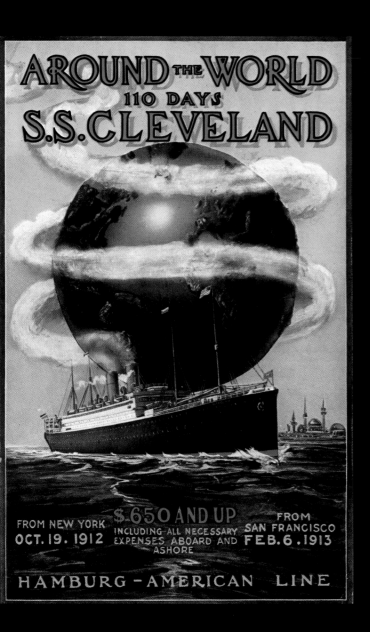

Signed gaily, "Love from Eleanor," a postcard mailed from a White Star liner (far right, middle) catches the high spirits of a steamer sailing in the early years of the 20th century. Sometimes the mood held: "Fine voyage," says the card above hers. And sometimes it didn't: "Land in sight after an awful trip," grumbles the one below.

Artists, too, captured the heady excitement of steamer trunks trundling down a cobbled wharf . . . sea dogs turning stern-to as a liner heads seaward on a timetable cover . . . revelers disporting on a program for a shipboard musical revue.

Gone now is the *Cleveland* that wreathed the globe in her smoke; gone, too, is the $650 around-the-world fare quoted on her timetable. Mermaids live only in myth— and on a menu cover of an elegant liner that might indeed have lured them up to frolic. Collectors now prize even a baggage label (below), for these are vignettes of paper that have outlived ships of steel.

PROGRAM

RedStarLine
PASSENGER LIST
Antwerp
Dover
New York.

Antwerp
Boston.

American Line New York Southampton

NORDD. LLOYD, BREMEN.

R. P. D. „Königin Luise".

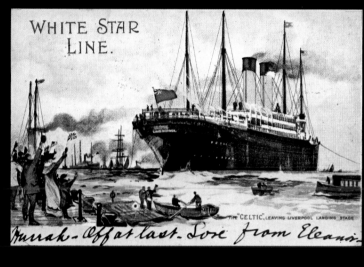

WHITE STAR LINE.

THE "CELTIC", LEAVING LIVERPOOL LANDING STAGE

Hamburg Amerika Linie

„Amerika" Damensalon.

Norddeutscher Lloyd
BREMEN.

Dampfer „BARBAROSSA", 4. Januar 1899.

272 *A bilingual breakfast and a portrait of the ship graced a menu aboard the North German Lloyd's* Barbarossa *in 1899. Steaks, chops, ham, cheese—to modern eyes it reads like a dinner menu. But the bounteous breakfast had become for some the best meal of the day. One liner passenger wrote lyrically of "certain sputtering and hissing sounds . . . backed up by sundry savory sniffs," their promise at last fulfilled as stewards lifted the polished covers. "After having duly paused awhile," he counseled, "choose between Cognac and Schiedam for a chasse."*

Frühstück.

Bananen. Mandarinen Ananas.
Hafergrütze.   Maisgries
Frische Milch und Sahne.
Gelée.   Marmelade.   Ingwer.
Geb Seezunge, Rémouladen-Sauce.
Beefsteak.   Hamburger Steak.
Hammelcôtelettes
Fricadellen.
Gebackene Kalbsnieren.
Salz-Kartoffeln, Brat-Kartoffeln
Spiral-Kartoffeln
Yorker Schinken und Speck
Verlorene Eier auf Toast.
Eier auf Wunsch.
Eierkuchen mit Tomaten
Rührei mit Spargel
Buchweizenkuchen
K a l t : Roastbeef. Sülze.
Chester- & Edamer-Käse.
Brödchen Kaffeebrod Hörnchen.
Kaffee   Thee   Chocolade   Cacao

Breakfast.

Bananas Mandarines Pine-apples
Oatmeal.   Hominy.
Fresh milk and cream.
Jelly.   Marmalade.   Ginger.
Fried sole, rémoulade sauce.
Beefsteak.   Hamburg beefsteak.
Mutton chops.
Meat balls.
Fried cal's kidney.
Boiled potatoes.   Fried potatoes
Spiral potatoes.
Yorkshire ham and bacon.
Poached eggs on toast.
Eggs to order.
Omelet with tomatoes
Scrambled eggs with asparagus.
Buckwheat cakes.
C o l d : Roastbeef. Brawn.
Chester- & Dutch-cheese.
Rolls.   Biscuits.
Coffee   Tea   Chocolate   Cocoa

WILH. JÖNTZEN, BREMEN.

afloat. She had five funnels, six tall masts, more than 58,000 square feet of canvas—which, fortunately for her crew, she rarely had to use. The merits of paddles and screw propellers were still being debated, but Brunel's ship had both, with separate engines for each: the wheels like Ferris wheels, the screw as big as a windmill. She fascinated and terrified contemporaries with her size and power. But to Brunel, she was his "great babe."

The huge dimensions of the *Great Eastern*—whose original name, in fact, was *Leviathan*—were not the product of megalomaniac fancy. They were dictated by the task she was designed for: to convey 4,000 passengers (or, if need be, 10,000 troops) and 6,000 tons of cargo from England to India or Australia, carrying all the coal she would need to make the passage without refueling.

It was not Brunel's fault that her owners decided, after long delays in launching and fitting out, to enter her instead in the North Atlantic stakes. There she lumbered along against more experienced and confident Atlantic runners, a magnificent misfit competing in a trade for which she was never intended. She was faster than average for her day; about 13 to 14 knots was her average speed. But she was no sleek, nimble ocean racer.

She was certainly spacious and well appointed, but comfortable only in good weather. Naive hopes that great size would render her immune to the action of wind and sea were soon disappointed; she rolled like a wallowing sow. There was something grotesque about her. That great bulk was hard to handle; she had a voracious appetite for coal; she was dogged by persistent bad luck.

"Live like a king," exulted one brochure—and so they did. With regal air these first-class passengers on the Kaiserin Auguste Victoria in 1906 view dishes fit indeed for a king. Most fares included meals, but here on the Hamburg American Line, many could choose tickets "Without Meals" and dine in a posh restaurant on no schedule but their own. Some found that unsettling; one woman fretted between diners on one side munching meat and vegetables, "and on the other side, they were eating ice cream and nuts!"

Numbers Noah never knew filled the transatlantic arks. An artist arrayed a dock with cargo, food, and water, and rank on rank of passengers poised to move mountains at mealtimes. A liner might need 100 tons of beef per crossing.

A proper Victorian pair take a turn around the weather deck. Promenading kept many from boredom—and others from rest when their deck chairs stood in the walkers' way, or their cabins echoed the footfalls of early risers tramping the deck above.

So far to go, so little to do. But turn-of-the-century folk were used to entertaining themselves. So they filled the idle hours with homespun fun. Children needed no social director (though some liners gave them one); they romped as in any schoolyard (top) or dragooned Daddy into a game of catch (bottom). Grown-ups needed none either; perch a passenger on a deckhouse with a concertina (middle), and a dance was sure to begin. Those still bored of joys at journey's end. On this cruise (below), "Xmas in Europe" lay ahead.

A heavy gale, when she was westbound in 1861, smashed the ship's boats and much of the upper works and battered her reputation beyond repair. Passengers told hair-raising stories of furniture skidding from one side of the grand saloon to the other. The cow house, a passenger recalled, was an early casualty; one cow ended hanging upside down through the skylight of the forward saloon.

More serious, both paddle wheels were disabled, and a rudder pin snapped, allowing the rudder to flap uncontrollably. While the ship's officers dithered over the cause of the rudder failure, a passenger with an engineering background figured out what must have happened and offered a plan to fix it. Not until his officers had thrown up their hands did the captain bring himself to accept the advice of a mere passenger. A man was then lowered from the stern, where the great ship's pitching and wallowing alternately dunked him in the ocean and yanked him dripping aloft until he finally jury-rigged a replacement for the broken pin. At last the ship limped into Queenstown under propeller alone.

To crown it all, *Great Eastern*'s voyages rarely made a profit. And costly repairs plunged her owners so far into debt that she could not earn her keep. She passed from one group of owners to another, and lost money for them all.

Her hour of glory came when she laid the first successful transatlantic cable in 1866. In her huge grand saloon, stripped of its sumptuous furnishings, she could carry—as no other ship could—a single strand of cable that would stretch across the ocean floor from Ireland to Newfoundland. But then, with the cable laid, what was she to do? She made a few

Far from the frolic and finery, black gangs—so-called for their grimy work—sweated in stifling stokeholes to feed a liner's fires. On one crossing they might shovel their way through 22 trains of coal—30 cars per train, 10 tons per car. No one in a liner's crew worked harder and no one was paid less.

276

more unprofitable Atlantic crossings, then went back to cable laying for a short time. She spent most of her remaining years berthed in the Mersey River as a floating funfair, a humiliation that her creator was not to share. Isambard Kingdom Brunel had died shortly after her launch.

In 1889 she went to the breakers for scrap, a ship born out of time, a prodigy. No other ship of her tonnage was built until nearly 50 years after her launch. Even the most valuable feature of her design—a cellular double bottom—was not imitated for a generation after her.

Ironically, this was a vigorous time in steamship development. More and more Americans were visiting Europe and could afford to travel in comfort. Immigrants were leaving Europe for America in numbers that made them worth competing for. New steamship lines came into being, among them Britain's White Star Line, with its big, fast, rather flashy ships and its loud, persuasive advertising. Its *Adriatic* was the first ship to be lit by gas—but the stuff leaked and reeked. Cunard's *Servia* in 1881 was first to be lighted throughout by electricity.

Early in its history, the White Star Line achieved a grim distinction in the wreck of the *Atlantic* off Nova Scotia in 1873, with heavy loss of life. It was one of the worst shipping disasters of the century. But the line survived—as years later it would survive a much worse disaster, the sinking of its superb new liner, the *Titanic*.

In the years between the 1860's and the 1890's, first iron, then steel, replaced wood in the hulls of all big ships. Paddles disappeared; screw propellers became standard. As ships got bigger and the strain on

single screws began to cause broken shafts and lost propellers, twin screws came into use. As confidence in steam increased, the need for auxiliary sail diminished, and masts were cut down to the size needed for signal and lookout purposes. By 1890, squared yards in steamships had become an old-fashioned oddity. More drastic still, a few years later the companionable thud of the old reciprocating engine gave way to the hum of the steam turbine.

Charles Algernon Parsons, besides being an English engineer of genius, had a talent for showmanship. Having worked for years to develop a marine steam turbine, he chose the best occasion of the century to display it: the Naval Review off Portsmouth,

England, that celebrated Queen Victoria's Diamond Jubilee in 1897. His unique vessel, the *Turbinia*, had been specially built to test the turbine drive now howling inside her. She was 100 feet long with only 9 feet of beam, lean and sharp as a pencil. She had breezed through weeks of trials; now she must perform in the glare of public scrutiny.

At the chosen moment, she nosed out from the marshaled rows of spectator craft and dashed off at unheard-of speed, flames belching from her funnel as she darted among the rows of anchored old warships. Having made her point, she shut down her engines and returned meekly to her place. So the biggest, oldest, most conservative (and perhaps, at

that time, most obsolescent) of the major navies of the world was brought face-to-face with a remarkable device that could—and did—revolutionize the propulsion of power-driven ships.

A reciprocating engine—an "up-and-downer" in sea slang—is powered by pistons moving up and down inside their cylinders. A turbine is a rotary engine in which a jet of steam is directed onto blades set at an angle in a drum. The force of the steam turns the drum. The turbine, logical partner of the screw propeller, brought a tremendous advance in efficiency, speed, smoothness, and above all, fuel economy. Suddenly ships bigger than the *Great Eastern,* much faster and vastly more profitable,

Neoclassic figures disporting overhead, a formal garden on one wall, fresh flowers amid marble columns and garlanded chairs—Aquitania's restaurant was a feast for the eye. The ship's interiors borrowed from many styles; a publicist said she was a "Temple of Taste."

The lap of luxury, Aquitania's first-class lounge seated its guests in splendor. A liner cruise had convinced designer Arthur Davis that most passengers were landlubbers—so he gave them a fine hotel like those ashore with few reminders that they were at sea.

began coming down the ways. The steam turbine ushered in the golden age of the transatlantic liners.

It also restored a somewhat faded British preeminence in the liner trade. Around the turn of the 20th century, the Germans were the pacemakers in the passenger business. In those years the Blue Riband—the coveted trophy for the fastest Atlantic crossing—was bandied back and forth between the big German liners: the North German Lloyd *Kaiser Wilhelm der Grosse, Kronprinz Wilhelm,* and *Kaiser Wilhelm II,* and the Hamburg American *Deutschland.* They all had up-and-downers, but were highly efficient, well-run ships. They were fast, and they had interior furnishings that overwhelmed the eye with Wagnerian magnificence.

In the face of this competition, White Star opted for spacious comfort over speed and glamour. Its *Oceanic* of 1899 was a fine ship, and the first to exceed the *Great Eastern* in length, though not in tonnage. But she was not particularly fast.

Cunard bided its time. The *Carmania,* the line's first turbine-driven ship, was a highly successful though not record-breaking experiment. But then, in 1907, the Cunard Line put into service the two ships that, more than any others, became symbols of the golden age, archetypes of marine excellence.

The *Mauretania* and the *Lusitania* were sister ships, differing only in interior decoration and a little in speed. Each ship was driven by four turbine-powered propellers and surmounted by four tall stacks, hallmarks of dignity and power. In the entire saga of the North Atlantic, only 14 four-funneled liners were ever built. So potent a symbol was the liner's mighty stack that some smaller ships added a

Final Hours Of a "Floating Babylon"

It was the first watch of the new day—April 15, 1912—and the North Atlantic lay as still as bathwater. Through the chill night air drifted the jaunty rhythm of a ragtime band. And out across the icy water, scores of stunned survivors caught the incongruous melodies as they huddled in lifeboats, watching in disbelief the death of an elaborate dream.

"God Himself could not sink this ship," said a deckhand to reassure a worried passenger. His boast would soon ring hollow, yet a few days earlier it had seemed a certainty as the White Star liner *Titanic* readied for her maiden voyage from Liverpool to New York. Now she lay dead in the water, slowly flooding since 20 minutes before midnight, when a towering iceberg had torn a 300-foot gash in her underbelly. Decks thronged, lights ablaze, she had become a great steel Atlantis slowly slipping into the sea. Yet, even with her foredeck awash, many still thought her unsinkable and let 13 of her 20 lifeboats lower away with room for more.

Earlier that evening the freighter *Californian* had stalled in the ice field. Her wireless operator had tried to warn the *Titanic*—but First Operator Jack Phillips cut him off and went back to sending private messages. Now Phillips tapped out a steady plea for help—but the *Californian*'s operator had shut down his radio and gone to bed. And Phillips got no answer from another vessel, whose lights appeared to be no more than ten miles away, perhaps a fishing boat without a radio.

About 12:45 a.m. the first lifeboat was lowered; women and children had to be urged to board. Many still would not believe the ship could sink, and preferred to stay and chat. An hour later people were crowding the boats beyond capacity.

Peril inspired uncommon bravery. Mrs. Isidor Straus would not board a boat without her husband, one of 11 millionaires aboard. John Jacob Astor watched his pregnant teen-age wife depart, then calmly lit a cigarette. Benjamin Guggenheim and his valet changed into evening clothes; "We've dressed in our best," he said, "and are prepared to go down like gentlemen."

Some of the rich had paid more for their suites than the average American earned in four years. For four days, first-class passengers had reveled in a Parisian café, a Turkish bath, a gym, a lounge styled after the Palace of Versailles—a world of dreams that came crashing down as the stern reared high for the final plunge. Everything movable—29 boilers, five grand pianos, 30,000 fresh eggs—broke loose and smashed against the bulkheads. At 2:15 a.m. the lights winked out. The music stopped. At 2:20 the stern vanished as the *Titanic* began its two-mile plunge to the bottom.

Chief Baker Charles Joughin, perhaps the last man off, stepped from the stern just as the sea swallowed it. Legend says the alcohol he had guzzled since the collision helped him stand the icy water until his rescue at dawn. For some 1,500 others there was no reprieve. Only one lifeboat even attempted a rescue mission; survivors in the other boats huddled amid the wails of the drowning hundreds until the night fell silent. In one boat sat White Star chairman J. Bruce Ismay, one of only 119 males plucked from the boats by the liner *Carpathia*. Ismay would spend his last 25 years as a haunted recluse in an Irish mansion.

The artist lit this scene with a melodramatic moon and a tumble of clouds. But the night was clear. And in *Titanic*'s death agony, reality held drama enough.

Stark headlines (below) told a terrible truth after a day of rumor and disbelief. Officials, "optimistic in the extreme," for hours would not admit that lives were lost. The ship was in tow, said one story; all had been rescued, said another. Even this edition erred: 705 survived. For more than 1,500 who did not, a subhead echoed like a dirge: "Rescuers There Too Late."

283

"Bon voyage!" rings out from a thousand throats as the French Line's France eases from a New York pier in the early 1930's. In such a ship, how could the wish fall short? "The Château of the Atlantic," she was called—and she earned the compliment with gilded paneling, a staircase three stories high, and a menu to tempt the most jaded tastes. One of her British admirers doubted "that any craft since Cleopatra's fabled barge knew such visual extravagance."

dummy stack, or even two; the space inside might be used as a kennel for the passengers' pets.

The *Lusitania* was sunk by a German submarine in 1915, and today is remembered chiefly for the manner of her end. But veteran travelers still recall her sister, the *Mauretania,* as a vibrant and living ship.

The *Mauretania* was a handsome vessel—handsome rather than beautiful—a ship of breeding, combining size and dignity with the simplicity and grace of a yacht. On her eastbound maiden voyage, she won the Blue Riband from the *Lusitania* and held it for two decades. For years on end she arrived at one side of the ocean or the other within a range of time that rarely exceeded ten minutes.

Yet these qualities do not explain why she was loved by a whole generation of passengers. Franklin D. Roosevelt, a sensitive and observant man familiar with ships, came as near to an explanation as anyone: "Every ship has a soul. But the *Mauretania* had one you could talk to. At times she could be wayward and contrary as a thoroughbred. . . . At other times she would do everything her master wanted her to, with a right good will. . . . She had the manners and deportment of a great lady and behaved herself as such."

For most passengers, the reason for liking the *Mauretania* was simpler: They always had a good time on board. A well-trained crew, with superb esprit de corps and professional pride, saw to that. To be sure, this was before the day of the zany distractions that in later ships were to fill every minute of the passenger's time, if he submitted to them. But already there were swimming pools, gymnasiums,

music, dancing, wide decks to promenade and sunbathe on, magnificent appointments, superb food, attentive and cheerful service.

The great Cunard ships did not carry luxury to preposterous excess. Restrained perfection was their ideal. In the *Mauretania* one could not—as in the *Kaiser Wilhelm*—catch one's own live trout in big tanks on the awning deck and have it cooked to order. But one could certainly live at a standard of comfort equaled by only a few of the grandest of grand hotels ashore, with the excitement of being at sea as an added stimulus.

There was more to it than that, however. The well-heeled but inexperienced traveler could be persuaded that his steamer ticket was a temporary admission to high society. The Cunard Line was expert at this kind of persuasion. The snob appeal was reinforced, not only by the rigid division of accommodations and deck space between first, second, and third class, but also by the elaborate hierarchy of the captain's table and the tables presided over at dinner by the other senior ship's officers. Many an arriviste was willing to pay good money to travel among the minor royalties, financiers, captains of industry, film stars, and pugilists who peopled the grand saloon.

The captains of the great liners—superb seamen with many years of experience—had to be social arbiters as well. They did not so much preside as hold court, and most of them seem to have taken a simple pleasure in the company of the rich and influential and in the splendor of their surroundings. The doyen of these august personages in the golden age was Sir James Charles, a portly and much decorated figure, for years commodore of the Cunard Line. When he had the *Aquitania,* those privileged to dine at his table got a note informing them of the hour of dinner and the dress to be worn. One dined not at one's own convenience, but at the commodore's.

Not all the liner captains relished the role of dinner-table autocrat. One of them even had all the chairs removed from the captain's table except his own, to spare himself the inevitable flood of predictable questions about the ship, the crew, the weather, even the tailors of London.

In exasperation, another liner captain armed himself with a well-rehearsed spiel, which he unleashed upon the querulous passenger in a crescendo of trivia. "I have crossed the Atlantic four hundred and twenty-two times this will be my four hundred and twenty-third I have not been shipwrecked or cast away on a desert island or been burnt at sea or marooned or shanghaied or caught by sharks and I don't want to be the ship is doing fifteen knots and could do more if she were going faster you will be able to go ashore as soon as we are alongside the jetty and not before and if you have anything you want to smuggle I don't want to know about it and I don't know the best way to get it ashore without paying duty I hope to retire from the sea some day *Is there anything else you would like to know?"*

Passengers now judged ships mainly by the food, the service, the comfort. Safety, punctuality, and speed were taken for granted. A little too lightly, perhaps, since these sometimes conflicted. The ship was on a tight schedule; the company's profits and the captain's reputation depended on maintaining that schedule; and when conflict appeared the schedule usually won. A liner in fog would double the

lookouts, close the watertight doors, make a token reduction in speed, and carry on. Doomsayers occasionally uttered a warning. As early as 1890 an editorial writer gloomily predicted that "one of these record breakers will break a record he does not wish to break, and then, too late, a howl will go up over the whole civilized world of the criminal folly of driving steamers at full speed through dense fogs and waters filled with icebergs." As usual, no one paid much attention. But on occasion the doomsayers proved to be right.

The very name *Titanic* suggests hubris, a brash vainglory displeasing to the gods. And the notion that gods had been tempted ran through many of the comments after the event, along with the more routine reactions: the shocked horror at the loss of life and the incredulous indignation that so superb a creation could prove so vulnerable. Other ships had been sunk by icebergs; but the *Titanic* was then the biggest passenger ship afloat, White Star's shining answer to the Cunard sisters, the most up-to-date, the most sophisticated in design. Because of her elaborate system of watertight compartments, many thought her unsinkable. In April 1912 she was on her maiden voyage, with a passenger list unmatched for influence and wealth.

No ship is unsinkable. A combination of chances against million-to-one odds destroyed the *Titanic*. Icebergs are usually visible for miles. But the lookouts did not see this one until too late. Probably it had recently keeled over, as icebergs will, and was showing its dark underside. If the *Titanic* had

285

Poster artists took a bow —or three—to tempt the transatlantic traveler of the thirties aboard. A generation earlier, artists had often limned the liner as a triumph of technology, its brute power told in soaring funnels, massive hulls, and ingenious machinery. But by the 1930's the liner was seen not as a workhorse but as a thoroughbred, sleek and fast and elegant. In the culture of the times it had become tastemaker; architects ashore aped its lines as decorators gave interiors the feel of the sea or the look of the liner. In the great ships, technology and art found common ground.

rammed the ice head-on, her watertight compartments would probably have kept her afloat. But at the last moment the lookouts did see the iceberg, and the officer of the watch ordered a sharp turn. The ship began to swing around and struck the ice a glancing blow. The impact was so slight that many passengers hardly felt it. But the underwater shelf of the berg laid open the liner's starboard side for 300 feet, a surgical slice through five watertight compartments and part of a sixth. She began to settle by the bow, and in less than three hours she was gone.

In the accounts of survivors the most striking feature of the scene was its eerie calm. The sea was still; the passengers were quiet and orderly; the lights burned steadily. The ship's orchestra played on deck until the end; their final selection was the Episcopal hymn "Autumn," and none of them survived to play another. The total capacity of the ship's lifeboats, incredibly, was only about half the number of passengers and crew on board—and yet, at first, there was no rush to board the boats.

When the old Cunarder *Carpathia* arrived and began picking up survivors, the ship had sunk. Those who had remained on board, some 1,500 of them, died within minutes in the icy water. The captain, as custom required, was among them.

The sinking of the *Titanic* was one of the greatest peacetime disasters in the history of the sea. Its consequences were felt throughout the world. Courts of inquiry were unable to fix blame; the disaster was an accident. It led to new regulations requiring ships to carry enough lifeboats for all on board and to keep a 24-hour radio watch; to a more southerly liner track across the North Atlantic; and to an ice patrol that

A mélange of myth and maritime history crowds this detail from a massive set of four gold-on-glass murals that complement the Normandie's *grand saloon, the largest public room that ever went to sea. A light fixture hides at left amid panels four feet high, each weighing over 50 pounds.*

continues to this day. It led to impressive acts of commemoration and atonement. And it produced at least one piece of imaginative literature, Thomas Hardy's "The Convergence of the Twain":

> *Dim moon-eyed fishes near*
> *Gaze at the gilded gear*
> *And query: "What does*
> *this vaingloriousness down here?"*

No one tried to tackle the root cause of the trouble: the tyranny of schedules. Spurred by clock and calendar, the liners continued to flirt with disaster.

In 1914 a greater disaster began: World War I. Many passenger liners were requisitioned at the outset. Some of the largest, including the *Aquitania* and the *Mauritania,* were employed as hospital ships or as troop transports. Smaller liners became armed merchant cruisers, and some of them met fighting ends. Some that continued to carry passengers were also lost, mostly by submarine attack. The *Lusitania* was one of the earliest of these.

On May 7, 1915, a German submarine lurking off the Irish coast spotted a great four-funneled liner. Only a week before, the Imperial German Embassy had warned in the New York newspapers that "the zone of war includes the waters adjacent to the British Isles; that . . . vessels flying the flag of Great Britain, or any of her allies, are liable to destruction in those waters and that travellers sailing in the war zone on ships of Great Britain or her allies do so at their own risk." In modern minds such a warning awakens grim memories of World War II, when the sinking of unarmed merchant vessels without warning became an almost daily event. But back in 1915

such action was considered almost unthinkable.

Some 1,600 passengers had boarded the *Lusitania* in New York on the very day the warnings were published. On May 7, when the ship made her landfall off Ireland at the Old Head of Kinsale, she was steaming at economical speed—21 knots or less— and was not zigzagging. Those who had missed or chosen to ignore the German announcements now loomed like sitting ducks in the crosshairs of a German U-boat's sights.

Torpedoed without hesitation, the *Lusitania* was torn by explosions from within. She sank with an appalling suddenness, and nearly 1,200 people died with her. Did her boilers blow up, as an inquest indicated—or did the explosions come, as rumor insisted, from contraband ammunition? Mystery and controversy still haunt the ill-fated *Lusitania*.

When the war was over, the shipping companies acquired German ships seized as reparations. And they began refurbishing their battered old ships for a return to normal business, converting them from dirty coal to cleaner oil. Again the advertising brochures beckoned the traveler aboard. "Today," said one, "ocean travel has taken its proper place as a special aspect of the very special art of living pleasantly. . . . The transatlantic week, from pier to pier, can be—should be—one of the gala weeks of life . . . one of those rare and preciously *perfect intervals,* snatched from the grudging gods."

But business refused to return to normal. The heedless rich were fewer in number and, for the time being, less rich. And in the old days, while first-class travel brought glamour and publicity to the shipping lines, *(Continued on page 301)*

A Regal Liner,
Truly
A Palace Afloat

Labyrinth of luxury, the classic Cunarder *Queen Mary* shows a liner's intricacy in a cutaway painted when she was new. Ingenious ducting kept the lower decks ventilated and led the smoke from boiler rooms to funnels through the walls of the saloons. Four screws and 200,000 horsepower could move her 81,000 tons at 32 knots.

The key below omits such features as stairs and elevators.

Mainmast *1;* Ventilators *2, 3, 4, 5, 6, 7;* Sports areas *9, 23;* Tank room *10, 11;* Directional aerials *12;* Semaphores *13;* Searchlights *14;* Chart room *15;* Wheelhouse and bridge *16;* Captain's and officers' quarters *17;* Veranda grill *18;* Engineer officers' quarters *19;* Engineers' wardroom *20;* Cinema projection rooms *21, 29;* Gymnasium *22;* Wireless room *25;* State-rooms and suites *26, 28, 56, 59, 62, 73, 76, 77, 80, 96, 97, 100;* Smoking rooms *30, 33, 84;* Pantries *31, 34, 39;* After-end of long gallery (port side) *35;* Ballroom *37;* Starboard gallery *38;* Stage of lounge *40;* Lounge *41;* Storage areas *42, 58, 61, 68, 86, 177;* Writing rooms *43;* Main hall and shopping area *45;* Drawing room *46;* Altar *47;* Children's playrooms *48, 102;* Bar and observation lounge *50;* Docking bridge *52;* Tourist lounge *53, 69;* Tourist writing room and library *55;* Third-class garden lounge *64;* Cargo hatch *65;* Fore-

mast *66;* Crow's nest (electrically heated) *67;* Suites and bedroom accommodation *71, 89, 91, 94, 109, 111, 129, 131, 133, 158, 159, 160, 161, 167;* Purser's office *79;* Hairdresser's *82, 92, 99;* Forecastle and anchor capstan *87;* Crew quarters *88, 106, 107, 127, 128, 156, 157, 165;* Third-class lounge *103;* Mail rooms *104, 163, 173, 175, 176, 179, 201;* Tourist dining saloon *113;* Baker's shop *114;* Vegetable-preparing room *115;* Kitchens *116, 154;* Grill *117;* China pantry *118;* Bar *119;* Private dining rooms *120, 122;* Restaurant *121;* Third-class dining saloon *124;* Third-class accommodation *126, 148, 150, 155, 162;* Capstan gear and crew's space *127;* Alcoholic beverage storage *134, 169, 171;* Perishable food stores *136, 138, 139, 140, 141, 142, 143;* Fruit-ripening room *137;* Grocery store *144;* Hospital and dispensary *145, 146;* Printer's shop *147;* Oil-filling station *149;* Dressing rooms of swimming pool *151;* Swimming pools *152, 168;* Kosher kitchen *153;* Specie room *164;* Baggage rooms *166, 174, 178, 200;* Garage *172;* Rudder *180;* Propellers *181, 182;* Shafts and shaft tunnels *183;* Engine rooms *184, 185;* Fan rooms *186, 197;* Boiler rooms *187, 191, 192, 195, 196;* Air-conditioning plant *188;* Generator rooms *189, 193;* Power station *190, 194;* Water-softening machinery *198;* Tanks *199;* General cargo *202;* Double bottom *203.*

A proud Queen Mary *slices the waves off New York Harbor in this portrait painted in 1959 (left). Like minnows around a dolphin, a dowdy pilot boat approaches while the Ambrose Lightship—long since retired—holds high its guiding light.*

Once she ruled the open seas. Now the Queen Mary *sails on a wave of nostalgia as a hotel, meeting center, and museum in Long Beach, California. There in a sleeping room —one of four rooms and a luggage closet that* made up a first-class suite— tour groups admire a marquetry panel that once graced a third-class lounge. The panel is said to contain woods used throughout what was once called "the ship of beautiful woods." Unicorns in gilded gesso and musicians in polished bronze adorn the liner's main lounge.

Passengers in second and third class could enter it only for church services—a rare chance to ogle the rich and their posh surroundings. Few saw the busy wheelhouse (lower right). At sea such brass would need a daily polishing.

How They Went
Showed
Who They Were

Today we would call them the jet set—the wealthy, the elite, the darlings of popularity. But in the heyday of the great ocean liners they traveled with a genteel grace long since left in the slipstream of the cramped and scurrying airliner. For the ship became a city at sea—and the first-class passenger list was its social register.

Rival steamship lines courted celebrities and flooded the newspapers ashore with all the trivia of their doings afloat. Fans in the 1930's followed with breathless fascination the shipboard honeymoon of film stars Joan Crawford and Douglas Fairbanks, Jr. (F), or the seagoing shenanigans of comedienne Beatrice Lillie and a vaudeville veteran named Paul Hartman (H). Though vaudeville was fading fast, Hartman would find a new lease on stardom in a fledgling marvel called television.

Canny publicists made sure a liner took along a good photographer. His eager gaze would surely spot the deck chairs of the Henry Fords (D) or actress Helen Hayes and her daughter, Mary MacArthur (E). Aviatrix Amelia Earhart (G) kept an eye on the sky, a dapper Maurice Chevalier (B) kept an eye on the ball—and celebrity-watchers kept an eye on them both. A luxury liner was a publicist's paradise.

What better place to photograph the glamorous Ginger Rogers (C) than at poolside with a big beach ball and a fetching swimsuit? Even more appropriate was actor-playwright Noel Coward's pose at the rail (A), for seasickness plagued him even in calm waters. Clever cameramen made shots that identified the shipping line; a life ring or a bath mat under a dainty foot would do. Fame did the rest, as those without it scrambled to sail with the stars.

B

A

C

D

F

H

E

G

Their glory forgotten, liners
sailed the tides of war as
troopships. Once greyhounds
racing for records, they now
zigzagged to foil submarines;
the pattern below took two
hours, then was repeated.
GI's in life vests jam Queen
Mary's deck to cut casualties
in case of attack—an affront
this Queen never suffered.

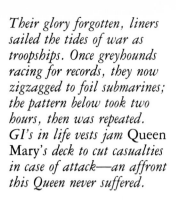

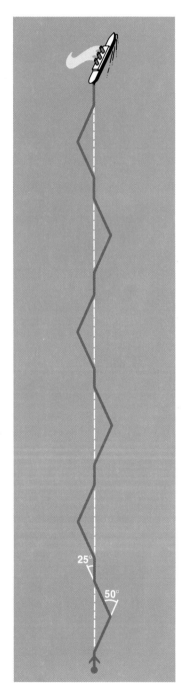

25°

50°

American soldiers dine—or, in military argot, mess— 2,000 at a time in the Queen Mary's onetime first-class restaurant. Bunks like bookshelves packed them into once-roomy cabins; 12 could sleep, or try to, in a room meant for a wealthy few. Thus refitted, the Queen Mary could hold 16,000 troops.

immigrants had contributed much of the companies' revenues. But the United States had severely restricted immigration, and that action virtually killed the steerage trade.

So the early twenties were a lean time for passenger shipping. And Prohibition made it especially difficult for an American ship to earn her keep. Passengers avoided "dry" ships as if they had been plague ships. "As you sail away," beckoned a French Line brochure, "far beyond the range of amendments and thou-shalt-nots, those dear little iced things begin to appear. . . . Utterly French, utterly harmless—and oh so gurglingly good!"

The way out of these doldrums lay in adapting to social change. If there were fewer rich men willing to pay for luxurious travel, and fewer immigrants, there were many more people of moderate means who wanted to travel in modest comfort, and many more students who wanted to get abroad cheaply. To cater to them, more modest classes had traditionally been available between the gilded splendor of first and the spartan facilities of steerage. But why not also upgrade the old steerage class and rename it "tourist"? It might even be possible to persuade the public that "tourist" travel was chic.

Companies began to build a new generation of great liners. North German Lloyd led the way with the *Bremen,* and a little later the *Europa*—both ships a little clinical in their fittings, but easily the fastest ships afloat in the late twenties and early thirties. Both went into service before the Great Depression slowed the shipping business. The French Line was less lucky with its peerless *Normandie,* but the French government kept her going with an immense

Reigns Of the Atlantic Queens

	Name		Maiden Voyage†	Length (Ft.)	Gross Tonnage	Service Speed (knots)	Name Change	Last Voyage†	Fate
Great Britain									
Cunard Line	Mauretania (I)*		1907	790	31,938	25		1934	1935 scrapped
	Lusitania*		1907	790	31,550	25		1915	1915 torpedoed and sunk
	Aquitania		1914	902	45,647	23		1949	1950 scrapped
White Star Line	Olympic		1911	882	45,324	21		1934	1937 scrapped
	Titanic		1912	883	46,329	21		1912	1912 hit an iceberg and sank
Cunard-White Star Line	Queen Mary*		1936	1,020	80,774	29		1967	museum and hotel at Long Beach, California
	Queen Elizabeth		1946	1,031	83,673	29		1968	1972 destroyed by fire
	Queen Elizabeth 2 (QE2)		1969	963	65,863	28.5			still in service
Germany									
Hamburg American Line	Deutschland (III)*		1900	684	16,502	22	1911 Victoria Luise; 1920 Hansa (II)	1924	1925 scrapped
	Vaterland (I)		1914	950	54,282	23	1923 Leviathan (United States Lines)	1934	1938 scrapped
	Bismarck		1922	956	56,551	23	1922 Majestic (II) (White Star Line); 1937 HMS Caledonia	1936	1939 burned and sank
N. German Lloyd Line	Kaiser Wilhelm II (II)*		1903	707	19,361	23	1917 Agamemnon (U. S. Government); 1927 Monticello (U. S. Shipping Board)	1914	1940 scrapped
	Europa*		1930	937	49,746	27	1946 Liberté (French Line)	1961	1962 scrapped
France									
French Line	France (II)		1912	713	23,666	24		1932	1935 scrapped
	Ile de France		1927	793	43,153	23		1958	1959 scrapped
	Normandie (II)*		1935	1,029	79,280	29		1939	1942 destroyed by fire
	France (III)		1962	1,035	66,348	34	1980 Norway (Norwegian Caribbean Line)	1974	cruise ship
Italy									
Italian Line	Rex*		1932	880	51,062	28		1940	1944 bombed and sunk
	Conte di Savoia		1932	815	48,502	27		1940	1943 bombed and sunk
United States									
United States Lines	America (II)		1946	723	33,532	22	1964 Australis (Chandris); 1978 America (Venture Cruise); 1978 Italis (Chandris)	1978	sold for hotel ship
	United States*		1952	990	53,329	35		1969	awaiting sale at Norfolk, Virginia

*Blue Riband   †Transatlantic   †Transatlantic

loan. She was launched in 1932, and in the opinion of many admirers she was the greatest passenger ship ever built.

Her life was tragically short. In the course of conversion into a troop transport in New York, she caught fire. The fire fighters, hampered by brisk winds and freezing temperatures, poured so much water into her that she capsized. She was then not worth the cost of restoration and eventually was scrapped in 1946.

The two great Cunard ships, the *Queen Mary* and the even bigger but slightly slower *Queen Elizabeth*, lacked the slim, elegant beauty of the *Normandie* and probably never evoked quite the enthusiastic affection she did. But they commanded immense respect. The *Queen Mary* had served only three years on the Atlantic run, and the *Queen Elizabeth* was still fitting out, when World War II erupted. Both ships became troop transports, each of them capable of carrying a whole division.

They sailed alone, without convoy, trusting for their safety in speed and secrecy. People along the Clyde still recall vividly the appearance of these great gray ghosts at their moorings off the Tail of the Bank. They moved with the silence and stealthy speed of elephants in forest cover. No one ever seemed to see them come or go. Early in the morning one or the other—never both at once—would be there; a few mornings later she would be gone. They led charmed lives—or was it good security, good handling qualities, superb seamanship? They handled like yachts and rode like picketboats. On one occasion—after the war, back on the passenger run—the *Queen Mary* arrived in New York to find

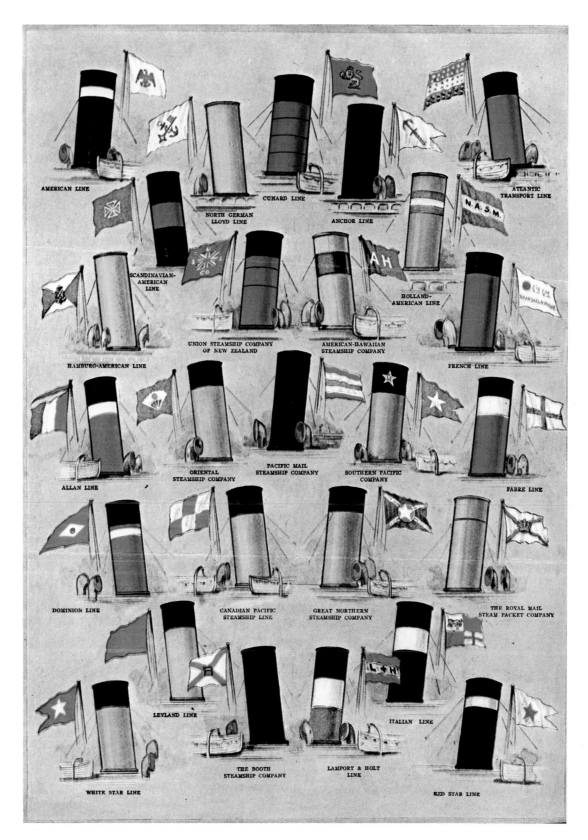

Lore and legend rode aloft on the flags and funnels of the shipping companies. Custom varied in the days of sail; a vessel might fly the flags of her owners, her master, or her expedition leader. By the early 1800's, companies dominated sea trade. Banners called house flags fluttered from their fleets like trademarks. Early steamers, their stacks often hidden by sails and rigging, added a pennant to show they were steam powered, a custom still honored in modern times. Funnels finally flew the colors too, as do these from around the turn of the 20th century.

303

New York near mid-century got a last grand glimpse of glory: Independence, *then* America *(II),* United States, Olympia, *the aircraft carrier* Intrepid, Mauretania *(II),* Sylvania, *and the* Queen Elizabeth *with her tugs. Of these, only the* Sylvania, *renamed* Fairwind, *still sails.*

304   the tugs all on strike. Her captain, G. T. Marr, sent lines ashore in his own boats and berthed his ship, all 81,000 tons of her, with his own engines. A miscalculation of a foot or two might have carried away the whole pier.

The *Queens* rendered another 20 years of transatlantic service, but by the 1960's they were carrying fewer and fewer passengers. Air travel was cheaper and faster; fewer people would pay to travel slowly and comfortably. The *Queen Mary* was sold in 1967 to become a museum and hotel; her sister caught fire and sank in 1972 at Hong Kong.

The *Queens* were not quite the last of their kind. The steely, efficient *United States* broke the *Queen Mary*'s Blue Riband record in 1952, and holds the record still. The *Queen Elizabeth 2* is a compact, computerized successor to her great namesake. The queenly *France* and the elegant ships of the Italian Line were notable additions to the postwar transatlantic liner fleet.

It seems unlikely that ships will ever again be the regular means of crossing the Atlantic. Gone is the time when travel meant the thrill and risk of weeks on the open sea. Gone are the days when an adventurous youth could ship out for two years before the mast. No longer does the majesty of the sailing ships enrich our commercial life. No more do the great liners furrow the waves in mighty fleets, cleaving to the tyranny of schedule, predictable and proud. Today's big passenger vessels have launched a golden age of their own, as cruise ships. The era of the transatlantic liners may be past, but nothing can diminish what these titans of sail and steam have bequeathed to the lore and romance of the sea.

Nautical Terms

Most nautical terms listed here are explained in the text and appear in the index. Some of the major types of sailing vessels—and their principal spars and sails—are illustrated on pages 228-229. Selected ancient and medieval vessels appear on pages 32-33. See also cutaway drawings on pages 66-67, 82-83, and 116-117.

306

Aback. A condition in which the wind blows on the forward side of a sail, tending to pivot or drive a ship backward.

Aft. The stern, or after, end of a ship or boat.

Balanced Rudder. A rudder with part of its area forward of the pivot point.

Battens. Wooden strips used to stiffen a sail; commonly seen on Chinese junks.

Beat. To work a vessel into the wind by taking successive zigzag courses, or tacks.

Belaying pin. A wood or metal pin to which the running, or adjustable, rigging is secured. Often used as a club in shipboard brawls.

Bend. To secure a sail to a yard or other spar. To tie the ends of ropes together.

Bilge. The lowest part of a ship's hull, near the keel, where water seeping aboard collects and can be pumped out.

Billet. An assigned place to sleep, usually determined by a crewman's rank or position.

Binnacle. The protective housing in which a ship's compass is kept.

Block. A mariner's pulley. Blocks with a line running through them form a tackle.

Boom. The spar that holds the foot, or bottom, of a fore-and-aft sail.

Bow. Forward end of a ship.

Bowsprit. The heavy spar projecting from the bow of a sailing ship.

Braces. Lines attached to the yardarms which control their angle to the wind.

Bulkhead. A wall or partition within a ship's hull.

Bulwark. A solid rail enclosing a ship's upper deck.

Bunt. The middle section of a yard or of a square sail.

Buntlines. Lines attached to the foot of a square sail that enable it to be hauled up to the yard for furling.

Capstan. A winch, usually located on the forecastle, with a vertically mounted shaft, used to heave anchors or hoist yards. See windlass.

Careen. To heave down, or tip, a vessel on its side so that the bottom can be cleaned and repaired.

Channel. A wooden platform projecting from the hull of a sailing vessel that spreads the shrouds and keeps them clear of the bulwark.

Chock. A U-shaped fitting, usually mounted on a ship's bulwark, through which passes a line or mooring hawser.

Claw off. To sail toward the wind in order to avoid running aground.

Cleat. A T-shaped fitting to which a line is belayed, or fastened.

Clew lines. Lines that control the lower corners of a square sail.

Coaming. The elevated lip of a hatchway or other deck opening.

Copper. A soft-metal sheathing attached to the underwater portions of a hull to keep it from fouling and to protect it from shipworms.

Counter. The sloping, curved underside of a vessel's hull aft of the sternpost.

Crimp. One who recruits men for a merchant ship through trickery, intoxication, or other devious means.

Crossjack. Pronounced crowjik; the lowest horizontal yard on the mizzenmast.

Davits. Cranes projecting over a ship's side by which its boats are raised or lowered.

Deadeye. A round wooden block, pierced by three holes, used to set up shrouds and stays.

Draft. The depth of water required to float a boat or ship.

Fairlead. A fixture or fitting that guides a rope in the desired direction.

Falls. The lines by which a ship's boats are hoisted or lowered from their davits.

Fathom. Six feet of water depth.

Fine entry. A sharp, concave bow.

Fore. The forward, or bow, end of a ship or boat.

Forecastle. Pronounced fo'c'sle; the raised deck at a ship's bow. Also the crew's quarters.

Furl. To roll up and secure a sail to its yard or boom.

Gaff. The spar set at an angle to the mast that supports the head, or top, of a fore-and-aft sail.

Gantline. A line used to raise and lower a man or a sail.

Gaskets. Short lengths of rope used to secure a sail that has been furled.

Gripes. Lashings that hold a boat securely in its davits or on deck.

Gunwales. Pronounced gunnels; the uppermost strakes of a hull that form the rail or bulwark.

Halyards. Ropes used to hoist sails and yards.

Handspike. A wooden bar used as a lever or crowbar on shipboard.

Hawser. A heavy line, or rope, used to tow a vessel or tie it to a dock.

Heave to. To halt the forward movement of a vessel by swinging it bow first into the wind.

Hold. The lower spaces of the hull used for cargo stowage.

Hull. The body of a vessel.

Jibboom. The spar fastened to and extending beyond the bowsprit of a sailing ship.

Jibe. To swing off unexpectedly on another tack while running with the wind, causing the boom to swing violently from one side of the ship to the other.

Jump ship. To desert or improperly leave a ship.

Keel. The backbone of a vessel. From it rise the frames, or ribs, and the stempost and sternpost.

Knee. A right-angled length of wood or iron used to support beams perpendicular to one another.

Knot. A measure of speed equal to one nautical mile per hour.

Landfall. The first sighting of land when coming in from the sea.

Lee. The side sheltered or facing away from the wind.

Leeward. Pronounced looward; downwind, situated away from the wind.

Maiden voyage. A ship's first voyage after it has passed sea trials and has been accepted for service.

Masthead. The top of a mast.

Nautical mile. A linear measure of distance equal to approximately 6,080 feet, or 1.15 statute miles.

Pitch. The fore-and-aft rocking motion of a ship that rides head on into the waves.

Poop. The raised deck at the stern of a ship.

Port. The left-hand side of a vessel, as you face the bow. Formerly called larboard.

Press-gang. A group of men empowered to force able-bodied men into naval service aboard a warship.

Quarterdeck. The upper deck from the mainmast to the stern.

Rake. The angle from the perpendicular of a mast, funnel, stem, or sternpost.

Reach. To sail with the wind blowing from the side.

Reef. To reduce the sail area exposed to the wind. To "shorten sail."

Reeve. To pass the end of a rope through a hole or opening.

Roll. The side-to-side movement of a vessel riding parallel to the waves.

Round to. To bring a ship's bow into the wind, as when heaving to or anchoring.

Run. To sail with the wind astern or nearly so.

Run the easting down. To sail in an easterly direction before a westerly wind.

Secure. To tie or make fast so that unwanted movement cannot take place.

Sheets. The lines used for trimming or easing a sail.

Shrouds. Rope or cable rigging that provides lateral support for a mast.

Spar. A general term applied to a ship's masts, yards, gaffs, and booms.

Starboard. The right-hand side of a vessel, as you face the bow.

Stays. Fixed ropes or cables that support a mast fore-and-aft.

Stem. The foremost upright timber of a ship's bow joined to the keel.

Stern. Rear end of a ship.

Sternpost. The vertical timber attached to the after end of the keel.

Stokehole. The compartment in which a steamship's boilers are located.

Stow. To put gear in its proper place.

Strakes. The horizontal side planks of a wooden vessel.

Tackle. Often pronounced taykle; the ropes and blocks, or pulleys, rigged to lift a heavy weight.

Thwart. The transverse seat in a boat.

Topmast. The section of mast immediately above the lower mast.

Topgallant mast. Pronounced t'gallant; the topmost section of a three-section mast.

Transom. The transverse planking that forms the stern of a boat or ship.

Tumble home. The inward curve of the upper part of a ship's hull that makes the upper deck narrower than the lower decks.

'Tween decks. Any deck between the upper and lowest decks.

Waist. The upper deck of a ship between the poop and the forecastle.

Warp. To move or haul a vessel, usually by winding in its anchor cable.

Watch. The duty periods into which a seaman's day is divided.

Way. The movement of a ship under power or sail, as in "under way."

Weather deck. A deck unshielded from the elements, usually the uppermost deck or decks.

Weigh. To raise the anchor.

Windlass. A winch with a horizontal shaft used for hauling heavy objects. See capstan.

Windward. The side or direction from which the wind blows.

Yard. A spar that crosses the mast and from which a sail is set.

Yaw. A combination rolling and pitching motion, as when a vessel quarters the waves.

Yellow metal. A copper-zinc alloy used to sheathe the underwater portion of a wooden hull.

Museums and Ships to Visit

The saga of man's encounter with the sea lives on in museums around the world. London's Science Museum, the Museum of the City of New York, Washington's Smithsonian Institution, and others offer maritime treasures. This sampling represents the countless museums that specialize in chronicling man's life at sea.

NORTH AMERICA

Penobscot Marine Museum Searsport, Maine. Paintings, prints, photographs, logbooks, maps, charts, models, shipbuilding tools, navigation instruments, whaling memorabilia, knot work.

Maine Maritime Museum Bath, Maine. Paintings, photographs, models, nautical instruments, trade goods, seamen's possessions.

Peabody Museum Salem, Mass. Paintings, photographs, models, scrimshaw, figureheads, fishing gear, navigation instruments, shipbuilding tools, shipboard lighting devices.

Francis Russell Hart Nautical Museum Cambridge, Mass. Ship plans, paintings, prints, drawings, photographs, models, engines.

Whaling Museum New Bedford, Mass. Paintings, prints, logbooks, maps, models, ship carvings, whaling relics, reproductions of whaling craft shops. Whaling museums also at Cold Spring Harbor and Sag Harbor, N.Y., and at Chatham, Nantucket, and Sharon, Mass.

Mystic Seaport Museum Mystic, Conn. Re-created 19th-century seafaring community. Craftsmen fashion mast hoops, barrels, ship carvings. *Charles W. Morgan,* last surviving wooden whaler; square-rigger *Joseph Conrad;* fishing schooner *L. A. Dunton;* sloops *Nellie, Estella A, Annie, Emma C. Berry.*

South Street Seaport Museum New York, N.Y. Nineteenth-century waterfront "street of ships." Photographs, models, ships' gear. Square-riggers *Peking* and *Wavertree,* schooner *Pioneer,* fishing schooner *Lettie G. Howard, Ambrose* lightship.

Philadelphia Maritime Museum Philadelphia, Pa. Maritime heritage of the Delaware River Valley. Prints, paintings, maps, models, scrimshaw, whaling implements, figureheads, underwater exhibit. Floating barge houses a boatbuilding workshop and Delaware River small craft.

U. S. Naval Academy Museum Annapolis, Md. Paintings, prints, models, nautical instruments, flags, weapons, uniforms, personal memorabilia of naval officers, John Paul Jones mementos.

Chesapeake Bay Maritime Museum St. Michael's, Md. Paintings, logbooks, models, antique engines, navigation instruments. Sailing log canoes, log-built bugeye *Edna E. Lockwood,* skipjack *Rosie Parks.*

Navy Memorial Museum Washington, D. C. Paintings, artifacts, and exhibits trace two centuries of U. S. naval history.

The Mariners' Museum Newport News, Va. Paintings, engravings, photographs, hall of models, gallery of miniature models, figureheads, ship decorations and accessories, navigation instruments, weapons, uniforms, medals, flags, sailors' handiwork and personal belongings, tools, whaling and fishing equipment, scrimshaw, lighthouse and lifesaving apparatus.

National Maritime Museum San Francisco, Calif. Paintings, prints, photographs, models, navigation instruments, scrimshaw, figureheads, marine steam engines, recordings of old-time shipowners and seafarers. Cape Horner *Balclutha,* lumber schooner *C. A. Thayer,* steam schooner *Wapama,* walking-beam ferry *Eureka,* paddle tug *Eppleton Hall,* steam tug *Hercules,* scow schooner *Alma.*

Maritime Museum Vancouver, B. C., Canada. Photographs and artifacts trace the maritime history of British Columbia and the northwest Pacific. *St. Roch,* first ship to navigate the Northwest Passage both ways.

Maritime Museum of the Atlantic Halifax, N. S., Canada. Models, paintings, and exhibits illustrate wooden shipbuilding and the age of sail; reconstructed ship's chandlery.

Fisheries Museum of the Atlantic Lunenburg, N. S., Canada. Fishing exhibits, mementos of the racing schooner *Bluenose.* Dory schooner *Theresa E. Connor,* fish dragger *Cape North,* rumrunner *Reo II.*

Bermuda Maritime Museum Sandy's Parish, Bermuda. Exhibits range from relics of island whaling days to jewels salvaged from shipwrecks. Dinghies, pilot gigs.

Museum of Military and Naval History San Juan, Puerto Rico. Maps, models, weapons, flags, and uniforms housed in a 1595 coastal defense fort.

SOUTH AMERICA

Museu Naval Rio de Janeiro, Brazil. Models, uniforms, personal belongings, and other artifacts tell the story of Brazil's Navy.

Museo Naval Viña del Mar, Chile. Paintings, photographs, models, fishing relics and equipment.

Museo Naval de la Nación Buenos Aires, Argentina. Paintings, maps, models, uniforms, arms, and battle flags depict Argentine naval history.

EUROPE

National Maritime Museum Greenwich, England. Paintings, maps, photographs, Admiralty ship plans, models, figureheads, stern carvings, ship fittings, Harrison's and Kendall's chronometers, globes, astrolabes, relics of Nelson and Cook, royal barges, swords, medals, uniforms. Old Royal Observatory.

Town Docks Museum Hull, England. Paintings, models, fishing and shipping relics, figureheads, whaling memorabilia.

Exeter Maritime Museum Exeter, England. Welsh coracles, Irish curraghs, Cornish fishing lugger, pearling dhow from Bahrain, sampans from Rangoon.

Vikingskipshuset Oslo, Norway. Ninth-century Gokstad, Tune, and Oseberg ships, and the Viking artifacts buried with them.

Norsk Sjøfartsmuseum Oslo, Norway. Exhibits show development of ships and man's use of the sea. Polar exploration ship *Gjöa.*

Statens Sjöhistoriska Museum Stockholm, Sweden. Paintings, charts, models, nautical instruments, weapons, uniforms, relics of the China trade. Warship *Vasa.*

Ålands Sjöfartsmuseum Mariehamn, Finland. Paintings, figureheads, ships' bells, nautical instruments. Bark *Pommern.*

Handels-og Søfartsmuseet Helsingør, Denmark. Paintings, photographs, charts, models, navigation instruments, lifesaving apparatus, shipbuilding tools. Greenland umiak.

Vikingeskibshallen Roskilde, Denmark. Viking ships salvaged from a fjord: a deep-sea trader, ferry, longship, merchant ship, warship.

Centralne Muzeum Morskie Gdańsk, Poland. Exhibits detail the growth of Poland's maritime economy and technology.

Deutsches Schiffahrtsmuseum Bremerhaven, West Germany. Exhibits range from the 14th-century Bremen cog, the only surviving example of a major medieval merchantman, to a luxury cabin from an ocean liner. Three-masted bark *Seute Deern;* steam whaler; *Grönland,* sailing ship that carried first German expedition to the North Pole.

Nederlands Scheepvaart Museum Amsterdam, The Netherlands. Paintings, prints, engravings, photographs, atlases, charts, ship plans, models, tools, navigation instruments, globes, weapons, medals, seals, flags, ship ornaments, English and Spanish booty.

Marine Museum Den Helder, The Netherlands. Photographs, models, and weapons of the Royal Netherlands Navy.

Nationaal Scheepvaartmuseum Antwerp, Belgium. History of European navigation from prehistoric times: paintings, photographs, maps, models, sailors' handiwork, ship decorations, uniforms, medals.

Musée de la Marine Paris, France. Paintings, relics of French navigators, ancient models, yachting exhibits.

Musée de Saint Malo France. Paintings, maps, models, ships in bottles, trade goods, and sailors' souvenirs housed in a dungeon.

Musée de la Marine Marseilles, France. Exhibits detail the maritime history of Marseilles as well as France's colonial empire.

Museo Naval Madrid, Spain. Manuscripts of Spanish explorers, 16th-century navigation books, charts, paintings, models, sculpture, weapons, globes, medals.

Museo Maritimo Barcelona, Spain. Paintings, charts, engravings, maps, sculpture, models, ships in bottles, anchors, weapons, seamen's knots.

Museu de Marinha Lisbon, Portugal. Paintings, models of discoverers' ships, royal barges, figureheads, guns, uniforms.

Civico Museo Navale Genoa-Pegli, Italy. Paintings, engravings, charts, models, figureheads, artillery pieces, nautical instruments.

Museo Storico Navale Venice, Italy. Paintings, photographs, models, anchors, weapons.

Museo del Mare Trieste, Italy. Charts, logbooks, models, fishing equipment, navigation instruments.

Pomorski Muzej Dubrovnik, Yugoslavia. Paintings, maps, models, nautical instruments.

SHIPS TO VISIT

Grand Banks fishing schooner *Sherman Zwicker,* Boothbay Harbor, Maine; brig *Beaver II,* reproduction of one of the Tea Party ships, Boston, Mass.; U. S. Frigate *Constitution,* "Old Ironsides," Boston; *Mayflower II,* reproduction of the kind of merchantman that carried the Pilgrims, Plymouth, Mass.; *Rose,* reconstruction of a British Revolutionary War frigate, New Bedford, Mass.; reproduction of the Continental sloop *Providence,* John Paul Jones's first command, Newport, R.I.; square-rigged warship *Niagara,* Erie, Pa.; U. S. Frigate *Constellation,* fought Barbary pirates and in War of 1812, Baltimore, Md.; *Maryland Dove,* reproduction of one of two ships that carried Maryland's first settlers, St. Mary's City, Md.; *Philadelphia,* oldest surviving American warship, Smithsonian Institution, Washington, D. C.; reproductions of *Susan Constant, Godspeed,* and *Discovery,* merchantmen that brought the first English colonists to Virginia, Jamestown, Va.; square-rigged ketch *Adventure,* Charleston, S.C.; reproduction of *Bounty,* seized by mutineers in 1789, St. Petersburg, Fla.; copy of Gokstad Viking ship, Chicago, Ill.; three-masted schooner *Wawona,* Seattle, Wash.; *Queen Mary,* Cunard liner, now a museum and floating hotel, Long Beach, Calif.; square-rigger *Star of India,* San Diego, Calif.; square-rigger *Falls of Clyde,* Honolulu, Hawaii; *Nonsuch,* reproduction of a 17th-century ketch, Winnipeg, Man., Canada; H.M.S. *Victory,* Nelson's flagship, Portsmouth, England; *Cutty Sark,* last China tea clipper, Greenwich, England; *Gipsy Moth III,* yacht in which Sir Francis Chichester sailed around the world alone, Greenwich; H.M.S. *Discovery,* Scott's antarctic ship, London, England; *Great Britain,* pioneer iron steamship, Bristol, England; *Turbinia,* first turbine vessel, Newcastle upon Tyne, England; Thor Heyerdahl's transpacific raft *Kon Tiki* and transatlantic papyrus boat *Ra II,* Oslo, Norway; polar exploration ship *Fram,* Oslo; ironclad warship *Buffel,* Rotterdam, The Netherlands; Kyrenia ship, Greek hull from the fourth century B.C., Kyrenia, Cyprus; 4,500-year-old funerary boat of Cheops, near Cairo, Egypt.

Acknowledgments

308

We wish to thank the many nautical experts and historians in the United States and abroad who generously contributed time and knowledge to the making of *Romance of the Sea,* especially Lt. Comdr. J. A. Barker and Cpl. Dave Kirkby, H.M.S. *Victory;* Comdr. J. R. Blake, S.S. Great Britain Project; Laura F. Brown, Steamship Historical Society of America; Robert S. Brown, Venore Transportation Company; W. F. J. Mörzer Bruyns, Nederlands Scheepvaart Museum, Amsterdam; John P. Eaton and Charles A. Haas, Titanic Historical Society; Dr. J. H. Elliott, Princeton University; Kathy Flynn, Peabody Museum of Salem; Ulla Garell, Vasa Museum, Stockholm; Capt. Irving Johnson; Rear Adm. John D. H. Kane, Jr., Dr. W. J. Morgan, and John C. Reilly, Jr., Naval Historical Center, Washington Navy Yard; J. B. Kist, Rijksmuseum, Amsterdam; Karl Kortum, National Maritime Museum, San Francisco; Mary R. Maynard, Mystic Seaport Museum, Conn.; Dr. James G. Mead, Smithsonian Institution; Lois Olgesby, The Mariners' Museum, Newport News; Stephen M. Riley and Lionel Willis, National Maritime Museum, Greenwich; Dr. Edouard A. Stackpole, Peter Foulger Museum, Nantucket; Sir James Watt.

Bibliography

Books of wide scope we found useful included *Five Centuries of Famous Ships* by Robert G. Albion, *Colonial Vessels* and *Sloops & Shallops* by William A. Baker, *Illustrated History of Ships and Boats* by Lionel Casson, *American Small Sailing Craft* and *The History of American Sailing Ships* by Howard I. Chapelle, and *The History of Piracy* by Philip Gosse.

We also consulted original accounts of early explorations published by The Hakluyt Society, *The Oxford Companion to Ships and the Sea* edited by Peter Kemp, *The Ship* by Björn Landström, *The Influence of Sea Power Upon History 1660-1783* by A. T. Mahan, *The Age of Reconnaissance* and *Trade and Dominion* by J. H. Parry, *Command of the Sea* by Clark G. Reynolds, and The Seafarers series by Time-Life Books.

For information on the evolution of boats and ships we used *A History of Seafaring Based on Underwater Archaeology* edited by George F. Bass, *Archaeology of the Boat* by Basil Greenhill, *Water Transport* by James Hornell, *The Sea-craft of Prehistory* by Paul Johnstone, and *Archeology under Water* edited by Keith Muckelroy.

Works about the Great Age of Discovery included *The Life of Ferdinand Magellan* by F. H. H. Guillemard, *Admiral of the Ocean Sea* and *The European Discovery of America* by Samuel Eliot Morison, and *The Portuguese Pioneers* by Edgar Prestage.

For accounts of the trading empires we turned to *The Dutch Seaborne Empire 1600-1800* and *The Portuguese Seaborne Empire 1415-1825* by C. R. Boxer, *Conquest and Commerce* and *Portuguese Brazil* by James Lang, and *The Spanish Seaborne Empire* by J. H. Parry.

Sources for the Second Age of Discovery were *The Journals of Captain James Cook on His Voyages of Discovery* edited by J. C. Beaglehole, *The Exploration of the Pacific* and *The Life of Captain James Cook* by J. C. Beaglehole, *Greenwich Time and the Discovery of the Longitude* by Derek Howse, and *Captain James Cook* by Alan Villiers.

Books on the emergence of navies included *The Armada* by Garrett Mattingly, *John Paul Jones* and *"Old Bruin" Commodore Matthew Calbraith Perry* by Samuel Eliot Morison, *Nelson* by Carola Oman, and *Naval Warfare Under Oars* by William Ledyard Rodgers.

For material about fishing and whaling we used *The Cod Fisheries* by Harold Innis, *The Cod* by Albert C. Jensen, *The Sea-Hunters* by Edouard A. Stackpole, and *History of the American Whale Fishery* by Alexander Starbuck.

Assistance with the chapter on clippers came from *Greyhounds of the Sea* by Carl C. Cutler, *Clipper Ships of America and Great Britain 1833-1869* by Helen La Grange, *The Last of the Windjammers* by Basil Lubbock, and *The China Bird* and *The Tea Clippers* by David R. MacGregor.

References for the chapter on packets and ocean liners included *Square-Riggers on Schedule* by Robert G. Albion, *North Atlantic Seaway* by N. R. P. Bonsor, *Lives of the Liners* by Frank O. Braynard, *Sway of the Grand Saloon* by John M. Brinnin, and *The Only Way to Cross* by John Maxtone-Graham.

Illustrations Credits

The following abbreviations are used in this list:
(t)—top; (b)—bottom; (l)—left; (r)—right; (c)—center; ca—circa. Also BM—British Museum, London; BN—Bibliothèque Nationale, Paris; KWM—Kendall Whaling Museum, Sharon, Mass.; LC—Library of Congress; MHS—Maryland Historical Society, Baltimore; MM—The Mariners' Museum, Newport News, Va.; MMA—Metropolitan Museum of Art, New York; MSM—Mystic Seaport Museum, Conn.; NBWM—New Bedford Whaling Museum, Mass.; NGL—National Geographic Library; NGP—National Geographic Photographer; NGS—National Geographic Staff; NSM—Nederlands Scheepvaart Museum, Amsterdam; NMM—National Maritime Museum, Greenwich, England; NYPL—New York Public Library; PMS—Peabody Museum of Salem, Mass.; SI—Smithsonian Institution; USNA—U. S. Naval Academy Museum, Annapolis, Md.

All maps are by Robert Hynes and National Geographic Art. End sheets, Hezekiah Frasier, Colonial Williamsburg Foundation. Pages 4,5-*Pride of Baltimore,* Robert deGast. 6,7-*Mercator,* J. Baylor Roberts.

From Boats to Ships
8,10(t)-Raghubir Singh. 10(b), 11(t)-BM. 10,11-Loren McIntyre. 12-Adam Woolfitt. 13(t)-LC. 13(b)-Robert W. Madden, NGP. 14-Thomas Nebbia. 15(t)-Guy Mary-Rousselière. 15(b)-George F. Mobley, NGP. 16,17-Cotton Coulson, Susan Griggs Agency. 18-Herb Kawainui Kane. 19(l)-Frank Wandell. 19(r)-Walter Meayers Edwards. 20-John G. Ross. 21-Victor R. Boswell, Jr., NGP. 22,23-Farrell Grehan. 24-BM. 25-Ny Carlsberg Glyptotek, Copenhagen. 26-Bates Littlehales, NGP. 26,27-Jonathan S. Blair. 28,29-Adam Woolfitt. 29(t)-State Historical Museum, Stockholm: Ted Spiegel. 30-NMM. 31-BN. 32,33-Wayne McLoughlin, based on drawings by Björn Landström from *The Ship,* New York, 1967. 34-Robert Harding Associates. 35-W. E. Garrett, NGS. 36-Thomas J. Abercrombie, NGS. 37(l)-David Cupp. 37(r)-Marion Kaplan. 38,39-Dick Durrance II.

Across the Boundless Sea
40-School of Joachim Patinir, 1485-1524; NMM. 42-NYPL. 43-Bettmann Archive. 44-Attributed to Nuno Gonçalves, ca 1458; Museu Nacional de Arte Antiga, Lisbon. 45-Thomas Nebbia. 46-Bastiam Lopez; British Library, London. 47-Jim Wells. 48,49-James L. Stanfield, NGP. 49(t) & inset-Collection of Mr. and Mrs. Paul Tishman. 49(b)-Collection of Peggy Appiah. 51-Museum of Mankind, London: Derek Bayes. 52,53-James P. Blair, NGP. 54-Museu de Marinha, Lisbon: Thomas Nebbia. 55-Academia das Ciências de Lisboa.

56(t)-Sociedade de Geografia de Lisboa. 56,57-Marion Kaplan. 58(t)-Attributed to Ridolfo Ghirlandaio, 16th century; Civico Museo Navale Genova-Pegli. 59-NMM: Ship model built by Dr. Robert M. Rose, on loan to NMM: Adam Woolfitt. 60-Théodore de Bry, 1590; NYPL. 61-Adam Woolfitt. 62,63-Théodore de Bry, 1592; LC. 64(t)-Real Academia de Bellas Artes de San Fernando, Madrid. 64(b)-John Carter Brown Library, Brown University. 65-Gordon W. Gahan, NGP. 66,67-Lionel J. Willis. 68-MMA. 70-Bruce Dale, NGP. 71(l)-Yale University Library: Bruce Dale, NGP. 71(r)-David S. Boyer, NGS. 72,73-John White, ca 1580; BM. 74,75-Johann Théodore de Bry, 1601; NGL.

Riding the Trade Winds

76-"Ships Trading in the East" by H. C. Vroom, 1614; NMM. 78-Miniature from 14th-century edition of Marco Polo's *Le Livre des Merveilles*; BN. 78,79-Johann Théodore de Bry, 1598; NGL. 81-Théodore de Bry, 1596; John Judkyn Memorial, Freshford Manor, Bath. 82,83-Lionel J. Willis. 84,85-Gordon W. Gahan, NGP. 86,87-Lloyd K. Townsend, Jr. 87-Jonathan S. Blair. 88,89-Farrell Grehan. 90,91-David Alan Harvey, NGP. 91-BM. 92(t)-Culver Pictures. 92(b)-LC. 92,93-BN. 94,95-Gordon W. Gahan, NGP. 94(b)-Liverpool City Libraries. 96-BM. 97-Etching by J. Mulder, ca 1690; NSM. 98-Victoria and Albert Museum, London. 99-Detail of a painting by Emperor Hui Tsung, 1082-1135; Museum of Fine Arts, Boston. 100,101-"Dutch Fleet at St. Helena" by C. Verbeeck, 17th century; NSM. 102-Walter Meayers Edwards. 104-From *Civitates Orbis Terrarum*; MMA. 105-Gift of Mrs. Albert Blum; MMA. 106,107-H. C. Vroom, 1614; NSM. 107-India Office Library, London. 108-NMM. 109-Winfield Parks.

Quest in the "Other Sea"

110-Engraving after Sydney Parkinson, 1769; Collection of Luis Marden. 112,113-From *Voyages Round the World* by George William Anderson, 1784; NGL. 114(l)-John Webber, 1776; National Art Gallery, Wellington. 115-NMM. 116,117-Lionel J. Willis. 118-Eva Cropp. 119(t)-Sydney Parkinson, 1770; The Rex Nan Kivell Collection, National Library of Australia, Canberra. 119(b)-Virgil Kauffman. 120(l)-Alexander Turnbull Library, Wellington. 120(r)-David Moore, Black Star. 121-William Hodges, 1774; Cooper Bridgman Library, NMM. 122-George Forster, 1772; British Museum of Natural History, London. 122,123-William R. Curtsinger. 124-NMM. 125-David Hiser. 126,127-Aquatint after R. Dodd, ca 1790; NMM. 127-Luis Marden. 128-Sally Anne Thompson, Animal Photography. 129-Radio Times Hulton Picture Library. 130,131-"H.M.S. *Terror* in the Ice" by W. H. Smythe, 1788-1865; NMM.

Wolves and Shepherds

134-H. C. Vroom, 1617; Rijksmuseum-Stichting, Amsterdam. 136-Ted Spiegel. 137(l)-Nicholas Hilliard, 1581; Kunsthistorisches Museum, Vienna. 137(r)-Gordon W. Gahan, NGP. 138-Robert Adams, 1588; NMM. 139-"The Defeat of the Armada" by P. J. de Loutherbourg, 1796; NMM, on loan to Royal Hospital School, Suffolk. 140(l&c)-Statens Sjöhistoriska Museum, Stockholm. 140(r)-Winfield Parks. 141-"*Resolution*" by Willem van de Velde the Younger, 1667; Cooper Bridgman Library, NMM. 142-NMM. 143-Wayne McLoughlin. 144-Lemuel F. Abbott, 1798; Lloyd's of London. 144,145-Clarkson Stanfield, 1836; United Service and Royal Aero Club, London. 146 through 151-Adam Woolfitt. 152-William H. Meyers, 1842; Bancroft Library, University of California, Berkeley. 153-Etching after Samuel Collins, 1790; NMM. 154,155-"Midshipmen's Berth" by Augustus Earle, 1850; NMM. 156-From *Iconographic Encyclopaedia* by J. G. Heck, 1851; United States Navy Department Library. 157-PMS: Mark Sexton. 158-"*Grand Turk*" by Antoine Roux, 1815; PMS. 159(l)-Diorama by Dwight Franklin; USNA: Joseph H. Bailey, NGS. 159(r)-1814; The Historical Society of Pennsylvania, Philadelphia. 160-Kenneth L. Garrett. 161-Michel Félice Corné, 1752-1845; USNA. 162(t)-From the *Baltimore American and Daily Advertiser*, March 18, 1815; MHS. 162-"Catch Me Who Can" by W. J. Huggins, 1812; MHS. 162,163-Robert de Gast. 164,165-Wayne McLoughlin. 165(l)-Bruce Dale, NGP. 165(b)-NYPL. 166-NMM. 167(l),168,169-From *The Pirates Own Book*, Marine Research Society, Salem, Mass., 1924; LC. 167(r)-From *History of the Pirates of All Nations*, London, 1837; British Library, London. 168-Museum für Hamburg Geschichte: Fischer-Daber. 170-"Burning of the Frigate *Philadelphia* in the Harbor of Tripoli, February 16, 1804" by Edward Moran, 1897; USNA. 171-"Decatur's Attack on Tripoli" by Dennis Malone Carter, 1858; Naval Historical Foundation, Washington, D. C. 172-"Commodore Matthew C. Perry's First Landing in Japan at Kurihama in 1853" by Gessan Ogata, ca 1950; USNA. 172,173-Private collection. 174,175-Yochikazu Ichikowa, ca 1853; LC.

Sea Hunters and Harvesters

176-Lithograph by F. Martens after Garneray, ca 1835; KWM. 178,179-From *A Collection of Voyages and Travels* compiled by Awnsham and John Churchill, Vol. I, London, 1732; NGL. 180,181-From Mrs. Alexander Graham Bell. 182-NBWM. 183-MM. 184,185-NBWM. 186,187-Otis Imboden, NGP. 188-University of Alaska Archives, Fairbanks. 189-NBWM. 190(l)-NBWM. 190(r)-MSM. 191(tl&c)-NBWM: Nicholas Whitman; all others, MSM: Volkmar Wentzel, NGS. 192-NBWM. 193(l)-MSM: Volkmar Wentzel, NGS. 193(r)-NBWM. 194,195-"Shipping in New Bedford" by Albert Van Beest, 1855; NBWM. 195-ca 1850; NBWM. 196-NBWM. 197-From Herman Moll's map of North America, ca 1710; LC. 198 through 201-John de Visser. 202,203-Volkmar Wentzel, NGS. 204-NBWM. 205-From W. R. MacAskill. 206-NBWM. 206,207-"*Livonia* and *Sappho*" by Edward Moran, ca 1871; PMS. 207-New York Yacht Club: Victor R. Boswell, Jr., NGP. 209-David Alan Harvey, NGP.

Flying on Clouds of Canvas

210-Montague Dawson, © Frost and Reed Ltd., London. 213-ca 1780; PMS. 214-Nelson Gallery, Atkins Museum, Kansas City, Missouri. 214,215-The Historical Society of Pennsylvania, Philadelphia. 215-PMS: Mark Sexton. 216(t)-MMA. 216(b),217-PMS. 218,219-James E. Buttersworth, ca 1853; PMS. 219-Thomas Ender, 1818; Bibliothek der Akademie der bildenden Künste, Vienna. 220-Seamen's Bank for Savings, New York. 221-SI.

222-225-Adam Woolfitt. 226,227(b)-NMM. 227(t)-PMS: Mark Sexton. 228, 230-Wayne McLoughlin. 231-Norman M. MacNeil. 232 through 237-Alan Villiers. 238-J. Holst, 1902; Musée International de Long-Cours Cap-Hornier, St. Malo. 239-MM. 240-MSM: Volkmar Wentzel, NGS. 240,241-Ira Block. 242(l)-KWM. 242(c)-NMM: Bates Littlehales, NGP. 242,243-MM: Victor R. Boswell, Jr., NGP. 243(c)-National Maritime Museum, San Francisco: Christopher Springmann. 243(r)-Courtesy of The India House Collection: Victor R. Boswell, Jr., NGP. 244-Atlantic Mutual Insurance Co., New York. 245-F. E. Gibson. 246-Collection of Richard M. Boonisar. 246,247-H. S. Thorne. 248,249-National Maritime Museum, San Francisco. 250,251-Jaime Ortiz, Gailway Graphics.

"The Liner She's a Lady"

252-Ken Marschall. 254,255-Joseph Walter, 1840; NYPL. 255(l)-NMM. 255(c)-L. N. Rosenthal; LC. 255(r)-Stokes Collection, NYPL. 256-Hervey Garrett Smith. 257(t)-Cunard Archives, Liverpool University. 257(b)-From a drawing by J. S. King, 1844; MM. 258-NMM. 259-Adam Woolfitt. 260, 261-David Ditcher, figures by Joan-Marie Abley, 1976; S.S. Great Britain Project. 262(t)-Science Museum, London. 262(b)-International Museum of Photography, Rochester, N.Y. 263-Robert Dudley, 1866; MMA, on loan to SI. 264-Culver Pictures. 265-MM. 266-Cunard Archives, Liverpool University. 267-Jasper F. Cropsey, ca 1856; Newington-Cropsey Foundation, Hastings-on-Hudson, N.Y. 268-Museum of the City of New York. 268,269-LC. 270(l),270(r),271(c)-Collection of William A. Newman. 270(c),271(r), 272,275(r)-Collection of Business Americana, SI. 271(l),275(tl), 276(t)-Collection of Frank O. Braynard. 273(l),275(c&bl)-

Museum of the City of New York. 273(r)-Hapag-Lloyd, Hamburg. 274-Bettmann Archive. 276(b)-NMM. 277,282,283,286,287-Steamship Historical Society Collection, University of Baltimore Library. 278, 279-NMM. 280,281-Chris Mayger, 1975; New English Library, London. 281-*The New York Times*. 284-Collection of William E. Donnell. 285-LC. 288,289-Gift of Dr. and Mrs. Irwin R. Berman, 1976; MMA. 290,293-From *Illustrated London News*, on loan to Science Museum, London. 294,295-Jack L. Gray, 1959; PMS. 296, 297-Charles O'Rear. 298,299, 301(b)-Culver Pictures. 300-Cunard Archives, Liverpool University. 301(t)-U. S. Army. 303-SI. 304,305-Alfred Mainzer, Inc., Long Island City, N.Y.

Type composition by National Geographic's Photographic Services. Color separations by Chanticleer Company, Inc., New York, N.Y.; Graphic Color Plate, Inc., Stamford, Conn.; Offset Separations Corp., New York, N.Y.; Progressive Color Corp., Rockville, Md.; The Lanman Companies, Washington, D. C. Printed by Kingsport Press, Kingsport, Tenn.; R. R. Donnelley & Sons Co., Chicago, Ill. Bound by R. R. Donnelley & Sons Co. Paper by Mead Paper Co., New York, N.Y.

Library of Congress CIP Data
Parry, J. H. (John Horace), 1914-
Romance of the Sea.
Bibliography: p. 308
Includes index.
1. Navigation—History. 2. Ships—History. 3. Naval art and science—History. 4. Seafaring life—History. I. National Geographic Book Service. II. Title.

VK15.P4   387.5'09   80-29569
ISBN 0-87044-346-1   AACR2

Index

Text references appear in lightface type, illustrations in **boldface**, picture captions in *italic*.